Treatment of Autistic Children

WILEY SERIES ON
STUDIES IN CHILD PSYCHIATRY

Series Editor
Michael Rutter
Institute of Psychiatry
London

The First Year of Life
Psychology and Medical Implication of Early Experience
Edited by
David Shaffer and Judy Dunn

Out of School
Modern Perspectives in Truancy and School Refusal
Edited by
Lionel Hersov and Ian Berg

The Clinical Psychiatry of Adolescence
by Derek Steinberg

Longitudinal Studies in Child Psychology and Psychiatry
Practical lessons from research experience
Edited by
A.R. Nicol

Treatment of Autistic Children
by Patricia Howlin and Michael Rutter

Further titles in preparation

Treatment of Autistic Children

By

Patricia Howlin and Michael Rutter
Institute of Psychiatry, London

With

M. Berger
R. Hemsley
L. Hersov
W. Yule

JOHN WILEY & SONS
Chichester · New York · Brisbane · Toronto · Singapore

Library of Congress Cataloging-in-Publication Data:

Howlin, Patricia.
    Treatment of autistic children.

    (Wiley series on studies in child psychiatry)
    Bibliography: p.
    Includes index.
    1. Autism—Treatment. 2. Autistic children—Rehabilitation. I. Rutter, Michael. II. Title. III. Series.
[DNLM: 1. Autism, Infantile—therapy. WM 203.5 H865t]
RJ506.A9H68 1987   618.92'89'82   86–24628

ISBN 0 471 10262 8

British Library Cataloguing in Publication Data:

Howlin, Patricia
    Treatment of autistic children. — (Wiley series on studies in child psychiatry)
    1. Autism
    I. Title   II. Rutter, Michael
    618.92'8982   RJ506.A9

ISBN 0 471 10262 8

Printed and Bound in Great Britain by Anchor Brendon Ltd, Tiptree, Essex

Contents

vi

Series Preface

During recent years there has been a tremendous growth of research in both child development and child psychiatry. Research findings are beginning to modify clinical practice but to a considerable extent the fields of child development and of child psychiatry have remained surprisingly separate, with regrettably little cross-fertilization. Much developmental research has not concerned itself with clinical issues, and studies of clinical syndromes have all too often been made within the narrow confines of a pathological condition approach with scant regard to developmental matters. The situation is rapidly changing but the results of clinical–developmental studies are often reported only by means of scattered papers in scientific journals. This series aims to bridge the gap between child development and clinical psychiatry by presenting reports of new findings, new ideas, and new approaches in a book form which may be available to a wider readership.

The series includes reviews of specific topics, multi-authored volumes on a common theme, and accounts of specific pieces of research. However, in all cases the aim is to provide a clear, readable, and interesting account of scientific findings in a way which makes explicit their relevance to clinical practice or social policy. It is hoped that the series will be of interest to both clinicians and researchers in the fields of child psychiatry, child psychology, psychiatric social work, social paediatrics, and education—in short all concerned with the growing child and his problems.

The treatment of children with serious disorders of development necessarily brings together considerations of developmental and clinical issues—one of the key aims of this series. This volume focuses explicitly on this important topic in relation to the syndrome of infantile autism, a condition that involves abnormalities in the development of social relationships, communication skills, and play. Research findings on the nature of autism are used to plan a treatment programme in which there is an emphasis on working with parents in their own homes. The therapeutic strategies combine a wide range of behavioural methods with counselling techniques, the objective being to foster normal development as well as to reduce maladaptive behaviour. The book describes the methods employed and outlines how the immediate and long-term effects of treatment were evaluated through comparisons with other approaches. The findings offer both hope in terms of what can be accomplished and also cautions on the constraints that derive from the nature of the biological handicaps associated with autism. The response to treatment is used to raise further questions on those handicaps, as well as to consider how treatment methods may be improved in the future. The project provides a good illustration of the necessity for research and clinical work to progress together.

MICHAEL RUTTER

Acknowledgements

The work described in this volume owes much to many people. The treatment programme that we describe was established on a research basis with the support of a grant from the Department of Health and Social Security given to Michael Berger, Lionel Hersov, Michael Rutter and William Yule who were jointly responsible for all the initial planning. It represented a development of a long-standing interdisciplinary collaboration between psychologists (MB and WY) and child psychiatrists (LH and MR). In addition, however, Fraida Sussenwein made a major input to the treatment programme from the perspective of psychiatric social work. She served as a therapeutic consultant during the early years of the project, being succeeded by Daphne Holbrook during the later years. We are very grateful to both of them for their invaluable guidance and support (particularly with reference to parental counselling) and for their contributions to the joint thinking about treatment strategies and tactics.

Patricia Howlin and Rosemary Hemsley were the two clinical psychologists who undertook almost the whole of the therapeutic work with the families during the course of the research phase of the treatment programme; they were also responsible for the research measures (except when it was necessary to have independent evaluations).

When the research funding came to an end, the Board of Governors of the Joint Bethlem Royal and Maudsley Hospitals (and subsequently the Special Health Authority) generously made it possible for the treatment programme to be continued on a reduced basis. It is now, therefore, an integral part of the services provided by the Joint Hospital. Initially, this service was provided by Patricia Howlin (clinical psychologist) and Nuala Sheehan (psychiatric social worker), both on a half-time basis. More recently, Judith Lask (psychiatric social worker) took over from Nuala Sheehan; we are indebted to both of them for their contributions to the continuing development of therapeutic ideas. Michael Rutter has provided the main child psychiatric input to the services but both Lionel Hersov and William Yule have continued to make major contributions.

Patricia Howlin and Michael Rutter have been responsible for writing the book but the ideas expressed are the result of the joint contributions of all six authors, and have benefited from the thinking of the other colleagues to whom thanks have already been expressed.

We are also indebted to Nan Holmes, Julie Rickett and Helen Likierman for undertaking an independent evaluation of parent perceptions of the programme. Chapter 12 is based on their research.

Finally, we are most grateful to Helen Journeaux, Averil Baxter, Nicola Billinton and Jennifer Smith for putting the text onto the word processor and for dealing so patiently with our multiple redrafts.

Chapter 1

Introduction

Autism was initially described by Leo Kanner in 1943 when he wrote of a group of children 'whose condition differs so markedly and uniquely from anything reported so far, that each case merits ... a detailed consideration of its fascinating peculiarities'. These were the children whom he described as having 'inborn autistic disturbances of affective contact'; in other words, autistic children.

Fascination with the condition, its possible causes and the challenges it presents to treatment has persisted for over 40 years. But, although attempts to solve the enigma of autism have given rise to many myths there are, as yet, few solutions. In writing this book we have attempted to give a detailed account of how the manifold problems of autistic children may be tackled therapeutically. In addition we have carried out a systematic evaluation of the effects and limitations of treatment. The implications of these findings, in terms of theoretical and research issues, are discussed. And, finally, consideration is given to how these findings might affect future developments in the treatment and understanding of autism.

THE NATURE OF THE HANDICAP IN AUTISM

In his remarkably clear and concise account of the syndrome of early infantile autism Kanner (1943) noted three major features. The first was 'the children's inability to relate themselves in the ordinary way to people and to situations from the beginning of life'. A second distinctive feature was the failure to use language for the purpose of communication. A third characteristic was described as 'an anxiously obsessive desire for the maintenance of sameness, resulting in a marked limitation in the variety of spontaneous activity'. Play, too, was characterized by a preoccupation with stereotyped, repetitive activities, lacking any creative or social function.

Subsequent studies have confirmed Kanner's original descriptions of the children. It is now also apparent that autistic children show a wide range of non-specific problems, such as temper tantrums, fears and phobias, sleeping and behavioural disturbances, in addition to their more specific difficulties. It is clear, too, that far from having normal cognitive skills, as Kanner initially suggested, there are distinct and deviant cognitive patterns associated with the condition, as well as a tendency to overall mental retardation.

Although the diagnostic criteria for autism can be summarized quite succinctly, in terms of their abnormal social relationships, abnormal communication skills and abnormal stereotyped play patterns (see Rutter, 1978; Rutter and Schopler, 1987) such brief headings do little to convey the overwhelming extent of the handicap. Nor do they give any adequate account of the difficulties faced by parents. For, as will become apparent, each separate problem has many different components, and these in turn affect almost every aspect of the child's functioning.

THE LANGUAGE HANDICAP IN AUTISM

The failure to develop normal communication skills is now accepted as one of the most important features in the diagnosis of autism (Rutter, 1985a). Abnormalities of language are frequently reported by parents as being the first problem to give concern and extend into many different areas. The babbling sounds made by autistic infants are rarely as extensive in range or frequency as those made by normal babies. Patterns of babbling are also affected and the speech cadences that usually develop by the age of 9 to 12 months do not appear (Ricks, 1975). The autistic child fails to take part in the reciprocal 'prelinguistic conversations' that are typical of normal mothers and babies (Martlew, 1987), and he neither responds to nor initiates verbal or social interactions. The children's understanding of spoken language is usually markedly reduced; and a lack of symbolic gesture or mime is equally characteristic. They tend to make their needs known by taking the adult by the wrist, rather than by the hand. Even very simple gestures, such as pointing, are affected, and if autistic children do indicate their needs in this way it is usually with the hand rather than with the extended index finger. Rarely are such movements accompanied by mime, demonstration or symbolic gestures.

Although, as they grow older, comprehension skills may improve, almost all younger autistic children are impaired in their understanding of language. Thus, although they may be able to follow simple instructions if given in a familiar social context or with the aid of gesture, they are usually unable to follow instructions that lack these cues. More complex instructions, involving the combination of two or more ideas, also present many difficulties, and problems in dealing with abstract concepts tend to persist throughout childhood and into adult life.

Abnormalities in the Use of Language

Nearly all autistic children are retarded in their language development and some never acquire speech. However, not only are autistic children unusually delayed in their acquisition of speech, but their pattern of language development and their use of language is strikingly different, from both normal children and those with other language disorders.

Perhaps the most characteristic feature of all is the failure of autistic children to use speech for social communication. The autistic child tends to talk much less than a normal child of a comparable level of language development. And, unlike the normal toddler who chatters non-stop as he follows his mother about the house, autistic childrn will rarely do this. They show little desire to communicate for communication's sake; nor is there any evidence of the 'to and fro' quality of conversations that characterizes the speech of young normal infants from the very earliest stages of language development (Cross, 1977). The development of generative language is delayed, and repetitive and stereotyped utterances take the place of novel and creative ones. Delayed and inappropriate echoing is common and there are a variety of characteristic abnormalities, such as pronoun reversal, and abnormal, egocentric use of language.

Although in later childhood and adolescence, some autistic children, particularly those of normal intelligence, achieve an average level of language competence, abnormalities in language usage remain. Speech remains repetitive and stereotyped and many autistic individuals tend to converse by a series of obsessive questions related to their particular preoccupation at the time. Difficulties with complex or abstract language concepts remain. Abnormalities in delivery are common, and a monotonous flat tone with little lability, change of emphasis or emotional expression is characteristic. In many cases speech is staccato and lacking in cadence and in inflexion. Frequently, too, there is a formality of language and a lack of ease in the use of words leading to a pedantic mode of expression, almost as if the autistic person were speaking a foreign language. The understanding of non-verbal cues used by other people, such as gestures and facial expression, also remains severely affected.

THE NATURE OF THE SOCIAL HANDICAP

Early Development

As with the emergence of language, autistic children show the same combination of retardation and deviance in their social development. Unlike normal children, austistic children do not develop strong, specific attachments to their parents in the first year of life. As toddlers, they do not follow their parents around the house nor do they run to them after a period of separation. Even if hurt or upset they are unlikely to seek out their parents for comfort and very few autistic children develop the bedtime kiss and cuddle routines that are characteristic of normal children. There is a general failure to use smiling, gesture or physical contact in a normal way to respond to or to signal social intent. Even in the very young, it is evident that autistic infants do not take up an anticipatory posture or put up their arms to be picked up when their parents approach, in the way that normal infants do. Nor do they show the usual delight and interest if a familiar adult approaches.

'Eye contact tends to be very abnormal. Some children seem deliberately to avoid making eye contact with adults, although in other children it is the *way* in which eye to eye gaze is used, rather than the amount of eye contact, that is abnormal. Normal children use eye to eye gaze as a social signal in a highly discriminating way. They do not stare fixedly at adults' faces but instead will look particularly when they want to gain attention or when they are being spoken to. 'Gaze also varies according to the familiarity of the adult, and the emotional context of the situation (Tiegerman and Primavera, 1984). The autistic child, however, does not use eye gaze in a way that is sensitive to the requirements of the social situation.

' Many autistic children tend not to discriminate between people, so that they will approach a stranger almost as readily as their own parents.' However although failing to develop normal attachments, they do not necessarily physically withdraw from people as some of the earlier accounts in the literature claimed. For example, many autistic children enjoy rough and tumble games or being tickled. Nevertheless, although they may *respond* to gross physical contact of this kind, they rarely initiate it. Although they may attempt to gain an adult's attention in order to meet their immediate needs, they will rarely attempt to share their own experiences with an adult. For example, they are unlikely to point out objects that may be of mutual interest, nor are they likely to check whether an adult is sharing their own enjoyment in a particular activity (Sigman *et al.*, 1985).

Social Development in Later Childhood

As autistic children grow older they do develop attachments to familiar adults and many demonstrate affection towards their parents. By the age of 5 years or so, many of the early social impairments may be less in evidence. Nevertheless, serious social difficulties persist (Howlin, 1986b; Lord, 1984). In particular, there is a lack of reciprocity and social responsiveness in their interactions with peers. They rarely engage in cooperative group play, nor do they develop specific friendships with other children. Indeed, although by this time they may well approach adults for attention, they will continue to avoid contact with their peers, preferring instead to spend their time in solitary routines.

The Failure to Develop Normal Reciprocal Social Interaction

As autistic children approach the teenage years the lack of interest in other people, which is often evident in early childhood, tends to abate. They may well try to approach other children, and often, at least in the case of brighter children, will express a wish to make friendships. Unfortunately, their ability to do so is severely limited by a number of factors. First, they show a curious lack of empathy in their response to other people and frequently seem insensitive to other people's feelings, even if these are expressed quite strongly. There is very little reciprocity in their social interactions and very little responsiveness to the needs and concerns of others. In addition, the inability to interpret or appreciate non-verbal social cues persits well into adulthood. This leads to failure in appreciating the demands of social situations, and frequently result in quite unacceptable behaviour in public.

Abnormal Patterns of Play

Given the marked abnormalities in both their language and social development it is hardly surprising that autistic children also show very abnormal patterns in play and imaginative skills (Black *et al.*, 1975; Riguet *et al*, 1981; Ungerer and Sigman, 1981; Wing *et al*; 1977). Just as language processes are stereo- typed and impoverished, so, too, play is ritualistic and lacking in imagination. Typically, play tends to be repetitive, non-functional and non-social. Play patterns are rigid and limited, with little variety or creativity and few autistic children show normal enjoyment in dolls or trains or cars. Even if some in- terest is shown in conventional toys there is little appreciation of the symbolic functions of such objects. Thus, the autistic child may be interested in spinning the wheels of the car, or dismantling a doll's body, but he is most unlikely to set off on an imaginary journey with them. These deficits in play are most evident in those autistic children who also have severe language impairments. However, the abnormalities are not simply a function of language retardation and occur amongst children at much higher levels of cognitive and linguistic development as well. Indeed, it is the failure to show any normal interest in, or desire for, play that highlights most strikingly the cognitive, social and linguistic deficits of autistic children. The spontaneous development of social play, which is so apparent not only in humans but in the young of many other species, does not occur. Nor is there any evidence of the inventiveness shown by normal children in making play things out of virtually any object. Instead, involvement with toys or household objects is usually limited to arranging them in complex patterns or seemingly endless straight lines.

This lack of imaginative ability clearly affects the autistic child's ability to take part in the games enjoyed by normal children. It also inhibits the development of abstract symbolic functioning and, without any imagination or fantasy, life tends to remain concrete and steeped in routine. As they grow older their appreciation of literature, films and theatre is severely limited and usually remains at a very childlike level. Many older autistic individuals, too, report that when alone they have no thoughts other than those involving their immediate preoccupations or obsessions. This failure to play, either imaginatively or socially, may also adversely affect language development. Uzgiris (1981), for example, has suggested that play, particularly involving imitation, is crucial for communication and that, in normal infants, the shared experiences that develop from play constitute a necessary framework for language to emerge.

OBSESSIONAL AND RITUALISTIC BEHAVIOURS

Ritual and Routines

In place of normal play patterns, the autistic child, even as a very young infant, tends to exhibit highly stereotyped and ritualistic modes of interaction with the environment. A resistance to change, and a marked dislike of alterations in daily routine, are common. Thus, the autistic child may well insist on eating at exactly the same time each day, in exactly the same position at the table, and with exactly the same set of utensils. He may also insist that other people in the house behave in an equally rigid way. This dislike of change frequently extends to the physical environment, so that the child refuses to tolerate a piece of furniture out of place, doors left open in a particular way, or a curtain hanging in an 'unacceptable' fashion. Decorating or renovation by parents is often made impossible, either by the child's distress if this occurs, or by his deliberate attempts to remove the new wallpaper or furniture. Even activities that the child particularly enjoys can be ruined by this resistance to minor changes. For example, a trip to the zoo can become a disaster if one of the animals is moved to a different cage for some reason. Many children show considerable pleasure in musical programmes, such as 'Top of the Pops', but then will get highly distressed if the records played each week are altered.

As children grow older many of these rituals become even more pervasive and may well affect almost every aspect of daily life. For example, there are many instances of children who will walk only in a northerly direction, or will only take right turns, or will never go past a red front door—all of which can severely limit the extent to which they can be taken out. They may also become more insistent that other people take part in their routines. For example, they may try to insist that everyone in a group of adults sits with his feet pointing in a particular direction, or that they all eat in a specific way.

Rituals may extend to verbal routines, which can involve everyone in the family responding to repetitive questioning in an identical fashion. The child may refuse to let members of his family use particular words. Or he may insist that they take part in frequent and often prolonged question and answer routines, with *exactly* the same questions asked and *exactly* the same answers given on every occasion.

Obsessional Interests and Attachments

Although autistic children rarely show normal interest in toys they may well show a fascination with unusual objects, or unusual aspects of objects. For example, they may become obsessed with touching every lamp, phone box, or even door knob that they see whilst out walking. They may be fascinated by the feel of people's hair or their clothing, although showing little interest in them as people. Hence, they may deliberately set out to touch people's heads or fur coats or beards or whatever else gives rise to this fascination, no matter how socially unacceptable this may be.

As noted above, even toys are used in a very ritualistic fashion, and many children also show an obsessional interest in collecting objects. The particular items collected vary from child to child and may be anything from foreign coins or teddy bears to more bizarre items such as sink plungers, chair legs, tin cans or bus tickets.

In middle childhood and later many autistic children develop unusual preoccupations which they follow to the exclusion of other activities. Typically, these involve topics such as bus routes, train timetables, colours, direction, numbers or patterns. Marked attachments to particular objects are also common. Again, these tend not to be the cuddly teddies or blankets of normal children, but bits of grass, a piece of leather belt or picture postcards. Such objects tend to be carried everywhere by the child and their loss or removal results in extreme distress.

Stereotyped Movements

Often the objects to which the autistic child is obsessionally attached will also be handled in a specific way. Thus, they may be carried in a very precise manner between the thumb and the index finger or held up to the side of the childs' face. Stereotyped, repetitive movements are also common in the absence of attachment objects. Hand and finger mannerisms, such as twisting or flicking movements, are frequently carried out near the periphery of the child's vision. Whole body movements, or spinning themselves or other objects are typical, and often these movements can be extraordinarily complex. Many of the more mentally retarded autistic children also injure themselves by biting their wrists or hands or banging their heads, although this occurs less commonly in those of normal intelligence.

OTHER PROBLEM BEHAVIOURS

Although problems of social interaction, communication, play and obsessional behaviour are particularly characteristic of autism, autistic children frequently present a variety of other, less specific, emotional and behavioural problems. Many children, especially when young, have severe problems in sleeping and feeding. Thus, they may exist on very little sleep and may well be highly resistant to being put to bed at night or to sleeping alone. Extreme food fads are particularly characteristic, with children living on very restricted diets (such as Marmite sandwiches or sausages and crisps). Other problems may include marked overactivity (often developing into underactivity in adolescence), short attention span, tantrums and aggression, and fears and phobias. Obviously such problems are in no way specific to autism, in that they are found in both normal and other handicapped children, but they may well present some of the most serious difficulties in management at home.

COGNITIVE ABNORMALITIES

Just as *deviant patterns* of development, rather than simple delays, in language, play and social behaviour are characteristic of autism, so, too, the relationships between cognitive skills and deficits are highly unusual. It is apparent that although autistic children vary greatly in their intellectual ability—with IQ scores ranging from severely retarded to highly superior—about three-quarters show some degree of impaired general intellectual functioning. Initially, it was believed that this poor cognitive performance was a reflection of the child's social withdrawal but it is now apparent that this is not the case. Evidence from home movies (Rosenthall, Massie and Wolff, 1980) suggests that autistic children's sensori-motor intelligence is already impaired during the infancy period. There is no support for the argument that low IQ can be explained by lack of motivation or social withdrawal (Rutter, 1979). Nevertheless, although IQ scores obtained by autistic children have the same properties as those obtained by other groups (that is, they predict later scholastic achievement, occupation and social status and they show moderate consistency over time) the patterning of IQ scores tends to be different from both normal children and those suffering from mental retardation. Even in children whose memory and visuo-spatial abilities are relatively intact, frequently there are severe deficits in tasks involving symbolization, abstraction and conceptual processing. A series of experiments by Hermelin and O'Connor (1970) and Frith (1970a and 1970b) showed that autistic children have particular difficulties in making use of meaning in their memory and thought processes. They are also much more impaired in their ability to process complex temporal sequences as compared with both normal and mentally handicapped children. On the basis of these and other experiments, Hermelin (1976) has argued that the essential cognitive deficit seems to consist of an inability to reduce information by extracting crucial features, such as rules and redundancies. Whether, in fact, this is the case remains to be established. Nevertheless, it is clear that autistic children show a very characteristic pattern of deficits in cognitive functioning, and that this pattern is found both in those of normal non-verbal intelligence and in those who are more severely retarded.

PHYSICAL CHARACTERISTICS

Perhaps the greatest paradox of all is that these bizarre behaviours and deviant patterns of functioning appear in a child who looks perfectly normal and who shows none of the usual stigmata associated with severe mental handicap. Particularly when young, autistic children tend to be physically attractive, and although their facial expression may be unusually serious, they do not have the blank uninterested look of the non-autistic, but severely retarded children. They may appear interested and alert, even if this interest is restricted to highly stereotyped activities. In their gross motor skills, too, they may be skilled and dextrous.

It is this combination of marked abnormalities in some areas and yet relatively intact abilities in others, together with normal physiognomy and an apparently intelligent expression that presents such an enigma. The highly unusual patterning of skills and deficits has given rise to the notion that, somehow, if only the right key could be found, the solution to all the child's handicaps could be discovered. Unhappily, research into both the causes and cures of autism indicates only too clearly that no such key has been found. Nevertheless, the search for explanations of, and solutions to, the problems shown by the autistic child persists and remains a continuing source of controversy.

Chapter 2

Changing Theories and Styles of Treatment in Autism

Although Kanner's early descriptions of autism have stood up well to the test of time, there have been many subsequent changes in concepts; a multitude of different theories about the causes of the condition, and corresponding variations in treatment approaches (see Schopler, 1983).

AUTISM AS A PSYCHOGENIC DISORDER

To begin with, Kanner viewed autism predominantly as a social and affective disorder. He argued that the linguistic and cognitive skills of autistic children were essentially normal, and that the apparent deficits in these areas were attributable to their profound social withdrawal. In his earliest writings he considered autism to be a constitutionally determined, developmental disorder, and noted that 'we must . . . assume that these children have come into the world with an innate inability to form the usual biologically provided affective contact with people, just as other children come into the world with innate physical or mental handicaps'. At the same time, however, he also commented on the lack of warmth shown by many parents, and their tendency towards a 'mechanization of human contacts' (Kanner, 1943).

As time went on, Kanner began to speculate more openly on parents' possible contribution to the disorder. In 1954, he wrote, 'it should not be forgotten that the emotional refridgeration which children experience from such parents cannot but be a highly pathogenic element in the patient's early personality development'. Although Kanner stressed that 'the children's aloofness from the beginning of life makes it difficult to attribute the *whole* picture exclusively to parental relations', many other authors began to remark on the apparently cold, detached and obsessive traits shown by parents. Gradually, despite Kanner's emphasis on the primary biological nature of the disorder, notions of psychogenic origin increased in popularity. Hence, throughout much of the 1950s and 1960s the prevailing concept was of a condition in which disordered social functioning was a maladaptive response to an unfavourable environment, rather than one characterized by an innate deficit.

Psychotherapeutic Approaches to Treatment

Throughout this period many authors such as Bettelheim (1967), Boatman and Szurek (1960) and O'Gorman (1970) suggested, variously, that autism was due to a lack of stimulation, parental rejection, lack of parental warmth, or *Early Treatment* intrapsychic conflict resulting from deviant family interactions. Such theories were widely accepted throughout much of Europe and America and had a direct influence of the types of treatment offered to the families of autistic children. Psychotherapy, either directly with the child or indirectly with the parents, became the most widely accepted mode of therapy (Szurek and Berlin, 1956; Goldfarb, 1961).

Subsequent research, however, failed to support either the value of this particular aetiological concept or its related therapeutic approaches. These early theories of psychogenic causation had tended to be based on uncontrolled clinical observations, frequently involving very poorly diagnosed groups of children. Better controlled studies, such as those by Cantwell *et al.* (1978), found no evidence that the parents of autistic children suffered from any greater emotional or personality problems than parents of other groups of children. Environmental stresses were no more or less common than in other families; no general abnormalities in patterns of family interaction were found, nor was there any specific psychopathology related to the autistic child. Moreover, although it had been claimed that autism was due to psychosocial factors, the characteristic behaviours of the autistic child were clearly very different from those of children who *had* suffered from physical or emotional abuse or neglect (see Rutter and Lord, 1987; Skuse, 1984). In addition, even if higher rates of abnormalities in family functioning were found, it did not necessarily follow that parents were the primary cause of these. The reciprocal nature of parent–child interaction was rarely considered, and the possibility that the apparent deviance in parental behaviour might have resulted from the pathology of the child, rather than vice versa, was generally ignored.

Psychogenic theories, too, failed to explain the highly specific nature of the cognitive and communication deficits, particularly the extreme unresponsiveness to social contact that is apparent even in the early weeks of life. The association with organic factors, including the high rate of perinatal problems, the development of epilepsy in many children and other evidence of neurological or neurochemical disturbance, also conflicted with theories stressing the parents' role in aetiology (Rutter, 1985a).

As time went on, it became apparent that these psychogenic theories were largely unsupported by research evidence. It also became progressively clear that therapeutic intervention based on these premises had relatively little success. Although psychotherapy has been claimed to be effective both in the case of families who 'cause' the autistic condition from the outset, and those who, supposedly, are responsible for maintaining it subsequently (Berlin, 1978), there has been virtually no systematic evaluation of this form of treatment. Admittedly, one cannot conclude with certainty that it does not work;

nevertheless, there is little evidence, from either research or clinical experience, to suggest that it does do so.

AUTISM AS A FORM OF SCHIZOPHRENIA

Often associated with psychogenic concepts of causation was the view that autism was an early form of schizophrenia. Authors such as Singer and Wynne (1963) and Mishler and Waxler (1965) attributed the emergence of schizophrenia in adolescence to abnormal patterns of family interaction. Kanner himself noted the close resemblance between schizophrenic withdrawal and that found in autism. This led him to express the view that 'there is no likelihood that early infantile autism will at any future time have to be separated from the schizophrenias' (Kanner, 1951). However, it is now apparent, on the basis of many different findings, that this assumption is not correct and that autism cannot be considered as a form of early onset schizophrenia. Rutter (1972) summarized the principal differences between the two conditions.

First, the age of onset is very different. Schizophrenia generally becomes evident in the early to mid teens (or later), whereas autism is, by definition, present by the age of 3 years.

Second, the symptomatology is quite different. Autism comprises a failure of development, whereas schizophrenia involves the emergence of abnormal thought processes after a period of apparently normal development. Moreover, the characteristic delusions and hallucinations found in schizophrenia are extremely rare in autism, even in adult life.

Third, the courses of the two disorders are very dissimilar. Marked remissions and relapses are frequent in schizophrenia, but although, occasionally, there may be a deterioration in some individuals at adolescence, autism follows a much steadier course.

Fourth, there are striking intellectual differences between the two conditions. Mental retardation, which is commonly associated with autism, is much less frequently associated with schizophrenia. Nor do schizophrenics show the typical pattern of IQ scores found in autism—i.e. a marked discrepancy between verbal ability and visuo-spatial skills.

Fifth, the sex distribution is very different. Whereas, overall, schizophrenia occurs as frequently in men as in women, autism occurs at least four times as frequently in males as in females.

Organic factors, too, differentiate between the two disorders. Perinatal complications and epilepsy are far more common in autism (Deykin and MacMahon, 1979), and if epilepsy does occur in schizophrenia this is usually of a different type (typically of temporal lobe origin) and has a different age of onset from in autism.

Finally, family characteristics are markedly different. There may be some tendency for the parents of autistic children to be of higher than average social class but the parents of schizophrenics show more or less normal social class distribution. Schizophrenia is rare in the parents or siblings of autistic children, whereas it occurs in about 10 per cent of the first degree relatives of schizophrenic individuals. On the other hand, there is an increased risk of autism in families with an autistic child. Approximately 2 per cent of the siblings of autistic children are also autistic, a rate that is many times higher than that in the general population. In addition, although a family history of autism is rare, a family history of speech delay is much more common, being present in about one-quarter of cases. The siblings of autistic children are much more likely than the siblings of other handicapped groups (e.g. Down's Syndrome individuals) to have language disorders, learning disabilities or mental retardation (August *et al.*, 1983). The siblings of autistic children have also been found to have lower verbal IQs than expected on the basis of demographic variables (Minton *et al.*, 1982). Twin studies have also shown a very high concordance rate for either autism or severe cognitive impairment in twins. Thus, Folstein and Rutter (1977) found an 82 per cent concordance rate in monozygotic twin pairs and 10 per cent in dizygotic twin pairs. These findings all indicate important genetic influences in the pathogenesis of autism, although they also suggest that it is not autism as such that is inherited, but rather some broader predisposition to language and cognitive abnormalities. Hence, although the particular genetic model associated with autism is still unknown (see Folstein and Rutter, 1977, for a review of the genetic evidence), it appears very different from that associated with schizophrenia.

PHYSICAL APPROACHES TO TREATMENT

Although now more or less discredited, early theories about the possible link between autism and schizophrenia resulted, for a time, in their being treated in very similar ways. In the 1950s the use of physical methods began to replace more traditional psychotherapeutic interventions in both schizophenia and autism. Convulsive therapy, either pharmacologically or electrically induced, had a brief vogue. However, although Bender (1953) claimed that this was effective for children with both early and later onset schizophrenia, this was not supported by subsequent research. Work by Clardy (1951) suggested that ECT did very little good and might well do harm, and its use was fairly quickly superseded by drug treatments.

Many of the drugs used in the treatment of schizophrenia were also employed in the treatment of autism, but again their effectiveness proved limited. There is some evidence from the work of Campbell (1978) that drugs that result in deterioration in schizophrenia may be beneficial in the treatment of autism and vice versa. In the treatment of schizophrenia medication tends to have a relatively specific, antipsychotic effect, and there is good evidence that drug maintenance is crucial in preventing relapses. There is no such effect in autism.

Although autism and schizophrenia respond very differently to drug treatments there has been a continued search for a medication that might offer the same benefits to autistic children as the major tranquillizers have given to schizophrenia. A wide variety of drugs, from hypnotics and hallucinogens,

14

lithium and anti-depressants, to sedatives and stimulants have been used from time to time. However, adequately controlled drug trials have rarely supported the original, enthusiastic claims for success. Instead, although drugs may have limited, symptomatic effects that may be useful (e.g. in reducing tension or overactivity), they have no direct effect on the specific, pathological features of autism. The one reported exception to this was fenfluramine and its apparent effect in reducing serotonin levels, which are known to be raised in autism. However, more recent work now shows that the effects are minor and even these are unrelated to serotonin reduction (August *et al.*, 1983; Ritvo *et al.*, 1983). Moreover, undesirable side-effects are relatively common (Piggott *et al.*, 1986).

In summary, there now seem few grounds for accepting claims that drug treatment is an essential component of the total treatment of the psychotic child (e.g. Campbell, 1978). Indeed, what limited evidence is available seems to suggest that drug treatments are far from being essential and do very little to affect the basic disorder. Moreover, the medical heterogeneity of autism reduces the likelihood that any one drug could be effective in all cases. Medication may be useful in reducing some of the non-specific symptoms associated with autism. It is also probable that autistic children vary in their response to drug treatment, with some showing important benefits. Obviously, research into the most effective types of drug treatments must proceed. At the same time, however, we need to look in other directions for effective ways of helping autistic children and their families.

Unfortunately, many of the directions followed so far have been none too productive. Although megavitamin therapy and hormone treatments have been enthusiastically recommended by some authors (e.g. Rimland, Calloway and Dreyfus, 1978) there is little evidence that such treatments are beneficial. Neither is there much convincing evidence that less intrusive intervention methods, such as pet therapy, play therapy, music therapy, holding therapy and the like, offer any particular advantages.

However, changes in conceptual views concerning the nature of autism have, in recent years, resulted in more rational and apparently more successful approaches to treatment.

AUTISM AS A COGNITIVE AND DEVELOPMENTAL DISORDER

Although earlier accounts of childhood autism focused predominantly on social abnormalities, in the mid 1960s attention began to shift to the cognitive deficits associated with the disorder. Initially, the linguistic and cognitive abnormalities shown by autistic children were viewed very much as secondary handicaps. But follow-up studies such as those by Rutter and Lockyer (1967) and DeMyer *et al.* (1973) indicated that they were much more central to the disorder than had previously been acknowledged. As already noted, despite their normal appearance and the occasional presence of isolated skills (such as good rote memory or a facility for music, drawing or rapid calculation) the majority of autistic children are severely retarded, with more than half having IQs of less than 50. The importance of cognitive factors was supported by findings that the level of intelligence, together with the presence of language, is one of the best prognostic indicators and is a powerful predictor of later psychosocial outcome (Rutter, 1970; Lotter, 1978). Kanner (1943) suggested that these apparently low IQ scores were an artifact, attributable to the children's severe social withdrawal. Nevertheless it became apparent that intelligence levels remain relatively stable over time despite improvements in communication and social behaviour (Rutter and Lockyer, 1967). Bartak and Rutter (1976) also found that IQ was related to the presence of epilepsy, with retarded children showing a much higher rate of seizures developing during adolescence. Again, there could be no plausible explanation for this in terms of social or motivational factors.

In addition to the general delays in intelligence shown by autistic children, rather specific patterns of cognitive dysfunction were noted when they were compared with normal or mentally handicapped children of the same developmental level.

The characteristic deficits in skills involving sequencing, abstraction, and semantic meaning have already been noted. It was apparent, too, from the series of experiments by Frith (1971, 1972) and Hermelin and Frith (1971) that autistic children showed highly rigid and stereotyped response patterns on a wide range of cognitive tests.

Altogether, there is a very substantial body of evidence that autistic children suffer from specific and unusual cognitive deficits that have been present from an early stage in development (Rutter, 1983). At first, the focus was on language related intellectual impairments but it has become clear that this constitutes too narrow a view. This deficit is conceptual rather than linguistic and most especially it applies to the children's ability to make social inferences and to use socio-emotional cues.

EDUCATIONAL APPROACHES TO TREATMENT

The recognition that autistic children were neither schizophrenic nor suffering from psychosocial deprivation, but rather had a specific cognitive defect, had a marked influence on prevailing methods of treatment during the late 1960s and early 1970s. Neither drugs nor individual psychotherapy had proved particularly effective and both were being used less and less, particularly in Britain. Instead, there was an increasing focus on the measures needed to promote better social and linguistic development, as well as to improve cognitive functioning. Rutter and Sussenwein (1971) recommended that treatment, particularly in the areas of social communication, should begin as early as possible in order to avoid the development of further behavioural and obsessional problems which were then regarded as being secondary to the more fundamental deficit.

As educationalists in different countries began to stress the importance of appropriate teaching for autistic children, schooling facilities began to increase rapidly and expanded to include nursery education and day and residential schooling as well as post-school experience for older autistic individuals.

Research studies stemming from this milieu confirmed the view that improvements in autistic children tended to be associated with good individual attention at school. Rutter and Lockyer (1967), for example, found that even with as little as 2 years' schooling, autistic children made appreciable gains in their educational and social development. Other follow-up studies by Mittler *et al.* (1966), DeMyer *et al.* (1973), Lotter (1974) and Kanner (1973) have also found that the length of education is related to outcome. However, it should be noted that the amount of time spent in school is usually linked to the child's intellectual level, and hence a direct relationship between schooling and eventual outcome has still to be convincingly demonstrated.

Early educational programmes for autistic children tended to rely on psychoanalytic and regressive techniques, which were prominent in individual psychotherapy at the time. Gradually these began to be replaced by an emphasis on more direct teaching. Research by Schopler *et al.* (1971), Egel (1981), Rutter and Bartak (1973) and Goldfarb (1974) testified to the much greater effectiveness of highly structured teaching programmes as compared to more *laissez-faire* approaches.

BEHAVIOURAL APPROACHES TO TREATMENT

The Use of Behavioural Techniques

In parallel with the emphasis on appropriate educational facilities, the 1960s witnessed a proliferation in the use of behaviourally based methods of treatment. Pioneers in this field, such as Eysenck (1960) and Wolpe (1958), had noted the effectiveness of operant techniques across a whole range of adult disorders, and the value of such an approach in both psychology and psychiatry was becoming widely accepted. By the mid 1960s these techniques were being increasingly used in the treatment of a wide range of childhood problems, including those shown by psychotic children.

Operant procedures involve the use of principles derived from learning theory to increase desirable or decrease undesirable behaviours (Yule, 1985). A functional analysis of behaviour is carried out in order to identify the circumstances associated with increases or decreases in particular behaviours. Rewards or other forms of encouragement are then used to increase existing appropriate behaviours, whilst procedures such as withdrawal of social attention (or 'time out' from reinforcement) are used to reduce maladaptive or disruptive behaviours. The child's repertoire of alternative appropriate behaviours may then be increased by the use of prompting, shaping and fading techniques. Detailed reviews by Ullman and Krasner (1965) and Bandura (1969) highlighted the effectiveness of these methods with many different groups of children.

Early Experimental Studies

The application of behavioural techniques has broadened considerably over recent years. Early studies with autistic children were based on very narrow experimental paradigms using methods derived directly from Skinnerian conditioning and animal studies. For example, Ferster and DeMyer (1961, 1962) trained autistic children in a variety of tasks, such as key pressing or placing tokens in a slot dispenser. Reinforcement was dispensed if the children learned to meet the requirements of the experimental situation. The authors concluded 'that altering the reinforcement programme produced corresponding changes in the children's performance, similar to the effects of these procedures in animal and normal subjects'. Hingtgen, Coulter and Churchill (1967) used operant techniques to demonstrate that autistic children could be taught to discrimate between auditory stimuli and that they were capable of learning simple auditory-motor associations.

The prime concern of much of the work carried out during this period tended to be with the experimental niceties of operant technology rather than with the possible practical benefits of these techniques. Gradually, however, the principles derived from learning therapy began to be incorporated into therapeutic practice.

The Therapeutic Use of Behavioural Procedures

Initially, the treatment of autistic children tended to focus on areas secondary to the disorder rather than on the more fundamental deficits of social and communication skills. These early studies concentrated on the elimination of maladaptive behaviours. A variety of methods was used including 'time out' or extinction procedures, and the use of punishment techniques. Differential reinforcement of incompatible behaviours was used to improve the range of positive behaviours shown by the child. Amongst the behaviours apparently reduced by these techniques were self-injurious behaviours such as head banging and self-multilation, hyperactivity, and tantrums and aggression, both at home and at school (see Lovaas et al., 1965; Wolf et al., 1964, 1967; Wetzel et al., 1966; Jensen and Womack, 1967).

Gradually operant techniques began to be used to increase the behavioural repertoire of autistic children, and success was reported in training a variety of self-help, occupational and constructional skills (see Marshall, 1966; Koegel and Rincover, 1974; Martin et al., 1968). Operant procedures were also employed in an attempt to modify the more fundamental deficits shown by autistic children. Social interaction with peers and adults was increased, generally using reinforcement techniques but sometimes, as in the work of Lovaas et al. (1965), by the use of aversive measures such as electric shock. Reinforcement procedures were used, too, to encourage non-verbal communication and develop receptive language skills. One of the earliest successful attempts to teach autistic children to speak was reported by Lovaas (1966).

Subsequently, the effectiveness of prompting, fading and reinforcement techniques in establishing language skills in autistic children was reported in many other studies such as those by Risley and Wolf (1967), Marshall and Hegrenes (1970) and Stark et al. (1968).

The use of operant methodology in treating a range of behavioural and developmental disorders was given wide publicity, and by the end of the 1960s there seemed little doubt about the effectiveness of these precedures in ameliorating almost any behavioural problem. However, by the early 1970s it became apparent that there were many serious limitations to the reported studies, as reviews by Pawlicki (1970), McDonagh and McNamara (1973) and Yule and Berger (1972) indicated.

First, it was clear that almost all the claims for the effectiveness of behavioural treatment were based on single case reports. Admittedly, well-conducted single case studies have played an important part in the development of treatment methods in both psychology and psychiatry over the years. However, in the absence of control groups it is impossible to make adequate judgements about the relative effectiveness of different experimental procedures. It is also impossible to disentangle whether reported improvements are due to treatment effects or to the natural changes that accompany maturation and growth. The need for control groups is particularly crucial when dealing with developmental disorders. Language, and cognitive and social skills all tend to improve with age, even in autistic children, and without control data there is no way of knowing whether changes occur as a result of treatment or simply as a result of time. Without controlled studies, too, it was impossible to know whether behaviourally based treatments were any more or less effective than other forms of intervention. There was some limited evidence from the work of Ney et al. (1971) that behavioural treatments were more successful in the short term than less structured forms of intervention, such as play therapy, but the longer-term effects of treatment remained largely unexplored.

Not only were control data conspicuously lacking, the majority of studies around this time suffered from multiple other flaws in their experimental design. Adequate diagnostic and descriptive data on subjects were frequently lacking. Information about factors known to affect outcome, such as age, IQ and language level, was generally inadequate. Data presentation was, more often than not, entirely anecdotal. And, most importantly, the lack of any systematic manipulation of treatment contingencies (as in the use of multiple baseline or reversal techniques) meant that very little evidence existed to show that behaviours were, in fact, under direct experimental control. In addition to these basic faults, statistical analysis was generally inappropriate. Most studies relied simply on changes between pre-test and post-test measures of behaviour. If these improved 'significantly' the techniques were presumed to be effective. However, obviously this can lead to totally erroneous conclusions about the effects of treatment when developmental delays are involved.

Second, the effects of treatment programmes had almost always been evaluated in terms of changes in specific behaviours, rather than in terms of overall functioning. Thus, even in more sophisticated experimental studies such as those carried out by Guess and his colleagues (Guess *et al.*, 1974), the results reflected change only in highly circumscribed behaviours. On the whole, such studies focused on changes in the number of specific grammatical rules learned, or decreases in particular disruptive behaviours such as temper tantrums or head banging. The more general effects of, often very long-term, programmes on the child's behaviour and development were rarely described other than anecdotally. Even in those programmes that did attempt to assess wider areas of functioning, variability in the types of measures used made it impossible to evaluate comparative rates of improvement in various areas of development.

Third, these early studies paid very little attention to the effects of individual differences or developmental needs. Little information was provided about which children responded best to treatment or which behaviours were most amenable to change. Moreover, since few journals readily report unsuccessful case studies, there was no way of knowing whether particular behaviours, or certain types of children, proved more receptive to treatment than others. There were, it is true, a few indications that individual children varied in their responsiveness to treatment. Language programmes, in particular, seemed to have a very variable rate of success. Some children were reported as acquiring 'near normal language' after relatively short periods of treatment (Mathis, 1971). Other children having undergone much longer and more intensive training periods made relatively little progress as studies by Hewett (1965), Nelson and Evans (1968) and Halpern (1970) indicated. On the whole, however, given the general lack of information about subjects, it proved impossible to evaluate the characteristics that distinguished those children who made progress from those who did not.

Inadequate assessments of children and disregard of normal developmental processes also resulted in many programmes being developmentally inappropriate. Language training programmes, for example, frequently included syntactic structures that normal children of 4 or 5 years of age would be unlikely to master, yet attempts were made to teach them to autistic children well below this mental age (Gray and Ryan, 1973). Similarly, attempts to increase eye contact resulted in children being trained to use abnormally high levels of direct eye gaze (see Mirenda *et al.*, 1983). It is hardly surprising, therefore, that the effects of such programmes were not maintained and did not generalize to other settings.

Fourth, behavioural changes tended to be evaluated almost exclusively within the same context in which treatment took place. Despite considerable evidence that generalization to non-therapeutic settings rarely occurs without special intervention, many clinic based programmes failed to monitor children's progress once they returned home. In the investigations that did attempt to do so, as in the follow-up studies by Lovaas *et al.* (1973), it was all too evident that although substantial gains may have occurred during intensive in-patient treatment, these were frequently lost when the children returned to their normal environment.

Finally, follow-up evaluations (even if they existed, which in most cases they did not) usually covered an extremely short time period. Adequate follow-up assessments are crucial when dealing with a chronically handicapping condition such as autism. There is little value in carrying out rigorous and time consuming treatment procedures if the results last only for the duration of the intervention programme, or if there are no overall gains either to the child or his family. Autistic children, in particular, seem to have severe problems in maintaining or generalizing newly learned behaviours. Short-term follow-ups, therefore, are very likely to result in misleading judgements about the real benefits of treatment. Certainly, although a few studies had reported, anecdotally at least, fairly favourable short-term effects, the longer-term results of intervention proved disappointing. It seemed that although intensive treatment with autistic children could result in marked gains in many areas, including language and social skills, these gains were frequently poorly maintained once intervention was discontinued (Lovaas *et al.*, 1973).

CONCLUSIONS

In summary, the limitations of existing studies of behavioural intervention meant that many questions remained unanswered about what seemed to be a potentially valuable form of treatment. In setting up the present research project it was evident that at least five aspects of research design needed to be strengthened.

(1) Previous reliance on single case studies meant that data were lacking on the extent to which different treatment approaches varied in effectiveness. Nor was there adequate evidence that any of them provided results that were superior to those that were consequent upon maturation and the ordinary range of experiences. Thus, a controlled experimental investigation was required that would assess differences between matched groups of treated and untreated children.

(2) The hitherto narrow focus on particular, circumscribed behaviours meant that very little was known about the general effectiveness of treatment. A much broader based approach to treatment was needed, which would assess the effects of intervention across the whole range of children's functioning.

(3) In the past, overreliance on strict behavioural techniques had led to a disregard of approaches that considered children's developmental levels and individual differences. It seemed that a well based intervention programme should incorporate developmental as well as behavioural principles. The modification of treatment procedures according to the skills and deficits of individual children was likely to be important for the success of treatment.

(4) Previous reliance on measures taken only in the treatment setting meant little was known about the generalization of treatment effects to other social contexts or to behaviour that was not the specific target of treatment procedures. A multifaceted approach to evaluation was required if the

wider effects of treatment were to be properly evaluated. Thus, assessments needed to extend beyond individual child behaviours to family interactions at home and parental views of treatment.

(5) Inadequate follow-up assessments in previous investigations meant that a much longer term evaluation of treatment procedures was necessary. This was required in order to investigate whether the often rather limited effects of treatment lasted beyond the actual intervention period. Assessments that were broader in scope and conducted over a longer time period were also needed to find out whether relatively modest short-term changes did eventually have a more beneficial effect on wider areas of the child's functioning.

In the following chapter the ways in which we attempted to meet these goals are discussed.

Chapter 3

Designing a Treatment Programme*

TREATMENT GOALS AND TREATMENT STRATEGIES

The requirements outlined in the previous chapter had extensive experimental and practical implications for the present project. The need for a well-matched control group was evident from the outset, and this is discussed at greater length later in the chapter. Practically, however, the crucial goal was that we should be able to devise effective treatment programmes that were based on the particular needs of individual children and their families. This approach required that, instead of focussing on only one or two behaviours in isolation, we should aim to improve the child's general level of functioning at home and his overall interaction with the family. It also meant that instead of relying entirely on behavioural techniques, treatment should incorporate other relevant forms of intervention—including a general restructuring of the home environment, and attention to family problems and parental concerns.

Selecting Treatment Goals

Much of the early work with autistic children had concentrated on the development of speech and language. This had arisen partly because of the pervasiveness of the language handicap, and the view that many other difficulties, such as social problems and obsessional behaviours, were secondary to this. The development of language was also important for prognosis and it was apparent that unless language was acquired by the age of 6 or 7 years it was very unlikely to be acquired subsequently (Rutter, 1970). Without language, the outlook in later life, even for children of normal non-verbal IQ, was extremely pessimistic. However, although it was clear that attempts to improve communication would play a central role in treatment, it was apparent that language was by no means the only problem shown by autistic children. Indeed, for some children it was not possible even to begin language training until other,

---

*Although the project began in the early 1970s, the total duration was 6 years. During that time we incorporated any newly emerging data from other investigations that were relevant to our work. Many of our original hypotheses were substantiated by subsequent research, and studies appearing during the course of the project (as well as those that predated it) are cited in the text.

more disruptive behaviours had been modified. Many other problems, related both to the children's lack of skills and to the presence of maladaptive behaviours, also required attention.

Individual Assessment of the Child

Intervention began with a detailed assesssment of the child in terms of his developmental level, his patterns of strengths and limitations, and the main problems of concern to his parents. Developmental assessments were carried out by means of standardized tests designed to assess both verbal and non-verbal skills. These were supplemented by careful assessment of the child at home using informal assessments and standardized observation schedules. Further details of the child's problems were obtained from interviews with the parents at home. A functional analysis was an important precursor to treatment. This enabled us to get a better idea of how factors in the environment affected the child's behaviour, either for better or for worse, and how the environment might be restructured in order to enhance progress. The initial assessments also dealt with the impact of the handicapped child on the family, the availability of family resources and the presence of parental susceptibilities, as well as the existing provision for the child's education, relief help and holiday care. Each child was given a systematic psychiatric and medical assessment and details of any family history of developmental or psychiatric problems were also noted, for both therapeutic planning and genetic counselling. Whereas some of the more formal assessments were carried out in the clinic, home visits were needed to determine what the child was like in his normal environment and to establish what features of the home were relevant in planning treatment. For example, the physical characteristics of the home, how large or small it was, whether or not it had a garden, and whether it was sturdily furnished or full of antiques, could make all the difference in recommending certain sorts of treatment rather than others.

By means of these detailed initial assessments it was possible to formulate highly specific goals for treatment, incorporating information about the child's skills and weaknesses and the particular needs of his family. Parents' views and wishes were taken into account when choosing the particular treatment techniques to be implemented and in selecting the behaviours to be modified. In general the aim of intervention was to increase the child's *positive* skills and behaviours with the aim that these should eventually take the place of less desirable ones. However, in certain cases, often quite minor problem behaviours produced such feelings of irritation or annoyance in parents that it was necessary to reduce these before attempting to modify other areas of the child's functioning. In some families it seemed that parents had come to accept more global problems shown by their children but that new, often rather insignificant, behavioural difficulties resulted in much more concern. One mother, for example, was extremely irritated by her son's pronoun reversal; another felt that her main problem was teaching her enuretic and non-speaking child to understand colour-names. Both of these children showed a multitude of other problems, all of which seemed much more important to the therapists concerned. However, by helping parents to work on these minor and therefore often easily remediable problems first, it proved possible to give them much more confidence in the efficacy of the techniques recommended. This, in turn, increased their willingness to try out these procedures on more fundamental areas of deficit.

Choosing Treatment Strategies

A Developmental Approach to Intervention

As is already apparent, the use of operant techniques formed the basis of much of our work with families. The use of prompting, fading and reinforcement procedures was described in detail to parents, who were then given practical demonstrations of how these might be used to change their child's behaviour. If necessary, ways of eliminating maladaptive behaviours, such as by extinction or 'time out' techniques, were also discussed. The importance of evolving consistent styles of handling was stressed at all times, and once parents had been given the opportunity to watch the use of these technqiues in action, they were encouraged to carry them out themselves, with plentiful help and feedback.

Although operant techniques are useful in dealing with some of the specific difficulties shown by autistic children they were by no means the only methods used. As with any developmental disorder the ultimate aim of intervention must be the encouragement of normal development. It was necessary, therefore, for treatment procedures to incorporate knowledge about normal developmental processes, about the factors that facilitate optimal development, and what is known of the abnormal features that interfere with this. In order to foster normal developmental growth it was essential to create an environment that would be effective in encouraging progress in the right direction. For example, in developing language skills, operant techniques may be effective in increasing vocabulary but they may not facilitate the growth of other aspects of language, such as play and imagination. Instead, deliberate encouragement of other related behaviours may be required. Thus, ways of increasing the child's use of representational toys, his sequencing of imaginative activities and his opportunities to take part in imitative and social games were used to improve basic levels of language functioning (as opposed to simple speech production).

In extending social behaviours there was deliberate intrusion into the child's solitary activities in order to encourage cooperative responses. Adults needed to alter their own responses to the child to ensure that their communication with him was clear and unambiguous and to ensure that he was better able to interpret social and environmental cues correctly. In addition, appropriate attachment behaviours were most likely to be fostered by adults learning to respond effectively to the child's particular ways of expressing need, fear, anxiety or distress. Brief, but structured, periods of intensive and stimulating interaction with adults were used to increase social relationships.

Environmental Modifications

A degree of restructuring the child's existing environment was also needed in many cases. Thus, in order to improve language skills children were given as much opportunity as possible to use them. For example, simply ensuring that food was not readily within a child's reach might have the effect of increasing the chances of his asking for what he wanted. The language environment to which the child was exposed was modified so that communications to the child were easily comprehensible, as well as effective in attracting and holding attention.

Quite simple modifications to the environment were of use in reducing stereotyped or inappropriate behaviour patterns. Such behaviours may occur either if the child is understimulated, or if the demands made of him are excessive for his developmental level. Children were provided with a range of different, developmentally appropriate activities to facilitate the reduction of deviant behaviour. Rigid routines could also be reduced by ensuring that minor alterations to daily routine were deliberately introduced so that they might become an accepted part of the child's life.

Adapting Strategies to Meet Particular Needs

Instead of relying exclusively on behavioural approaches to treatment, parents were guided to make use of whatever other strategies seemed appropriate. Choosing the correct strategy is not necessarily an easy task, and only careful monitoring of changes in the child's behaviour will tell whether or not the choice has been the correct one. A careful functional analysis of problems, before intervention began, helped to identify factors that might be causing difficulties, and served as a basis for suggestions regarding appropriate modes of intervention. For example, if tantrums or other disruptive behaviours were used as an attention seeking device they might be appropriately treated by differential reinforcement or 'time out' procedures. However, alternative approaches were used if the mechanisms seemed different. Thus, if tantrums occurred only when the child was unoccupied, the appropriate solution might be to provide him with greater stimulation. If disruptive behaviour resulted from the child's fear of particular situations or objects the answer would be to treat the fears and anxieties directly. If tantrums occurred when the child was tired or hungry, the solution was fairly obvious. Finally, when the child's tantrums were a response to parental tiredness or irritability, treatment might focus on reducing parental stresses or improving coping strategies.

Involving Parents in Treatment

Parents were much involved in treatment from the outset. All decisions about which problems to work on and which procedures to use were influenced by the parents' own views of what was necessary and acceptable. In order that treatment might have more global effects on the child's general interaction at home, interventions were carried out in the home environment. Although a number of previous studies had involved parents as co-therapists, in most of these the parental role had been relatively minor, with most of the intervention being carried out in the clinic. However, as work by Schopler and his colleagues (1971), Patterson *et al.* (1973) and Clements (1985) had indicated, parents can play a very major role in therapy, becoming highly effective co-therapists. Moreover, reports by Browning (1971) and Lovaas *et al.* (1973) indicated that, unless parents were directly involved in treatment, the long-term gains to the child were likely to be minimal. For this reason, all intervention was carried out with the parents in the child's home. The particular problems to be worked on, the goals of treatment and the strategies to be used were decided upon through joint discussion between parents and therapists. The implementation of treatment procedures was then largely undertaken by the parents when the therapists were not present. However, it was made clear that parents were *not* expected to spend extensive periods each day working with their child. Instead, the basic aim of intervention was to help parents develop successful strategies for teaching new skills or reducing behaviour problems that could be applied whenever the opportunity arose. Rather than requiring them to spend a greater amount of time each day with the child, parents were taught how to structure their time more effectively. Time spent in intensive teaching sessions (although sometimes necessary, as in the case of language training) was generally restricted. Newly acquired skills would be encouraged instead whenever opportunities arose during the day. Similarly, we aimed to provide parents with effective and consistent management strategies that could be adapted to a whole range of problems as and when behavioural difficulties occurred. It was felt that this type of approach, as well as making fewer demands on parents, would also be likely to lead to a better generalization of skills by their children.

Support for Parents

Although advice about management was obviously essential to our work with parents, it was not in itself adequate to cope with the wide range of practical and emotional difficulties faced by families. Expert and skilled counselling was required to help parents understand and cope with the complex mixture of feelings of sadness, guilt, bewilderment and often hostility associated with having a severely handicapped child. Intervention to deal with marital and other difficulties frequently required a combination of behavioural and counselling approaches. Parents needed support and assistance to avoid becoming over-involved with the autistic child to the possible detriment of their own lives and those of the rest of the family. This, again, required a combination of counselling and advice about daily management as well as provision of more practical sources of help.

Finding appropriate schooling for the child was frequently an urgent concern in the early stages of intervention. Once this was established, close liaison between parents and teachers was encouraged as much as possible. This not only helped in increasing the amount of support for parents but also ensured that the autistic child received much more consistent treatment.

Links with social services were encouraged to ensure that parents received the practical and financial support to which they were entitled. Provision of short holiday placements or brief periods of planned respite care, for example, proved of enormous benefit to families under stress.

Finally, the feelings of isolation experienced by many families were greatly reduced by encouraging them to join the National Autistic Society. Help from the Society was invaluable in practical ways, such as how to find baby-sitters, holiday homes, local relief help, etc. By putting parents of autistic children in touch with one another the social benefits for families, who previously had been deprived of any normal sort of social life, were considerable. The mutual support generated by parents' groups also proved of great value.

The Extent of Intervention

The families involved in treatment generally lived within a 60 mile radius of Central London and, during the term of the project, contact varied according to distance and the severity of the child's problems. Generally, home visits were made at least once a week during the first 6 months of treatment. During these visits, of 2 or 3 hours, the results of ongoing treatment programmes were discussed and assessed, new procedures being recommended as appropriate. In the therapists' absence parents were encouraged not only to carry out recommended procedures but also to keep simple records of their effectiveness. By the end of the first 6 months of treatment most families showed considerable skill in carrying out and recording straightforward programmes. Over the following 6 months of treatment it was possible to reduce visits by therapists to approximately 2 or 3 a month. By the end of the 18 month period, visits were usually occurring at monthly intervals.

To begin with, two therapists tended to be involved in family work. This was necessary in order to show parents how the various techniques might be put into practice, whilst at the same time explaining the aims and rationale for what was being done. After the first few visits, one therapist took over the principal responsibility for each family. Additional support for the psychologist directly involved in therapy was provided by a consultant team of psychiatrists, psychologists, and a senior psychiatric social worker who met weekly with the home therapists to discuss treatment programmes and problems.

TREATMENT DESIGN

The Selection of Children for the Treatment

It was evident that inadequate information about children's handicaps, and the lack of any controlled comparisons, were major flaws in most existing programmes. Since variables such as IQ, language and level of behavioural disturbance were known to affect outcome, it was essential to have adequate information about such factors. Appropriate selection of children was also vital if we were to be able to make judgements about the differential effects of treatment. Too homogeneous a group, in terms of behavioural problems and cognitive, linguistic and developmental levels, would make it impossible to assess individual differences in response to treatment. Too heterogeneous a group, on the other hand, might result in difficulties in drawing general conclusions about the effects of treatment.

A certain number of restrictions in sample selection were necessary, in order to facilitate the assessment of treatment efficacy. Because our sample size had to be relatively small (and hence inadequate for the evaluation of possible sex differences) boys only were included in the project. Also, to reduce the possibly distorting effect of serious medical disorders or those requiring regular use of medication or special procedures, it was decided to exclude children with known medical conditions likely to serve as a direct cause of autism, those suffering from epilepsy at the time of referral, and those with clinically significant hearing or visual handicaps. It was also decided to confine the sample to those with an IQ of 60 or more. Previous follow-up studies (see Lotter, 1978) had indicated that severely retarded autistic children had an extremely poor prognosis. Treatment might improve the outcome but the effects of gross mental handicaps markedly constrained what could be achieved. Because the assessment of treatment effects would be made much more difficult if the variations in outcome were dominated by the effects of individual differences in the degree of handicap it was necessary to impose this IQ restriction. However, it should be emphasized that this decision was taken because of research needs and not because of treatment applicability. The procedures used are equally appropriate for more handicapped children, autistic and non-autistic.

There were no exclusion criteria with respect to behavioural and language problems. The children ranged from those who were mute and severely lacking in language comprehension to those who had a good grasp of grammatical rules but whose use of communicative language was abnormal. Similarly the sample included very withdrawn or passive autistic children as well as some who were outgoing, but extremely deviant, in their social responses. The range of behavioural, obsessional, and developmental problems exhibited by the children was extensive. At the beginning of treatment the ages of the children extended from 3 to 10 years; non-verbal IQ levels ranged from a minimum of 60 to over 120; and social class, although skewed towards the upper end of the range, included individuals in every class sector. Since treatment was to be carried out predominantly by parents, no child was in long-term residential care although some of the older ones attended weekly boarding school.

All children, in addition to fulfilling the inclusion criteria described above, met the diagnostic criteria for autism outlined by Rutter (1971, 1978). These were:

(1) *Onset before the age of 30 months.*
(2) *Impaired social development* that is out of keeping with the child's chronological and intellectual level and which shows a number of specific characteristics, including a relative lack of selective attachments, poor use of

eye to eye gaze to regulate social interactions, a lack of social reciprocity and a failure to form selective peer relationships.

(3) *Delayed and deviant language* that is out of keeping with the child's mental level and which involves deficits in language comprehension, abnormal use of language for social communication purpose, together with serious impairments in non-verbal communication and creative imagination.

(4) *Stereotyped and repetitive behaviours* as shown by rigid play patterns, abnormal preoccupations, unusual routines or rituals, abnormal attachments to objects and protests over environmental change.

Individual characteristics of the children are presented in Appendix 3.1. All the children had been originally diagnosed as autistic at the Maudsley Hospital by one of the consultants (LH or MR) directly involved in the project. The time that had elapsed before the children became involved in the home based project, however, varied from child to child. A number had been diagnosed some years prior to the project; others who had been diagnosed more recently began treatment almost immediately following initial assessment. The time period between diagnosis and subsequent involvement in the project ranged from less than 1 month to almost 5 years, with an average time lapse of 34 months. Group details of the age, IQ and language level of the experimental group of children are presented in Table 3.1.

Table 3.1
Mean Scores of Experimental Children in Initial Diagnosis and
Immediatley Prior to Treatment

	Mean	(SD)
Age when diagnosed	4 yr 10 m.	(1 yr 6 m.)
Age treatment began	6 yr 2 m.	(2 yr 5 m.)
IQ when diagnosed	89.1	(17.6)
IQ prior to treatment	86.8	(17.9)
Mecham language age when diagnosed	2 yrs 1 m.	(1 yr 8 m.)
Mecham language age prior to treatment	2 yrs 6 m.	(1 yr 8 m.)

The Selection of Control Groups

Single case research designs were used in the study when appropriate. However, they have too many limitations in the case of autism for them to constitute the main evaluation strategy. Experimental manipulations, such as multiple baseline techniques or reversal designs, are largely inappropriate for the study of developmental disorders. The use of multiple baseline techniques requires that several specific behaviours are identified and then modified selectively in a predetermined sequence (Yule, 1980). If individual behaviours remain stable until modified, changing only after the implementation of intervention procedures, this can be used to demonstrate experimental control. However, the value of this technique rests on the assumption that the behaviours involved are functionally independent. Thus, it is assumed that changes in one domain, such as language, will not affect other areas of functioning—such as tantrums or rituals. In children with global developmental and behavioural problems, however, this is frequently not the case. Instead, improvements in one area may have marked effects on other, apparently unrelated, aspects of their development.

Reversal designs are based on comparisons that rely on treatment periods interspersed with periods of no treatment. If behaviours change in the predicted direction as treatment stops or starts, intervention may be presumed to be effective (Yule, 1980). Such an approach necessarily ignores developmental processes (skills once acquired will not be lost simply because they are no longer the focus of treatment). It also assumes that behaviours are exclusively under the control of extrinsic reinforcers. However, clearly if treatment is effective, behaviours should not remain under direct experimental control and should generalize to non-training settings. In addition, parents may be very unhappy with this apparently 'stop–go' approach to treatment. If they find a way of coping that apparently works, they may be most reluctant to abandon it, simply to comply with research requirements. Few parents, for example, having successfully dealt with a severe sleeping problem, are likely to want to return to a series of broken nights in order to fulfil the niceties of experimental design.

It was evident that control groups would be required, and that these should be used to assess both the short-term and long-term effects of treatments.

A short-term control group was required for several different purposes. To begin with, a prospective, longitudinal design with direct case–control comparisons of behavioural changes over time greatly facilitates the measurement of treatment effects. It also carries the possibility of investigating the links between different facets of change, such as between alterations in parental behaviour and improvements in the child's functioning. Also, however, it is desirable to measure the short-term benefits of any intervention. If any treatment is to have much appeal for parents, it should result in at least some detectable gains in the early months. A short-term control group, therefore, was selected to assess the effects of treatment over a 6 month period. Although it has been planned to have equal numbers of families in each group, in the event only 14 families could be found who fulfilled all the necessary criteria. The children in this control group were matched with cases for age, sex, language level, IQ and social class. None was receiving any intensive form of behavioural treatment or home intervention, although most had some form of limited, sporadic professional care. However, in the majority of cases, such help was remarkably limited, with the exception of one non-speaking child who was undergoing intensive psychoanalysis.

Families in this control group were contacted through the National Society for Autistic Children and confirmation of the diagnosis was sought from the consultants involved. All the children included in the study fulfilled the criteria for autism cited above and details of the individual characteristics of the children are given in Appendix 3.2. Table 3.2 outlines the group characteristics of cases and short-term controls. None of the case–control differences was statistically significant (although the language scores of the control children were slightly higher than those of the cases). Control parents were also of slightly higher social class than the cases. This was probably a function of the fact that they were all volunteers, selected from families belonging to the National Autistic Society.

Table 3.2

Comparisons between Cases and Short-term Control Group Prior to Treatment

Measures	Cases (N = 16)		Short-term control group (N = 14)	
	Mean	(SD)	Mean	(SD)
Age at initial assessment	6 yr 2 m.	(2 yr 5 m.)	6 yr 5 m.	(2 yr 4 m.)
Non-verbal IQ at initial assessment	88.8	(17.9)	88.4	(24.8)
Mecham language scores prior to treatment	2 yr 6 m.	(1 yr 8 m.)	2 yr 9 m.	(1 yr 9 m.)
Language level:				
No. of children who were:				
Mute	6		5	
Single word speech	5		3	
Phrase speech	7		6	
No. of children in social class:				
I–II	8		8	
III	2		2	
IV–VI	6		4	

Because autism is a chronically handicapping condition, it was also necessary to assess the longer-term benefits of treatment. This was particularly the case in view of the uncertainty over whether behavioural interventions improved language and social development, or rather just aided the better usage of existing skills without influencing ultimate developmental progress or outcome. The original control group was not used for this purpose as it was considered unacceptable to withhold treatment over a prolonged period while at the same time expecting the families to cooperate with extensive observational, interview and self-recording measures. Accordingly, at the end of the 6 months assessment period, the short-term control group were offered such help as we could provide with limited resources. In the event, only three or four families availed themselves of this offer.

In choosing an alternative, long-term control group it was decided to select a group of children who had previously attended the Maudsley Hospital for treatment, but who lived too far away to be included in the treatment programme. All the families had been given behaviourally orientated advice on a limited outpatient basis but none had been involved in home based intervention. The therapeutic principles employed with this long-term control group were the same as those used in the home intervention group, but the families' distance from the clinic had meant that they could be seen only relatively infrequently. This type of approach allowed us not only to assess the longer-term effects of treatment, but also to determine whether any gains made by the experimental group might have been achieved with less intensive therapy. All the children in this group were intially seen and diagnosed by the consultant psychiatrists (LH and MR) who were directly involved in the project. Children in this group were individually matched with the experimental children and Appendix 3.3 gives individual details of the boys involved. Table 3.3 summarizes details of the group matchings in terms of age, IQ, severity of behavioural handicap and language level at the time of initial referral. Again, none of the group differences was significant. Language levels, IQ and ratings for behavioural disturbance showed a high level of correspondence in each case–control pair. However, control children tended to come from families of a higher social class than cases (probably as a reflection of the fact that such families are more likely to know how to gain referral to specialist centres distant from local facilities). Control children were also somewhat older then the experimental group. This was because most had been diagnosed some years before the experimental children, at a time when the early diagnosis of autism was less common. Some discrepancy in age at first presentation, therefore, was inevitable, but these age differences were taken into account in the final analysis of results.

Table 3.3
Group Matchings at Time of Referal

Measures	Cases (N = 16)		Long-term control group (N = 16)	
	Mean	(s.d.)	Mean	(s.d.)
Age at referral	4 yr 10 m.	(1 yr 5 m.)	5 yr 2 m.	(1 yr 5 m.)
Non-verbal IQ at referral	89.1	(17.6)	88.0	(17.8)
Mecham language score	2 yr 1 m.	(1 yr 8 m.)	1 yr 9 m.	(1 yr 4 m.)
Language rating (a)	10.6		11.7	
Behaviour severity rating (a)	38.2		34.6	
No. of children in social class				
I–II	8		10	
III	2		3	
IV–V	6		3	

Note
(a) See Appendix 3.4 for details of language and behaviour ratings based on the parental interview.

ASSESSMENT OF CHANGE

Because of the wide ranging scope of the intervention programme a variety of assessment measures was required and these needed to be sensitive to developmental progress and to changes in deviant behaviour. Although standard psychometric and language tests are valuable in assessing changes in children's level of competence, they do not adequately tap improvements in the *use* of skills. Additional measures were required that would reflect changes in the child's use of skills, in levels of competence in language and social relationships, and in the frequency and extent of behaviour problems. In assessing these changes a three-way approach to assessment was used:

(1) Standardized psychometric testing.
(2) Parental accounts of behaviour (by standardized interview measures).
(3) Direct observation.

Psychometric Testing

Many autistic children are difficult to test, and patience, ingenuity and persistence may be required. Nevertheless, we found that if the situation was appropriately structured, and if the tests were chosen to be appropriate for the child's level of ability, testing was possible and the scores proved to be reliable and valid indicators of later performance. Obviously, with most young autistic children items that required complex verbal instructions or a verbal response were avoided. However, in order to provide for comparibility between children, test procedures and approaches were kept consistent, while ensuring that the testing was done in a way to maximise the child's cooperation. In all cases, psychometric assessment (which was carried out by independent psychologists) was accompanied by detailed accounts from parents and teachers of the children's cognitive performance at home and at school, as well as by our own direct observations of the child.

The main IQ tests used were the Merrill Palmer scale (Stutsman, 1948) for children between the ages of 18 months and 6 years and the WICS for older children.

The child's language skills were also evaluated through standardized testing. The Mecham Scale (Doll, 1965), which is based on information from the parents, was used in matching children on language level initially. Follow-up assessments utilized the Reynell Developmental Language scales, which provide measures of both comprehension and expressive language (Reynell, 1969, 1977).

Information from Interview Data

A detailed interview was developed to obtain a full account of the child's language and social development, and the extent of his behaviour problems at home. This was largely based on the interview used by Rutter *et al.* (1970) in previous studies but also included a number of items from the schedules used by Wing and Gould (1979) in their epidemiological studies of autism. Because of the potential unreliability of retrospective reports, questions focused on the child's present level of functioning. The style of interview was based on that described by Rutter and Graham (1968) in the Isle of Wight studies. Thus, after a general discussion of the child's problems and progress, in which parents were able to air spontaneous complaints and problems, they were asked a series of systematic questions about different domains of children's behaviour. Codings were strictly standardized and were based on concrete examples of the nature or incidence of operationally defined behaviours. The severity and frequency of the behaviours were coded immediately after the interview. The schedule comprised 150 questions with the codings grouped into seventeen broad categories, which are detailed in Table 3.4.

Table 3.4
Categories of Language and Behaviour Assessed by Parental Interview

(1)	Language level and usage
(2)	Non-verbal communication
(3)	Language abnormalities
(4)	Language comprehension
(5)	General social responsiveness
(6)	Responsiveness to parents
(7)	Responsiveness to stimuli
(8)	Responsiveness to peers
(9)	Play
(10)	Abnormal responses to other adults
(11)	Obsessions/rituals
(12)	Mannerisms
(13)	Activity level
(14)	Mood
(15)	Behaviour problems at home
(16)	Behaviour problems outside the home
(17)	Developmental skills

Initial pilot studies indicated a high correlation between direct observations of the child at home and the severity of problems as reported by the parents. The reliability between independent raters was high and the measures also proved sensitive to changes over time.

(Details of the scoring procedures and the categories involved in the parental interview are fully described in Appendix 3.5.)

Direct Observation of Children's Behaviour

Direct observations of the child were used to provide information about the child's use of skills in his ordinary home environment. Because of the emphasis on the development of language, the most detailed assessments concerned changes in the child's use and level of language.

The observation system used was designed to measure both the *level* of children's language and *abnormalities* in language usage. This was important because, although virtually all autistic children are delayed in their language development, some language features, such as echolalia, that are abnormal later are quite normal in the early stages of language development. Thus, their interpretation is dependent, in part, upon knowledge of the child's developmental level. Syntactic and semantic features were noted separately and both were differentiated from language usage for social communication. These features develop roughly in parallel in normal children but this may not be the case in children with abnormal language development, as recent work by Bartolucci, Pierce and Streiner (1980) and Howlin (1984b) has indicated.

Measures of Language Level

A system of categorization was designed to tap the features specially relevant for the assessment of the language of young autistic children. The structures used in the analysis were objectively defined and showed high interrater reliability. All the language rules selected for analysis were based on normative data and

Table 3.5
Assessment of Children's Lanaguage Level: Measures of Syntactic Complexity

Morphemes	
'ing' progressive	(runn*ing*)
's' plural	(house*s*)
'ed' past	(want*ed*)
's' possessive	(mummy'*s*)
's' present	(run*s*)
Pronouns	(he,she,etc.)
Articles	(the, a, an)
Prepositions	(in, on, etc.)
Transformations	
Imperative	(Go away!)
Interrogative	(Are you going?)
'Wh' questions	(*Where* are you going?)
'Do' support	(*Do* you want to?)
Infinitive	(Are you going *to go*?)
Auxiliaries	(I *might* go)
Copula	(He *is* going)
Phrase level	
Complex sentences	(I have a hat and am running away)
Simole sentences	(I have a hat.)
Verb phrases	(running away)
Noun phrases	(the red hat)
Prepositional phrases	(on my head)

Mean morpheme length of utterance
[i.e. Total number of morphemes divided by total number of utterances.]

included structures that consistently develop early in the speech of normal children (Brown, 1973; De Villiers and De Villers, 1973). Table 3.5 outlines the particular rules that were assessed in this way. Details of reliabilities and definitions of categories are presented in Appendix 3.6.

Measures of Language Usage

In order to assess improvements in language functioning over the course of treatment, the system needed to reflect deviant aspects of language function as well as more language usage. The system used was described in full by Howlin *et al.* (1973a). Essentially, the measures covered fourteen different categories of utterance which fell into three main subgroups: (1) echolalic (both immediate and delayed) and other egocentric utterances; (2) socialized utterances, including prompted echoes and spontaneous remarks; and (3) non-verbal utterances and incomphrensible remarks.

Table 3.6 lists all categories used. The measures differentiated autistic and other linguistically handicapped groups of children, were sensitive to changes over time and were highly reliable (see Cantwell, *et al*, 1978). Further information about the definitions and reliability data for all categories used are presented in Appendix 3.7.

Table 3.6
Categories used in Analysis of Children's Functional Language

Echolalic and autistic utterances

(1)	Immediate repetitions of self
(2)	Immediate repetitions of other (exact, reductions and expansions)
(3)	Delayed echoes and stereotyped remarks (communicative and non-communicative)
(4)	Action accompaniments and thinking aloud
(5)	Metaphorical and telegraphic utterances

Socialized utterances

(6)	Prompted echoes (exact, reductions, expansions, mitigated and extensions)
(7)	Questions
(8)	Answers
(9)	Spontaneous remarks and comments
(10)	Directions or commands
(11)	'Automatic' utterances
(12)	Other (reading, etc.)

Other

| (13) | Non-verbal |
| (14) | Incomprehensible |

The Selection of Speech Samples for Analysis

Because language handicapped children tend to perform less well in a formal testing situation, all speech samples were collected during unstructured interactions with the mother at home. The mother was asked to interact with her child as she would ordinarily, and the observation sessions were scheduled for times when she was relatively free from other distractions. Recordings were not begun until the mother and child had become familiar with the presence of the observers, who remained as unobtrusive as possible during the recording periods. Pilot investigations indicated that a half-hour recording of the child and his parents, following an initial warm-up period, furnished a highly reliable estimate of the language used by the child and his parents throughout the day. These measures provided a good picture of the speech styles of children and of their parents and, in the absence of intervention, remained stable over repeated occasions (see Howlin *et al.*, 1973a).

Interactional Measures

The treatment programme had as its central feature an emphasis on helping parents to develop effective ways of promoting their children's normal development and of reducing deviant behaviour. Accordingly, it was crucial to monitor changes in parental behaviour in order to indicate those aspects of parental change that were most closely associated with improvements in the children.

Assessment of Mother's Language

Observations of parents' language to normal children have indicated that the way in which adults talk to children is strikingly different from adult conversation, in both tone and content. There are some associations between features of maternal speech and normal language development; in particular the use of questions, extensions and expansions of the child's speech tends to be positively correlated with language acquisition (see Howlin and Rutter, 1987). A frequent use of imperatives and negatives by parents, on the other hand, is associated with inhibited development (see Furrow *et al.*, 1979; Barnes *et al.*, 1983; Baker and Nelson, 1984). Although there is very little direct evidence to show that variations in maternal speech style affect normal children's language development either positively or negatively, work with linguistically delayed children suggests that certain language strategies, such as prompts, corrections and reinforcement, are associated with improvements in language development.

For the purpose of the present study, analysis concentrated on utterances that were associated with improved speech in language handicapped children. Utterances used frequently in the speech of mothers of young, normally developing children (e.g. questions, expansions and imitations) were also included. Remarks that were not directly related to children's use of speech (such as directions, general statements or interjections) were analysed separately. Utterances were divided into two principal categories: those designed to elicit, modify or reinforce verbalizations made by the child—so called 'language directed utterances' — and those designed to direct his activities or to provide more general information about his environment—'non-language directed utterances' (see Table 3.7).

Table 3.7
Categories Used in the Analyis of Mother's Speech

Language eliciting utterances
    (1) Questions
    (2) Answers
    (3) Imitations
    (4) Mitigated echoes
    (5) Reductions
    (6) Expansions
    (7) Directed mimicry
    (8) Prompts
    (9) Corrections
    (10) Reinforcements

Non-language directed utterances
    (11) Directions
    (12) Statements
    (13) Approval
    (14) Disapproval
    (15) Indirect modelling

Other
    (16) Interjections
    (17) Incomprehensible

It was hypothesized that language directed utterances would increase during the course of treatment, whilst non-language directed utterances should decline. The development of the language assessment procedures is described more fully by Howlin *et al.* (1973a). In summary, however, it was apparent that the measures used were applicable to parents of children with a wide range of language skills; they produced results comparable with other studies of parent/child interaction; interrater reliability was high, and, without intervention, the language profiles that emerged proved very stable over time for individual parents. This method of assessment has also been used subsequently in a modified form in a series of other studies of autistic children and their parents by Wolchick and Harris (1982). Full details of the categories used, and information about the reliability and stability of measures over time are given in Appendixes 3.8; 3.9 and 3.10.

Assessment of Mother–Child Interaction

Interactional measures were also needed to assess a variety of other aspects of children's functioning and maternal responses to them. Because of the particular problems faced by the families of autistic children none of the schemes available at the time were suitable for the present project; hence a new system was devised. Measures were required to discriminate between different families and to be sensitive to changes over time. Pilot work involved autistic children, children with sensory and physical handicaps, retarded children and those of normal intelligence. The age range extended from 3 years to teenage. Language abilities varied widely with some children mute, some with a few words only, and others with good speech. Pilot children came from families of different nationalities and language backgrounds and were of widely differing social class. By developing measures that could be used with such a heterogeneous group of subjects it was hoped that they would be sensitive to all the behaviours that might be observed during the experimental phase of treatment. The use of normal children in the pilot work was felt to be essential in that we did not want to concentrate entirely on deviant aspects of behaviour. The final version of the observation schedule comprised ten categories of child behaviour and nine categories of child communication. These are detailed in Table 3.8. Parental categories focused particularly on the content and style of communication to the child; the type of speech to the child (i.e. whether it was critical, directing, rewarding, etc.) was assessed, and the mother's responses to the child and her engagement with him in various activities were also recorded. The nature of any physical interactions, whether these were directing, hostile or affectionate, and instances of gestural communication were also monitored (see Table 3.9).

The children's behaviours and the adults' responses were recorded simultaneously. Observation sessions lasted for 90 minutes, and data were recorded both on audio tapes and on standardized assessment sheets. Two observers were always present in order to increase the accuracy of recordings

Table 3.8
Categories Used in the Observation of Children's Behaviour and Those Used in the
Assessment of Children's Communication

Behaviour	Communication
Not occupied	Total utterances
Task alone	Non-communicative verbalizations
Task with mother	Communicative verbalizations
Play alone	Non-communicative words
Play with Mother	Communicative words
Rituals/stereotypies	Non-communicative phrases
Object attachment	Communicative phrases
Out of room	Cries/distress
Disruptive/aggressive	Gesture
Non-cooperative	

Table 3.9

Categories Used in the Observation of Mothers' Behaviour and Those Used in the Assessment of Mothers' Communication

Behaviour	Communication
Ignoring child	Total speech to child
Interacting with observer	Praise
Interacting with other	Negative/criticism
No interaction	Confirmation
Out of room	Correction
Own task	Directions
Attention to child	Positive tone
Total contact with child	Negative tone
Neutral contact	
Directing contact	
Negative contact	
Positive contact	
Smiles	
Gesture	

and to avoid problems such as observer drift or reduced reliability over time (for more general discussions of the techniques and problems involved in naturalistic recordings, see Yule, 1980; Murphy, in press). Interrater reliability for all the measures was very high and details of these, together with details of the categories of behaviour observed, are presented in Appendixes 3.11 and 3.12.

Time Budget Measures

A standardized interview was used to assess the quality and quantity of interaction between mothers and children during the day. Many mothers were already spending large parts of their day with the autistic child at home at the outset of the project. Our aim was not to impose additional burdens on parents by insisting on greater involvement with the child. Instead, a major goal of intervention was to assist parents to use their time with their child more effectively. For this purpose it was necessary to establish how children were spending their days, how much of their time was spent in isolation or in interaction with other people, and what type of activities they were involved in throughout the day. A 'standard day interview', originally devised by Douglas *et al.* (1968) to document the activities of young normal children, was adapted for this purpose.

The original Time Budget of Douglas *et al.* (1968) had used a detailed interview with parents to ascertain the type and duration of the child's activities throughout the previous 24 hours. These activities were categorized to assess the intensity, duration and range of behaviours shown by parents and children. The results of our initial pilot investigations confirmed that the technique was

Table 3.10
Ratings for Intensity of Interaction

0 =	No interaction: mother and child involved in separate activities (often in different rooms)
1 =	Mother supervising/observing child from a distance. No direct interaction
2 =	Mother makes some attempt to engage child but this does not lead to interaction
3 =	Mother and child interacting together
4 =	Mother giving undivided attention to child; close physical and verbal contact

valuable in providing detailed information about a typical day for the autistic children and their families. Having established that the previous day had, in fact, been fairly typical of the child's routine, parents were asked about their activities over the preceding 24 hours. In order to establish the degree of proximity between children and parents through the day, parents were asked about the layout of the house and garden, and a simple plan was drawn, showing possible communication channels such as open windows, doors or food hatches. Any obstruction to vision, such as hedges and walls, were also noted.

The informant, usually the mother, was then guided through the preceding 24 hours, beginning with some easily identifiable events such as lunchtime. She was asked what the child had been doing at that time, how much verbal communication there had been between them, whether she could see and hear the child, and how long the activity between them lasted. The mother could then be prompted to describe the next identifiable activity and so on throughout the day. Accounts were linked as far as possible to specific activities, such as mealtimes or going to the shops, since this usually prompted more accurate recall of where the child had been and what he had been doing. Interviews were tape recorded, and additional notes were made about the time of day when the activity had occurred, who else had been there, and how much communication had taken place. For each behaviour coded, the position and accessibility of the child to other family members was noted. Thus, a parent or sibling might be actively involved in the child's behaviour; sitting in the same room but not interacting; or busy with their own tasks in a nearby room out of sight and hearing of the child. Using this information it was then possible to assess the intensity of interaction between parents and their children. Five different intensity levels were coded (see Table 3.10)

This type of assessment allowed us to rate the ways in which parents interacted with their child throughout the period when they were at home, or during any time when they were out together away from home. The only period not rated, when the parent and child were both at home, was when the child was asleep in bed. Otherwise the whole of the time that parents and children were at home was divided into these mutually exclusive categories.

Parental Coping Efficiency

Many intervention programmes with autistic children have shown that, once home support is discontinued, the maintenance of change can prove very difficult. The behaviour of both parents and children may rapidly revert to pre-treatment styles with the treatment initiated skills not being applied or adapted to deal with the onset of new problems. In order to ensure the persistence of treatment gains, parents need to be helped to acquire generally effective coping strategies together with an understanding of how to decide on the means of tackling new difficulties as and when they arise. In order to assess the success or otherwise of the treatment programme in this connection we developed an interview measure of parental coping skills.

Successful parental coping necessarily involves many different elements. Strategies that may be successful in reducing disruptive problems, such as tantrums, may not be the same as those needed to increase positive skills, such as verbal communication or play. Indeed, in some cases the former may actually interfere with the latter. For example, in our pilot work, one family found that limiting access to breakable items (such as cups and plates) proved an effective strategy in preventing their autistic son's tendency to smash crockery. However, since this meant that he was provided with only a baby's plastic bottle from which to drink, he had no opportunity to learn how to eat or drink in a manner appropriate to his developmental age.

Judgements about the effectiveness of parents' behaviour must be based on information about the child's actual progress or deterioration. The success of parental coping needs to be considered in terms of its effectiveness in promoting normal development or in reducing maladaptive behaviour, and not in terms of whether or not it coincides with some theoretical notion of what constitutes good management or of what 'should' work best.

On this assumption, our parental coping measures took into account eight main features:

(1) *Activity* Successful coping involves some type of action to alleviate the child's difficulties (to aid development or reduce problem behaviour).
(2) *Individuation* Parental behaviour should be tailored to the needs of the individual child (rather than rigidly pursuing some approach because it is supposed to be the 'right' thing to do or because it proved effective with some other child or in some other circumstances).
(3) *Response sensitivity* Parental coping style should be responsive to the effect on the child (that is, successful coping involves sufficient persistence to determine whether the approach is effective; followed by a change in approach if the coping style is not bringing about the desired consequences, and a continuation if it is working).
(4) *Strategy/tactics* Parents should have some general plan in mind, that includes some goal(s) for which they are aiming.
(5) *Safety/harmony* The parental behaviour should not result in persistent distress, the emergence of other problems, or undue restriction (an

approach that brought about behavioural control at the price of continuing fear, or constraints that significantly limited the child's opportunities for learning or for social development would not be regarded as successful coping).

(6) *Effectiveness* The parental tactic should be accompanied or followed by some changes in the child's behaviour in the desired direction.

(7) *Persistence* Successful coping should involve an appropriate degree of persistence in order to find some approach that succeeds in the objectives.

(8) *Goal appropriateness* The parental aims should be suitably adapted to the child's developmental level, and should include some realistic appreciation of what degree, type and rate of behavioural change is likely to be possible with their child at that time and in prevailing circumstances (that is, there should be neither undue pressure for the child to behave in ways inappropriately above his developmental level, nor too ready an acceptance that no gains are possible).

In order to assess their style of coping according to these eight principles, parents were systematically interviewed to obtain an account of what they actually did with respect to a predetermined list of possible problem areas. These comprised ten aspects of language, play and social development that tend to show autism-specific deficits; and thirteen types of behavioural difficulty, including those that are particularly associated with autism (such as rituals and obsessions), and those that arise in a wide variety of disorders (such as tantrums, sleep disturbance, fears, aggression, etc.). These are detailed in Table 3.11.

Parents were asked to describe how they had dealt with each of these problem areas (when applicable to their child), what they were seeking to accomplish, how they were attempting to do that, why they had adopted their particular tactic and why they had changed what they did (when that was the case). In order to relate parental coping to possible changes in the child's behaviour, systematic information was sought on the child's functioning 6 months earlier and concurrently. The interviews were tape-recorded and transcripts of the interview were then related by independent assessors (who were kept blind as to whether the subject was a case or control).

Three separate coping scales were employed. The first assessed the extent to which the parental behaviour was appropriate for the child's developmental level. The second assessed appropriateness of the degree of pressure used by the parents to influence the child's performance. The third provided an overall appraisal of parental coping skills, using the eight criteria listed above. Each feature was rated on a scale in which a low rating indicated highly efficient and adaptive coping strategies and a high rating reflected random, inconsistent methods of handling, an inappropriate level of pressure, or techniques that resulted in greater disturbance or distress. The use of several different scales, each assessing a separate dimension of parent behaviour, allowed coping to be judged as successful on one criterion yet not so on others. Thus, a parent might be using an appropriate amount of pressure for the child's development level but still be using a very inefficient technique that resulted in distress to the child.

Table 3.11
Coping Assessment: Problem Areas Assessed

Developmental items

(1)   Use of speech
(2)   Use of gesture
(3)   Comprehension of language
(4)   Ability to feed himself
(5)   Ability to dress himself
(6)   Independence at the toilet
(7)   Ability to wash and bath himself
(8)   Content of play
(9)   Ability to play with children
(10)   Attachment to other people

Disruptive items

(11)   Soiling
(12)   Enuresis—day or night time
(13)   Sleeping problems
(14)   Tantrums
(15)   Aggression to others
(16)   Self-injury
(17)   Destructiveness
(18)   Mannerisms
(19)   Ritualistic behaviour
(20)   Resistance to change
(21)   Attachment to objects
(22)   Phobias
(23)   Hyperactivity

THE INVOLVEMENT OF PARENTS IN TREATMENT

Following initial diagnosis, and once it had been established that a child fulfilled the criteria for inclusion in the project, families were approached and asked whether they wished to participate in the research project. It was fully explained that this would involve many assessments, interviews and observations, as well as return visits to the hospital for standardized assessments of the child. They were warned that observers would need to spend a considerable amount of time in the home and that parents' interactions with the child would be recorded. In addition, they would be required to keep diaries and records of changes in their autistic child's behaviour and would also be expected to find sometime during the day to spend alone with their child. In return for this intrusion on their time, the psychologists involved in intervention would visit the family at home on a regular basis and would advise on methods of management and techniques to develop new skills, especially those involving communication problems. The therapists would also attempt to provide help in arranging suitable education; they would liaise with other professionals as necessary and would generally offer support to the family over an 18-month period. Of all the families approached only one refused the opportunity to take part. Contact with the families varied according to the extent of their problems and their distance from the hospital. As already noted, intervention was generally most intensive during the first 6 months of treatment, becoming less frequent as time progressed.

The progress made by the children in the experimental group was monitored at 6-monthly intervals during the course of treatment. Comparisons with the short-term control group were made prior to treatment and then again following the first 6 months of intervention. Comparisons with the long-term control children were made at the end of the 18 month treatment period. In addition to the battery of standardized assessments described above, which was needed for detailed group comparisons, parents kept daily records of changes in their child's behaviour and also monitored changes following the implementation of specific behavioural programmes. The use of these more informal methods of recording enabled us to monitor the effectiveness of treatment over time. All parents were able to keep at least simple records of changes in their child's behaviour, and if behaviours did not show an improvement following the implementation of behavioural or other programmes, they could be modified quickly. Record keeping of this kind also proved highly reinforcing for many parents who were thus able to see for themselves that the time and effort expended on training programmes was, indeed, productive.

All parents in the project were extremely tolerant of the demands made upon them by therapists and in most cases were only too willing to carry out the recommended procedures. This high level of cooperation was, no doubt, due to the fact that treatment programmes were worked out carefully with parents in advance to ensure that the parents were entirely happy with the strategies recommended. Our aim was to adapt parents' *present* style of management in ways that would prove more effective and consistent, rather than completely to alter their style of coping. Parents were encouraged to restructure their time to use it more efficiently to help their child, and they were asked to set aside some 20 to 30 minutes each day for therapeutic purposes. However, it was made clear from the outset that parents should have ample time for themselves and for activities with their other children. This type of approach proved to be highly successful in maintaining parents' cooperation throughout the full 18 months of treatment.

The Role of Fathers in Treatment

The project was designed to improve *parents'* management strategies but in practice the main emphasis came to be on *mothers'* roles in changing the children's behaviour. Two fathers whose jobs allowed them a fair degree of flexibility played a very active part, but in most cases practical constraints markedly limited fathers' involvement. On the whole, mothers were responsible for day to day care and it was they who generally bore the major burden of coping with the child's problems.

Nevertheless, fathers were involved with their children at evenings or weekends and practical advice was offered on how they might better interact at these times. We sought to elicit fathers' cooperation in training programmes and tried to ensure that their approaches were consistent with the coping styles used by the mother.

Occasionally parents would disagree about the most appropriate form of intervention and in such cases our aim would be to evolve treatment methods that were acceptable to both parties—even if this involved a compromise on treatment effectiveness. It was preferable to have *both* parents using a slightly less effective technique than having one parent use a highly effective programme in which the other felt quite unable to take part. If parents simply could not agree on the particular treatment programme to be used we would try to encourage them to work on separate problem areas. In this way they were able to work effectively independently, even if they could not do so together. This technique worked well, for example, with a couple whose marriage had broken down. Although, they failed to agree on almost any other subject, they were united in their desire to do as much for their son as possible, and, working separately, they were able to deal successfully with a wide range of problems.

Because of the rather limited role of most fathers in treatment, assessment measures concentrated on mothers' behaviours and on the interaction between mothers and children. Ordinarily, there are differences between fathers and mothers in their styles of interaction with children (Wolchick and Harris, 1982). Nevertheless, our impression with these parents of handicapped children was that the fathers' response to the treatment programme was broadly comparable with that of the mothers. The one actively involved father whose interactions were assessed systematically over time changed in ways that were very similar to those shown by his wife. While we do not have evidence on whether or not children made greater progress when fathers played a more active role in treatment, it was evident that mothers who felt that they were being given practical support by their husbands were more willing to continue with treatment programmes.

Chapter 4

Fostering Language Development

Autistic children suffer from a wide variety of language problems including a general retardation in language development, deviant language features and a relative failure to use language or social communication. Each of these features requires a somewhat different set of treatment strategies which will be described in turn, beginning with the steps needed to increase simple skills in spoken language.

AIDING THE UNDERSTANDING OF LANGUAGE

Prompting and Fading Techniques

Many techniques may be used to develop new language skills. The early stages of treatment for autistic children with very little use or understanding of speech need to rely heavily on the use of prompting techniques. In essence, these involve some form of guidance that explicitly shows the child what is to be taught—in terms of the use of words or what words mean. Prompting is important in teaching novel responses to children whose behavioural repertoire is extremely limited. It ensures that correct responses are learned from the outset, and reduces the risk of the child developing undesirable or inappropriate behaviours. This is of considerable importance when teaching autistic children, who, if they learn an incorrect response, may well persevere with it. Bricker and Bricker (1972) pioneered the use of prompting techniques to increase understanding of language in very severely linguistically impaired children; their methods have been used with benefit in many treatment programmes, including our own.

In the preliminary stages of a programme designed to increase simple comprehension skills the child should be given a clear, simple command such as 'come' or 'sit' and then physically guided to carry out this action. Gradually, physical prompts or cues are withdrawn, or 'faded', until the child is able to respond to the spoken command alone. In the early stages of treatment it is often helpful to have two people working with the child, one of whom gives the command, with the other prompting him through the required action. Then, as less and less physical guidance is required, it is possible for teaching to be carried out by one adult alone. Once the understanding of simple commands is acquired in this way, new instructions that are more relevant to the individual child and his family can be introduced using similar methods.

As children become able to respond to a few commands in context, prompting techniques can also be used to teach the child to recognize particular object names. Thus, the child may be presented with an object that is of particular interest to him, such as a car or ball, and told to 'point to' or 'give me' the ball or car or biscuit or whatever object is chosen. At the same time physical prompting is used to ensure that the child reaches towards or points to the correct object. Gradually the amount of physical guidance proffered is reduced until the child is able to follow the verbal instruction alone.

When single items can be identified correctly in this way, the range of objects from which the child has to choose can be gradually increased. Thus, to begin with, the child might be required to identify 'ball' when this is the only object on the table. The next stage would involve teaching him to select the ball from a choice of *two* objects. Initially the objects on display would be made very different from each other in shape, function, colour and name. Physical prompting would then be used to ensure that the child chose the correct object on command. Errorless learning is particularly important in these early stages, and the teaching situation needs to be structured in such a way as to ensure that mistakes are kept to a minimum.

Gradually, however, as the child's responses become more reliable, direct physical prompts can be faded. For example, instead of actually putting the child's hand on the correct object, the therapist should eventually need simply to point towards it. Prompting can subsequently be reduced even further until the adult has only to look at the object in question in order for the child to respond. Then, in the final stages of the programme, as the child comes to respond to the verbal instruction alone, all non-verbal prompting should be removed.

Once the child is able to discriminate between very different pairs of objects in this way, more complex discriminations can be trained. Using the same sort of techniques children can be taught to discriminate between objects with similar sounding names or of similar size and colour, e.g. between a toy 'cat' and a toy 'car', or a 'ball' and a 'book'. Once this stage of language comprehension is reached, and physical prompts are no longer required except for teaching new or unfamiliar words, it is important to move on to teaching in more naturalistic settings. Instead of limiting training to set teaching times with a few specially selected objects, the child should be encouraged to identify an increasing number of items in his daily environment. Thus, he might be requested to point to a variety of different pictures in books, to select particular toys from his toy cupboard, or to point to items of food at the dinner table.

Inadvertent Prompting

Although deliberate prompting is an extremely useful technique in language training, as in training many other skills it is important to be aware of the power of inadvertent prompts. For example, unless training objects are systematically varied in size, colour and position, the child may well learn to select items 'correctly' not by name, but on the basis of other cues. Thus, the word 'car' may be responded to correctly, not because the child understands the name but because he learns that the object required is always red in color, or is always on the left of the therapist. Children may also become very sensitive to inadvertent cues given by the adult. Looking towards an object at the same time as naming it, for example, is a very natural response. However, if the child is to learn the object name in the absence of non-verbal cues, it is important that he does not become reliant on such prompting. Again, if training is extended to more naturalistic settings, the presence of incidental cues can be avoided more easily than in one-to-one training sessions with a very limited number of items.

The Use of Reinforcement

No matter how effective prompting procedures prove to be in the early stages of treatment, progress will only be maintained if, at the same time, the child is 'reinforced' for his attempts to cooperate. One of the fundamental principles of operant methodology is that behaviour is altered by its consequences. Some consequences will increase the likelihood that the behaviour will continue or recur. Those consequences, defined in terms of their effects, are termed positive 'reinforcers'. In general such reinforcers are pleasant and hence often they are called rewards. Nevertheless, it should be emphasized that a positive reinforcement need not necessarily be something that appears pleasant to other people. Sometimes apparent punishments can be rewarding, especially for autistic children who do not necessarily respond in the normal way to adult attention or other stimuli! The practical issue with each child is to determine which consequences increase and which decrease the likelihood *for him* that a particular behaviour will persist.

It will be appreciated that the 'theory' of reinforcement is in a sense tautological since reinforcers cannot be defined in terms that are independent of their effects. Nevertheless, this limitation does not matter in practice. What is important is the recognition that the consequences that immediately follow a behaviour will make a substantial difference to whether or not the individual continues with it or stops. Moreover, there is a high degree of predictability, over time and across situations, in the consequences that are and are not reinforcing for any one child. The principles are simple, concise and very helpful as elements in a treatment programme. In practice, however, finding effective reinforcers for handicapped children with a limited range of skills and interests can prove difficult. If the child shows no desirable behaviours, for example, how can he be reinforced? Conversely, if he shows no interest in conventional rewards, how can appropriate behaviours be encouraged?

What is rewarding to any individual child is a matter of empirical observation and not something to be decided by theory. However, particularly when teaching new skills such as language, it is essential to ensure that the training procedures are inherently pleasurable for the children. Thus, the materials and activities used in language training should, themselves, be interesting and rewarding so that they constitute intrinsic reinforcers. If developmental processes are to be enhanced through training, it is essential that they are not under the complete, direct control of external reinforcers; rather the child must come to *want* to use the skills because they are enjoyable or useful to him. If newly taught behaviours can be made enjoyable in their own right, the need for extrinsic reinforcers will be minimized. Indeed, the use of unnecessary 'rewards' for activities that children want to do for their own sake may actually take away some of the enjoyment and make it less likely that the behaviour will continue (Lepper, 1981).

Unfortunately, it is not always possible to ensure that the tasks themselves are sufficiently fun to be self-motivating and, particularly for children with minimal comprehension and communication skills, other reinforcers may need to be sought. Nevertheless, it would seem important to try to avoid the food rewards that proved the mainstay of much of the early clinic based language work with autistic children. Because of the problems of reducing such rewards over time (some autistic children may be extremely resistant to even minor changes in their 'Smartie' rations), the potential damage to the child's teeth, and the fact that many children have eating problems anyway, food rewards—except at mealtimes—must generally be viewed as undesirable. Instead, the use of alternative, tangible rewards needs to be explored. In the case of autistic children it is particularly important not to rely on conventionally accepted notions of reward; observations of the child are necessary to determine which reinforcers are most likely to be effective.

Such assessments, in the present study, led to the selection of a wide range of reinforcers. Several potential rewards would be identified whenever possible, since not all the predicted reinforcers proved effective, and others tended to lose their potency after a time.

The 'Premack Principle'

Often it was found that the most effective reinforcers were associated with the child's obsessional activities. For example, Graham, an 11 year old, was rewarded for his cooperation during language sessions by giving him bits of plumbing equipment. He would then spend many hours putting these together and dismantling them, and the promise of further equipment would encourage him to take part in future teaching sessions.

This use of behaviours, that occur frequently, such as obsessional activities, to reward and increase infrequent but more desirable behaviours, such as appropriate verbal responses, was first described by Premack in 1959. It is particularly valuable in the case of autistic children, who, as noted, may show little interest in conventional rewards such as praise, toys, etc., and for whom effective reinforcers can be very difficult to find. Again, the use of the Premack Principle involves close observation of the child in order to determine what he prefers to do when left alone. Any preferred, high frequency activities can then be used to reinforce less preferred low frequency ones. Although for many children in the study the high frequency activities tends to be stereotyped or obsessional in nature, these could be used effectively to build up more desirable skills (see Murphy, 1982).

A number of parents expressed concern lest this type of reinforcement might encourage repetitive, obsessional activities rather than reducing them, but such anxieties proved unwarranted. Instead, as the children's enjoyment of their newly taught skills increased, the need to indulge in obsessional activities decreased. Gradually the children became more responsive to conventional reinforcers and to adult attention, and began to spend longer and longer periods of time in constructive and appropriate activities. For example, Ben's co-operation in language sessions was reinforced initially by allowing him to play with his 'twiddlers' (which were anything from bits of grass or string, to belts or silk ties). As his simple language skills increased, the use of his 'twiddlers' began to decline and although he was never entirely without these, his dependence on them lessened considerably.

Ensuring the Effectiveness of Reinforcers

In the initial stages of treatment, particularly when trying to develop new skills, it is important to ensure the continued effectiveness of rewards. In order to do this, the child's access to them should be restricted as much as possible so that he is only allowed his favourite book, or bit of favourite string and so on, following a period of cooperative activity. Limiting access to specific tangible reinforcers in this way helps to ensure that the child is more easily able to understand the connection between receiving a reward and the production of desirable responses. It is also important that, whatever reinforcers are used by parents, they should be given *immediately* the child responds appropriately and that they should be given *every time* he responds. In order to emphasize this point Hemsley and Carr (1980) have suggested that reinforcers should always be given with a 'CICC'—that is, they should be clear, immediate, consistent and given contingently on the desired behaviour. This acronym proved extremely useful, particularly with parents who sometimes found it difficult to respond quickly and emphatically to their child's attempts to communicate.

The Reduction of External Reinforcers

Frequently, in the early stages of teaching a new skill, it is necessary to use tangible reinforcers to reinforce the child at every stage of the programme. As learning progresses, however, both the frequency and the nature of the reinforcers may be changed. Thus, once a behaviour is well established, parents may begin to reinforce the child intermittently, or after increasingly lengthy periods of cooperation. Or, they might reinforce alternate responses, rather than every one, and then move on to reinforcing one in three or one in four of the child's responses, until reinforcement is on a much less regular basis.

Intermittent reinforcement of this kind is more in keeping with what happens naturally in ordinary circumstances; it reduces the closeness of the reliance on external rewards, and in the long-term it has been shown to be more effective than the use of reinforcement each and every time a behaviour occurs (Bandura, 1969). Nevertheless, in the language training of autistic children we found that a fairly frequent reward schedule was required initially. The move to intermittent reinforcement is crucial but it should not be made prematurely.

Every form of tangible reward (including idiosyncratic ones such as the use of plumbing equipment mentioned above) was *always* paired with adult attention from the very outset. In this way it was hoped that, eventually, the child would come to respond to social reinforcement alone. Wherever possible, too, treatment programmes aimed to ensure that the skill being taught should eventually become self-reinforcing for the child so that extrinsic rewards are no longer required in order to maintain the behaviour. It was evident, for example, for many children that the use of simple spontaneous speech came to be intrinsically reinforcing in its own right, and external reinforcement from adults became less and less necessary.

Simple Command Training

These basic techniques of prompting and reinforcement were used to increase comprehension in 5 year old Patrick, who initially showed almost no understanding of language. He did not respond reliably to his own name, although he would occasionally respond to the command 'No' if this were given in a loud, firm voice. To begin with, simple, easily executed movements, such as 'sit' and 'stand', were introduced. These could be clearly demonstrated by his mother, who was able to prompt him physically to carry out the action immediately the command was given. At the same time immediate reinforcement (in Patrick's case, a bit of string) was given for cooperative responses. Gradually, physical prompting was reduced until he was able to respond to the verbal command alone. New commands were then introduced, and once gross motor actions were under verbal control, finer movements could be introduced. Actions such as 'clap' or 'wave', for example, were taught as part of a game sequence with his mother. 'Push' or 'throw' were taught in relation to playing cooperatively with cars and balls. By this stage, too, Patrick had come to enjoy these simple 'play' activities and the interaction with his mother so much that the need for additional reinforcers, other than praise and verbal encouragement, was minimal. His mother, too, enjoyed being able to gain his cooperation. Indeed, ensuring that parents, as well as children, receive some rewards and encouragement during teaching sessions is important since progress in the early stages of training tends to be slow and arduous, the first few commands often taking many weeks to acquire. Thereafter, however, learning seems to progress more rapidly and parents can go on to teach the child to understand many different words and more useful, everyday instructions.

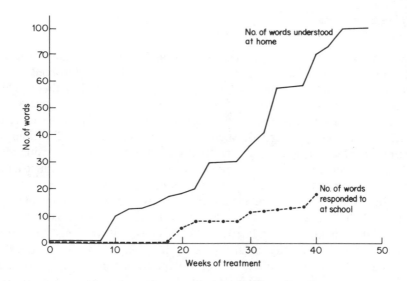

Figure 4.1 Acquisition of receptive vocabulary in 4 year old Patrick

Once Patrick was responding to a number of simple, one word commands, more complex commands of greater help in daily living were introduced. These included instructions such as 'Pick it up', 'Fetch your coat', 'Go to the toilet'. Each stage of the training procedure was similar, with the child being given physical guidance initially to ensure that he followed a command immediately and without errors. Then, gradually, physical guidance was reduced until he was able to follow the verbal command alone. Verbal reinforcement and immediate access to his 'twiddlers' was given consistently by his mother in the early stages of training. And, as already noted, the language activities themselves were also made as pleasurable as possible for him. Eventually, once appropriate responses were well established, non-verbal reinforcement was slowly reduced and although his mother continued to praise his efforts, this praise was given on a more and more intermittent schedule. Figure 4.1 shows the pattern of improvement in Patrick's comprehension over a year of treatment. It also illustrates, however, how few of these skills transferred spontaneously to his school, where comprehension training was not undertaken.

It was noticeable, in Patrick's case, as with many others, that when he first learned to respond to very simple instructions, the relationship between him and his parents began to improve dramatically. Perhaps for the first time, parents were able to control their child's actions through speech and the child himself could make some sense of the language impinging on him. This frequently resulted in a marked increase in social interactions and a corresponding decrease in tantrums and obsessional or ritualistic behaviours.

Shaping Procedures

Although reinforcement techniques play a crucial role in treatment, they are useful only if appropriate behaviours already exist to be reinforced. If such behaviours do not exist the child must be helped to develop them. This is frequently best done by building on existing (not necessarily very useful) skills that can be 'shaped' into more productive activities. Shaping is an extremely effective technique if carried through efficiently. However, as Tsoi and Yule (1980) pointed out, shaping is an art. 'It is the art of the therapist, using all the skills and ingenuity at his or her disposal, in getting the child to produce a novel response. Fortunately, it is an art form which has some ground rules.'

The fundamental ground rule is an initial analysis of the components of the particular behavioural goals to be achieved, followed by a systematic appraisal of the child's existing skills and deficits. On this basis, the therapist can develop a plan of how to modify existing skills in such a way as gradually to approach the ultimate objectives. Careful planning is crucial for the success of shaping programmes, since each step of the training procedure needs to be worked out in great detail. Gelfand and Hartmann (1975) suggested that the art of shaping is to 'think small': never to proceed too rapidly, nor by too great steps. Thus, each new step should follow closely from the previously established behaviour, so that the child is barely aware of the ever increasing demands being made of him.

In the early stages of training, it may be necessary to pair shaping procedures with prompting, either verbally or with physical guidance, to ensure that the child does not meet with failure at any stage. Immediate reinforcement, too, is also likely to be necessary. However, as the child becomes more proficient, the amount of prompting required can be reduced. External reinforcers should also be able to be dispensed with over time if each stage of the programme is carefully structured and ensures that the child is given immediate and well defined feedback on his performance. Although laying the first 'bricks' in a programme designed to shape increasingly complex behaviours can be slow and arduous process, once the early foundations are laid, more complex elements of the task can be introduced more rapidly.

The steps of each shaping programme must be kept small, but the ultimate goal of training should always be kept in mind. It is important that the child does not remain fixed at one level for prolonged periods of time. Instead he should be moved on to more and more useful skills step by tiny step. The child's progress at each stage will require careful monitoring so that, if learning proceeds more quickly than expected, the child may be moved through several stages of the programme in rapid succession. Conversely, if progress to another stage does not occur as rapidly as predicted an intermediate step may need to be introduced into the programme.

THE DEVELOPMENT OF EXPRESSIVE LANGUAGE

Shaping is a particularly valuable technique for the development of simple language skills in children who have some comprehension of language and who can also make a few spontaneous sounds. In increasing the child's repertoire of sounds a combination of prompting, reinforcement and shaping procedures is generally required.

To begin with, physical guidance may be needed to teach the child how to form his mouth into the correct shape and how to omit particular sounds. Open vowels sounds such as 'oo' or 'ah', which are simple to demonstrate and prompt, tend to be the easiest to train initially. At first, any effort that the child makes to produce the sounds should be rewarded, but gradually, at the same time as physical prompts are reduced, the child should be rewarded only for closer and closer approximations to the required sound. Once a range of discrete sounds can be reliably elicited in this way, the next stage is to combine these or 'shape' them into more complex sounds or word approximations. For example, if the child can already make the sounds 'k' and 'ah' separately, he can be taught to chain these together to form an approximation to the word 'car'. If he is able to make single sounds such as 'ma' or 'da' these, too, can be shaped into approximations for 'mamma' or 'dadda'.

A combination of prompting and shaping procedures proved successful in establishing a simple labelling vocabulary in 7 year old Jamie. Training in the early weeks focused on the imitation of mouth movements because of his apparent difficulties in producing certain sounds. This use of physical and verbal prompting resulted in a rapid imitation of simple sounds. By the end of 3 weeks of treatment he was reliably able to copy *all* consonant and most vowel sounds. His mother then began to 'shape' these sounds into word approximations. The names of several objects that were of particular interest to Jamie, such as 'cup', 'mat', 'brush' and 'baby', were rapidly established in this way. However, in naming items that he was less interested in he still tended to give the initial letter-sounds only. Additional prompts were needed to ensure that he produced the final syllable of words. Nevertheless, whereas to begin with his mother needed to pronounce the final sound clearly herself, by the end of 2 months of treatment prompts had been faded sufficiently so that she simply had to mouth the appropriate vowel or consonant sound. By the end of only 2 months of treatment Jamie was able to use approximately a dozen words, both in order to make his own needs known and to answer simple questions such as 'What is that?'

Individual Differences in Response to Training

The use of shaping procedures proved valuable in developing language skills in many of the children in the project. Initially, as in the training of comprehension

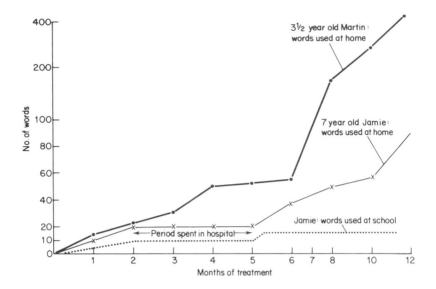

Figure 4.2 Acquisition of expressive vocabulary in boys aged 3½ and 7 years

skills, progress tended to slow. Gradually, however, the rates of acquisition of words began to increase. Nevertheless, the ultimate level of vocabulary reached varied considerably from child to child. Figure 4.2, for example, compares the development of vocabulary in Martin, a 3½ year old boy, with that made by an older boy, Jamie, using very similar treatment techniques. Although initially mute when treatment began, by the time he was admitted to school 9 months later, Martin's expressive language age, as measured by the Reynell language scales, was only slightly below his chronological age. By contrast, progress in the older boy was much less marked although vocabulary did increase steadily.

Moreover although Jamie made gradual progress over the course of a year, with his vocabulary increasing to over fifty words, his speech showed little of the flexibility that began to appear in Martin's utterances. The younger boy, for example, quickly and spontaneously learned to link two or more words together to generate novel utterances. This skill was never acquired by Jamie. The older boy's use of language also tended to be much more restricted. Thus, he would ask for things he wanted (mainly food) but he would never use words spontaneously to describe objects or comment on his surroundings. An additional problem was that few of the words he used at home generalized to untrained settings. As Figure 4.2 indicates, although his use of words continued to increase gradually at home, he showed much less progress at school, where there was little emphasis on the development of language. Similarly, during a period spent in hospital, when training was discontinued, no increase in vocabulary occurred.

As in other studies of autistic children, it appeared that unless useful language had been acquired by the age of about 6 or 7 years subsequent language skills were generally very limited. Although several of the older children in the project developed a simple labelling vocabulary following the implementation of training techniques, they rarely used these abilities spontaneously. The complexity of their utterances remained very restricted, and few showed any evidence of generating novel utterances.

Even amongst the younger children there were considerable individual differences in their rates of progress. To a large extent, the speed with which children acquired a labelling vocabulary in the early stages of training tended to predict the level of linguistic competence eventually attained. Martin, for example, whose rapid acquisition of vocabulary has already been described, was able, by the end of a year of treatment, to generate many new utterances. That is, he could combine individually learned words in novel ways to formulate untaught phrases and sentences. He also began to acquire new words incidentally and without any need for structured teaching. In addition, he was able to ask for objects that were not immediately present in his environment. Eventually, too, he was able to tell his parents a little about what had happened when he was away from them at school or on holiday. In contrast, Gary, who was of similar age, and apparent language level, showed a much slower rate of language acquisition initially and never progressed beyond the use of the specific structures taught.

THE MAINTENANCE AND EXTENSION OF LANGUAGE USAGE

Although the basic procedures of prompting, shaping and reinforcement proved valuable in teaching simple comprehension and expression skills, a variety of different approaches were also required when it came to increasing the complexity of language.

Changing Parental Speech Styles

Clearly, if language training were to be effective, it could not be restricted to brief but intensive periods of teaching. Instead, the child needed to be exposed to a language environment that would encourage his existing speech skills as much as possible throughout the day. Studies of normal children and their parents have identified a number of aspects of parental language that seem to be associated with improved, or delayed, language development on the part of their children (Howlin and Rutter, 1987; Wells and Guttfreund, 1987). High rates of imperatives, demands or negative remarks tend to be accompanied by somewhat slower language development in children. Parents who use higher rates of prompts, corrections, reinforcements, and particularly expansions or extensions of their children's utterances, tend to have children whose language development is relatively advanced. Obviously, caution should be exercised in assuming causality from these relationships, in that children will affect parents' speech as well as vice versa. However, certain styles of maternal speech do seem to affect language development more than others. There is also some evidence that the general style of verbal interaction used by mothers of autistic children may be less than optimal when eliciting or encouraging language. Wolchick (1983), for example, in her observations of normal and autistic children and their parents, found that non-language oriented utterances were significantly higher amongst parents in the autistic group. Gardner (1976) reported that mothers of autistic children were less successful in obtaining cooperative responses from their children than were parents of normal children. Horosborough *et al.* (1985) found that although mothers of autistic children were generally effective in adapting their conversational style to the linguistic abilities of their children, some of these adaptations were more successful than others. For example, the high frequency of questions used by the mothers in this group resulted in a high rate of responses from their children. Although discourse was better maintained in this way, however, these strategies also allowed more opportunity to the autistic child to respond with syntactically unrelated utterances.

Although it is clear that mothers of normal children are well able to adjust their speech according to the language level of their children, successful adaptation may be much more difficult when the normal, reciprocal qualities of conversational exchange are lacking. Interaction with an unresponsive, language impaired autistic child is far more difficult than interacting with a normally garrulous, socially motivated child. In some cases, parents in the present study adopted a rather immature style of conversation, which was perhaps effective in maintaining the child's cooperation, but not necessarily in improving his language level. Stevie's mother, for example, almost never used pronouns in her speech. She referred to herself and her husband as 'mummy' and 'daddy', rather than 'I' or 'we'. Instead of using the pronoun 'you', she tended always to address Stevie by his proper name. There was thus very little opportunity for him to learn to use pronouns correctly. Instead, he tended to avoid these and to use proper names, in much the same way as his parents did. If he did attempt to use pronouns these were usually confused and incorrect.

In contrast, other parents, particularly with children whose speech was very limited, seemed almost to have abandoned their attempts to gain the child's attention. Kevin's mother, for example, talked constantly to him, but in streams of long, often disconnected and complicated sentences. As it was often difficult for the therapists themselves to keep track of her constant flow of speech, it seemed likely that Kevin himself understood virtually nothing of the speech addressed to him. Many other parents, although adapting their language level more successfully to the child's linguistic skills, failed to respond to their child's incorrect or stereotyped utterances in more direct ways. Thus, very little correction tended to be given for inappropriate, immature or idiosyncratic utterances. Nor were children taught, by the direct use of prompts, to use more appropriate forms of speech.

Many parents, therefore, needed to be helped to develop more efficient ways of responding to their children's verbalizations. They were encouraged systematically to correct, immature or inappropriate utterances. They were also taught how to prompt the child to use more developmentally appropriate speech and were given feedback on how they might adapt their own speech more effectively to the child's level. For example, in dealing with Stevie's parents it was pointed out that although their rather 'babyish' style of interaction had probably been very helpful at an earlier stage of his development, it was currently less effective in encouraging more mature language usage. Parents such as Kevin's mother, on the other hand, were encouraged to simplify their sentence structures. In such cases it was important to teach parents to speak much more slowly and clearly and in ways which made it easier for the child to associate the spoken word with particular objects, instructions or activities.

Techniques derived from operant methodology, such as the use of reinforcements and corrections, were used to encourage suitable speech whenever this seemed appropriate. Findings from studies of normal psycholinguistic development were also incorporated wherever possible. Thus, parents were encouraged to respond to their child's utterances by elaborating or expanding on his speech in such a way as to provide him with a model for using more complex syntactic and semantic structures, as well as responding with a 'good boy' or 'that is right'.

Because of the lack of reciprocity and the severe developmental problems shown by autistic children it is unlikely that 'normal' styles of verbal interaction would be adequate to ensure optimal language development. A very different linguistic environment from that in which normal children develop is needed. Amongst other things this will require a much greater degree of structure and a much more intensive use of reinforcement, prompts and corrections by parents. However, in striving to achieve more normal language usage, factors that seem to be important in normal mother–child interaction should not be neglected. Successful language therapy needs to combine techniques derived from experimental studies of abnormal populations, with natural strategies identified in the course of studying normal mother–child interaction.

The Generalization of Language Skills

The failure to show generalization is a common problem even with normal children, if skills, not previously in the child's repertoire, are taught by the use of operant techniques (Patterson et al., 1973). Autistic children seem to have a particular inability to transfer skills learned in one setting to other situations or to other people and hence it was important to encourage generalization as much as possible. In the early stages of training, parents were taught to ensure that the child's response to a particular object name was not dependent solely on the presence of a specific item. For example, if the word 'cup' was taught, the child would be trained to respond to a variety of different cups, such as toy cups, mugs or pictures of cups. In developing a naming vocabulary, too, it was important to make sure that the child could label correctly any item from a particular class of objects, and that he would not attribute a particular label, such as 'chair' or 'book', to just one specific chair or book.

Since problems of generalization may also occur in transferring the skills learned with one therapist to another, parents were encouraged to involve as many other members of the family as possible in training. However, although it was generally possible to encourage other family members to work successfully in this way, it was not always possible to involve outsiders. Some schools were extremely willing to cooperate in extending the treatment carried out by parents. Others were less disposed to do so, and in the case of language training, cooperation by schools tended to be crucial for effective generalization. In Patrick's case, for example, the number of words and commands he understood increased steadily at home over a period of a year, as Figure 4.1 indicates. At school, however, where there was little emphasis on language training, progress remained very limited. Patrick was one of the three children in the experimental group who, although showing greatly increased comprehension skills, made no progress in the use of the expressive language over time. It is most unlikely that this was mainly because of the school's failure to cooperate in treatment; rather it is likely that Patrick's profound language deficit imposed constraints on what could be achieved. Nevertheless, more support from the school would certainly have been welcomed by his mother, and might have increased the rate of acquisition of a receptive vocabulary, even though the ultimate level of language reached may have remained much the same.

Environmental Modifications

In addition to encouraging parents to use styles of verbal interaction that would be most likely to foster language development, emphasis was placed on making the child's environment as conducive to language use as possible.

Even in the earliest stages of imitation training, it was made clear that all the child's 'words' should be associated *from the start* with familiar objects. Thus, it was essential that the objects used in training were those which the children had daily opportunities of naming and using. They were also, whenever possible, items which were of particular interest or relevance to the children, so that attempts at naming could be instantly reinforced by actually obtaining the object. Once children learned that their attempts at naming, no matter how primitive, could immediately increase their control over their environment, the motivation to use speech could be greatly increased, and other extrinsic rewards then proved much less necessary.

In addition, minor modifications to the children's environments were made to ensure that they could not easily gain access to desirable items without verbalizing their needs in some way. Many autistic children become extremely adept in ensuring that their needs are met without using any language at all. In many cases, parents will respond almost instantaneously to a shriek or cry from the child. In other cases, food or other items are simply left within easy reach so that the child does not have to communicate at all to obtain them. Asking parents to remove such items from the children's immediate reach, so that they were obliged to verbalize in order to have access to them, frequently resulted in a considerable increase in existing language skills.

If a child is born with a profound language deficit, and does not learn to speak for many years, the inherent difficulties involved in using language may well outweigh any extrinsic reinforcers. Even if a child *can* speak when pressurized or placed in a highly structured teaching environment, he is unlikely to do so in other settings where the 'press' to speak is much less, or if his needs can be obtained with less effort. If language skills are to be maintained and generalized, it is essential to make certain that they are of immediate, practical value to the child. Hence, it is vital that the language skills taught allow the child to attain goals that would be very difficult for him to acquire by other means. In other words, it is important that the language taught provides the child with much more immediate and effective control over his environment. The language skills taught must have what Goetz *et al.* (1983) have termed 'functional competence' for the child. The apparent failure of many language programmes may be a function of the lack of any practical value to the child of the skills taught and not a problem of lack of generalization as such. If the speech acquired is not functionally useful then the 'pay-off' for not using language will almost certainly outweigh any extrinsic encouragement to do so. Thus, lack of success may be due more to inadequate attempts to motivate the child to use his skills than to inherent difficulties of generalization.

Incorporating Psycholinguistic Approaches in Teaching

There is still considerable controversy as to whether language in handicapped children follows the same developmental patterns as in normal children; nevertheless, the weight of evidence seems to suggest that the linguistic rules acquired easily by normal children are also the easiest for language delayed children to acquire. In view of this, all the language training programmes were based, as far as possible, on findings from research into normal language development. Thus, in simple expressive training, the sounds or sound combinations taught were those that appear earliest in the speech of normal children. When work on single words began, nouns relating directly to the child's own interests were taught first. These included the names of family members, pets, food, cars and clothing, all of which are among the earliest items of vocabulary to appear in normal speech.

As soon as children progressed from using single word utterances, attempts were made to foster a more elaborate and creative use of language by teaching the syntactic and semantic rules that are acquired early in the development of young normal children. A number of early studies with autistic children had reported on the successful teaching of simple grammatical rules and in the present study shaping procedures were used to increase the complexity of children's utterances. Thus, once a fairly extensive noun vocabulary had been established, other parts of speech were gradually introduced and combined with existing elements in the child's repertoire. By using simple combinations of nouns and verbs, the child was able to describe his own actions and those of others around him, whilst the use of simple adjectives helped to increase general descriptive skills.

Each stage in the teaching programme followed a similar course. When new speech forms were introduced these were taught in the same gradual way: prompting the child to imitate the correct structure, rewarding his attempts for doing so, and then gradually reducing prompts until he was able to use the words spontaneously. When the child was able to use many single words, these would be shaped into more complex utterances such as adjective *plus* noun *plus* verb. Again, when words began to be paired together, the focus was placed on teaching semantic relationships that appear in the early phrase speech of normal children. The main rules taught were possessives (as in 'Johnny's hat'), locatives ('on the chair'), noun plus action ('Mummy sleeps'), action plus object ('hit ball') and demonstrative and attributive phrases ('that book', 'red car', etc.). The morpheme rules taught were also those that appear early in children's speech: i.e. the 'ing' ending of the present progressive (running, jumping, etc.), the 's' ending on plurals and possessives (cups, mummy's, etc.) and simple verb tenses. Structures that are known to present problems for young normal children before the age of 4 or 5 were avoided. The transformations taught, again, were those that are normally acquired early, such as the use of imperative and question forms (see Brown, 1973; De Villiers and De Villiers, 1973; Clark and Clark, 1977, for a discussion of early language development).

A number of training 'rules' that seemed to be important in facilitating normal language learning were also incorporated within the training programmes. Amongst these 'rules', that appear to be common to many cultures, is the fact that semantically and syntactically consistent structures are acquired earlier and more easily than irregular ones. Phrases involving a simple noun–verb–object order are acquired before those involving more elaborate ordering. Full forms of a structure (such as 'I am', 'you are') tend to be used before contracted forms (such as 'I'm', 'you're', etc.). Finally, short but syntactically correct sentence models seem to be more effective for teaching them than abbreviated sentence forms (see Slobin, 1973, for a fuller discussion of these 'rules').

Although few of the autistic children in the present study acquired the facility to generate novel utterances with the ease and flexibility of normal infants, the teaching of language rules in this way seemed to have at least limited success. Thus, those children who did acquire phrase speech showed similar patterns of acquisition to normal children. They also showed the errors of overgeneralization of rules that are characteristic of normal children. Thus mistakes such as 'sheeps' 'wented' or 'thems' occurred frequently. Such mistakes indicated that children had learned the basic morpheme rules, although they had not necessarily learned specific instances of when these rules are *in*appropriate. Like normal children, who frequently make up their own words in the early stages of language acquisition, autistic children would apply morpheme endings appropriately to their own neologisms. Stevie, for example, complained that the radiator in his room had been 'utting' at him—'utt' being his word for the noise radiators make. Martin spontaneously described a barking dog as 'woofing', whilst Graham, instead of describing a pan of water as boiling, announced that

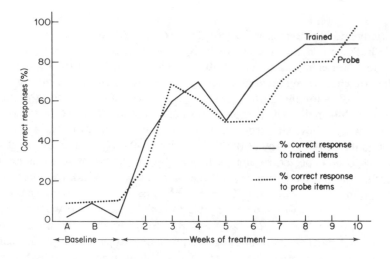

Figure 4.3 Use of singular and plural verb forms during training

it was 'hot raining', 'hot rain' being his own term for steam. Similar evidence of rule acquisition was found in all the children who began to use utterances of two or more words in length.

Children also demonstrated the ability to combine several syntactic rules in novel ways. Thus, children who were taught in formal teaching sessions to use plural and singular noun and verb constructions were then able to use these correctly in other settings. For example, children were able to use such rules when describing events that had happened during the day when their parents were not present. Occasionally specific probes to test generalization were built into training sessions. Whilst training 5 year old Matthew to use singular and plural noun and verb phrase cnstructions (i.e. 'it is a boy', or 'they are boys'), probe items, on which he had not been trained, were deliberately inserted into the session. Figure 4.3 shows the frequency of correct responses for both trained and untrained items; although accuracy was slightly less on the untrained items, the pattern of improvement was very similar for both sets of items.

Improving Conversational Skills; The Use of Role Play Techniques

As autistic children grow older and more competent in their use of spoken language, other deficits tend to become apparent. Language is frequently formal and pedantic, and often the older autistic child's language remains repetitive, obsessional and socially inappropriate.

Many of these subtle deficits have proved far more resistant to change than the grosser verbal handicaps of young children. However, role play techniques can be used to teach the older child or adolescent to increase his range of conversational topics. For example, he can be taught how to introduce himself in company and how to respond to common social questions—such as 'How are you', 'What's your name' and so forth. Specific rules may also need to be laid down about not engaging others in obsessional topics; not going on and on at great length when a single sentence reply is all that is required, and not indulging in repetitive questioning. Although such techniques can help young people to appear more 'normal' in the company of others, increasing conversational skills to a level where they can freely *initiate* sensible conversations is a far more difficult goal to attain. Many of the children involved in the present project were too young to be expected to engage in lengthy, independent social exchanges with unfamiliar adults. However, set rules about *whom* to talk to, *what* to talk about and how long to talk for, did prove of some value in making them more socially acceptable in shops or buses. Certain skills associated with successful social communication, such as looking towards or smiling at one's conversational partner, or indicating the particular objects being talked about by looking at or pointing at them, can also be taught to some degree. For older children the use of video recordings which could be played back to them as a form of feedback, proved very useful here. However, the finer modulation and 'meshing together' of these skills generally proved much more difficult to teach.

Improving Abstract Language Skills

The ability to deal with abstract linguistic concepts was beyond all the children in the study at the time of treatment (although some of the older ones now show greater evidence of abstract abilities). Nevertheless, in order to lay the foundation of simple abstract skills, it was found useful to teach children ways of expanding their existing language skills. Teaching synonyms, for example, was found useful, not only in increasing vocabulary but in helping children understand more about the flexibility of language. Metaphors, too, often presented problems.

Stevie, for example, was very upset by the use of metaphors and similes and tended to take their meaning literally. A remark such as 'It's raining cats and dogs' would result in his sitting by the window all day screaming 'Where's the cats, where's the dogs? It's not raining animals; it's raining water.' A dictionary was made up for him in which simple definitions of common similes were given; he was encouraged to write down his own definitions of similes or metaphors which he subsequently came across. Once he became aware that such utterances had a definable, albeit not a literal, meaning he accepted their usage, although he did then tend to bombard visitors with the most arcane similes he could find and demand their definitions of them.

Such strategies can have only very limited effects on the fundamental deficit in dealing with abstract concepts that is so characteristic of autistic children. However, if used in association with techniques to develop other areas of imaginative functioning, they may at least form a bridge that enables the less handicapped autistic child to pass from purely concrete functioning to the level of simple abstract concepts.

REDUCING ABNORMAL LANGUAGE USAGE

Although delays in the development of language are common to almost all autistic children, it is abnormalities in the use of language, rather than the failure to acquire speech, that is particularly characteristic.

In the early stages of normal language development speech may well be repetitive and echolalic to some degree. However, whereas in normal children such utterances tend to disappear around the age of 3 to 4, autistic children may persist in the use of such utterances for many years, often to the exclusion of appropriate spontaneous speech.

Differential Reinforcement Procedures

The use of reinforcement techniques to establish new and appropriate behaviours has already been discussed. However, reinforcement is also an extremely powerful agent for the maintenance of inappropriate behaviours. Many parents and teachers, having lived so long with the child's abnormal style of speaking, tend to respond to bizarre and stereotyped utterances as if they were entirely appropriate. In Simon's case, for example, the phrase 'Morris Mummy' was enough to indicate to the adults around him that he wished to go out, a desire that they would duly fulfil. In fact, Simon had perfectly good grammatical speech but the phrase had arisen when they lived out in the country and had an old Morris car. In those days the only way for him to go out was to be taken by his mother in the Morris, and hence the phrase had been entirely appropriate. Ten years, several cars, and a much greater degree of language sophistication later, this was scarcely the case, and yet this immature and stereotyped utterance still met with the required response from adults.

The power of differential reinforcement lies in shifting the attention or reinforcement that the child receives for inappropriate speech or activities to more behaviourally or developmentally appropriate ones. In other words, although the child is given the same *amount* of rewards and encouragement, their use is differentially patterned to ensure that only appropriate behaviour is reinforced whereas inappropriate behaviour is not. Obviously, if the child's repertoire does not include appropriate forms of utterance, these will have to be taught. Thus, differential reinforcement techniques will often need to be used in conjunction with prompts for the correct form of utterance. If the child is consistently prompted and rewarded for using the correct form of utterance, whilst inappropriate utterances go unattended, there is likely to be a marked increase in the use of appropriate speech. Some parents, having desperately tried to encourage their child to speak in the early years, were worried lest these techniques might result in their childen ceasing to talk again. However, as long as the child obtained adequate attention for appropriate speech, this did not occur. Instead, as inappropriate, stereotyped utterances declined, socialized and communicative speech showed a steady increase.

Duncan, for example, was a 5 year old whose speech was predominantly echolalic and repetitive. Pronoun reversal was common as in 'Do you want to

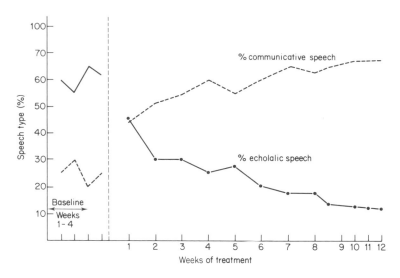

Figure 4.4 Changes in communicative and ccholalic speech during treatment

go out' instead of 'I want to go out' or 'Would you like to go to the swings now, Duncan?' When commenting on his own or others' activities he would use phrases that he had heard his mother or teachers use (sometimes to their considerable embarrassment). Although his mother showed a good deal of patience in dealing with the many behavioural problems shown by Duncan, she was intensely irritated by his echolalic and repetitive speech. Unfortunately, the irritation that she clearly felt over this resulted in Duncan receiving a great deal of attention for such remarks. At the same time, he received very little guidance as to how he *should* be speaking. It was suggested that his mother should alter *her* responses by prompting and reinforcing only the correct form of utterances. As she learnt to prompt and respond only to appropriate speech, echolalic remarks declined steadily. After 3 months of treatment, Duncan's speech was almost entirely non-echolalic, although occasional echoes still occurred if he failed to understand a question or if he became confused over pronouns. Figure 4.4. shows the steady increase in his socialized speech over this time.

Differential reinforcement procedures may also be valuable in reducing stereotyped or jargon utterances that are deliberately used to gain attention. Swear words are a particularly notable example of this, but autistic children may also develop their own idiosyncratic utterances. Seven year old Sam, for example, came from an extremely deprived family in which his mother strived hard to keep the very cramped flat in which they lived clean and tidy. In general, Sam used only single word utterances and received intermittent attention for these. However, he had learned that the one way of getting instant attention was to comment on the dirtiness of his environment. Thus, the only two-word phrases that he used began invariably with the word 'dirty' (as in 'dirty baby',

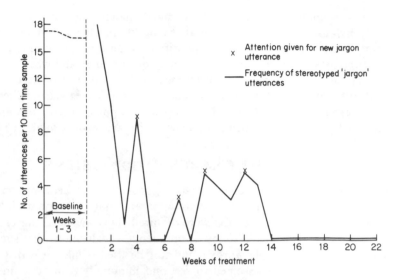

Figure 4.5 The use of 'extinction' to reduce inappropriate utterances

'dirty mummy', 'dirty carpet', etc.), the one adjective calculated to provoke his mother into a fierce rage. Despite severe punishments for this, the use of such phrases seemed to be increasing. Initially his mother found it very difficult not to respond to these deliberately provocative verbalizations. However, eventually, as nothing else appeared to be effective, she attempted to make use of differential reinforcement to encourage alternative and more appropriate speech. Once she was able to ignore the provocative remarks, whilst encouraging his use of acceptable speech, the frequency of Sam's 'dirty' speech reduced dramatically. Unfortunately, he found that he was still able to get attention by inventing new and equally infuriating phrases from time to time. These invariably met with an outburst of anger from mother, with the consequence that they increased rapidly in frequency. Gradually, however, as she learnt to ignore such phrases fairly successfully, and was able to attend much more consistently to appropriate speech, the use of jargon utterances almost entirely disappeared. (See Figure 4.5.)

Reducing Environmental Demands

Although echolalic and repetitive utterances are generally best dealt with by the use of differential reinforcement, it is important to be aware that their use may indicate that excessive verbal demands are being placed upon the child. Echolalia frequently reappears in situations when the child is unable to understand what is going on, or conversely, when his own verbal skills are inadequate for the demands of the situation. Much the same happens with young normal children, and occasional instances of echolalia may well be a sign that the child is unable to cope with the verbal demands made of him. In such instances, obviously, it is more appropriate to modify the demands made on the child rather than directly attempting to modify his utterances. Thus, if echolalia arises in circumstances where the child seems not to understand what is being said, the clarity and simplicity of utterances to the child may need to be improved. If echolalic and repetitive utterances occur because the child does not have the verbal skills with which to respond appropriately, prompting techniques will be required to ensure that such skills are made available to him.

AUGMENTATIVE COMMUNICATION SYSTEMS

Although much of our therapeutic work tended to concentrate on the development of *spoken* language it was apparent that for certain children alternative forms of communication were required. This was particularly so in the case of children who made so few spontaneous vocalizations that shaping procedures to develop simple words could not be used. Children with severe comprehension deficits also seemed to respond minimally to programmes to increase spoken language.

In choosing the appropriate form of alternative communication, procedures similar to those described for the development of verbal skills were followed. Thus, a *functional analysis* would be undertaken to determine the child's particular skills and weaknesses. *Prompting* and *fading* procedures would be used to develop new skills; and *shaping* would be used to develop the child's existing skills into some form of communicative response. *Reinforcement* would be used to increase the rate of the child's attempts to communicate. *Environmental modifications* would be imposed to ensure that the child used his newly acquired skills as effectively as possible. Finally, the generalization of communicative behaviours would be encouraged by ensuring that they were of *functional value* to the child, and that they were responded to in as wide a range of settings as possible.

The Use of Simple Gestures

On the whole, the more limited the child's general level of ability, the simpler the form of communication system taught.

For example, Gary was a 3 year old boy with a non-verbal IQ of 60 who made a few sounds but who could copy simple gestures fairly readily. Imitation of gestures was systematically encouraged by the use of physical prompts and reinforcement. In this way he was taught to copy simple signs for a number of objects that he frequently needed during the day; notably 'drinks', 'toilet', and his favourite activity, 'jigsaws'. Gradually, his mother's prompts were reduced until he could use such signs spontaneously to indicate his wishes. At the same time, he began to vocalize more when using these signs although the vocalizations were generally rather indistinct. Unfortunately, generalization was made difficult in this case because his mother was reluctant to insist that he use signs for a wider variety of objects. The range of signs he used remained extremely limited until he began to attend school, when more attempts were made to increase his signing. A few more signs were acquired here although, again, because of lack of generalized training, these remained few in number and were restricted to a few specific activities.

Teaching More Complex Forms of Non-Verbal Communication

Alternative communication systems can also be developed for children who have motor difficulties or who show little motivation to communicate by signs or gestures.

Four year old Thomas, for example, although having a non-veral IQ of over 120, showed virtually no understanding of spoken language nor did he show any particular desire to communicate. Because of his high level of non-verbal intelligence he was able to obtain more or less whatever he wanted by himself, and attempts to teach him to use either simple sounds or gestures to communicate had met with no success. Instead, his excellent visuo-spatial skills, and his overriding interest in complex patterns and picture matching, were used as a basis to increase his motivation to communicate.

To begin with, his picture matching activities were encouraged and reinforced (although, in fact, external rewards were generally unnecessary because of the great enjoyment he clearly obtained from such activities). Shaping procedures were then used to improve the potential usefulness of this skill. Thus, instead of simply matching pictures, he was taught to match pictures to familiar household objects (see Figure 4.6). The distance between the card and the relevant object was gradually increased until, by the end of 3 weeks, his mother could use the cards, together with a verbal instruction, to get him to fetch a variety of objects around the house. By the end of this stage of training, matching skills could be shaped into even more complex activities and he was rapidly taught to match pictures to written words. Then, gradually, pictorial cues were faded until he was able to match written words to the appropriate objects.

To begin with, the relationship between the written word and the object was taught in a formal teaching session, with written labels and related objects being placed on the same table. But, systematically the distance between the written labels and the objects was increased, until by the end of 2 months his mother was able to use written instructions to get him to fetch clothing and objects around the house. Single words were then expanded to two word phrases. Adjectives and verbs were introduced, and he was soon able to identify objects of different colour, size, gender and position. Thus, he could respond appropriately to written labels requiring him to identify 'big blue triangle' 'baby crying' or 'cat in box'. In addition to the child's own activities, puppets, dolls and pictures were all used to extend the scope of teaching sessions.

By the end of a year of treatment Thomas was able to respond to over a hundred written labels in this way. At the same time, his comprehension of verbal commands seemed to increase slightly. His verbal comprehension was

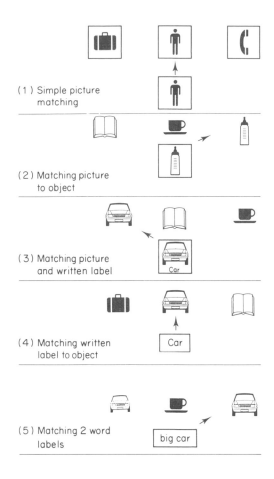

Figure 4.6 Steps in teaching a simple sight vocabulary

never as well developed as his comprehension for written materials; nevertheless, by the end of this period, he was able to respond to approximately twenty verbal commands without additional written cues. Thomas's understanding of spoken language has continued to improve since the intervention programme and he now responds entirely to spoken instructions. There has been no generalization from non-verbal to verbal forms of productive communication, although this has occurred in some published reports (see Kiernan, 1983, for a review of these). Thomas still remains virtually mute but he is now able to use a 'Communicator', on which he types out his needs very effectively, and he responds readily to other people's attempts to communicate with him.

Chapter 5

The Facilitation of Social Development

The social impairment in autism, like the language deficit, affects many areas of functioning. It also presents changing problems as the child grows older. In much the same way as with language programmes, therefore, treatment needs to be adapted to the specific needs and developmental level of the child. In dealing with young children the emphasis tends to be more on the use of techniques that are deliberately intrusive and highly structured in order to increase the frequency of social interactions. With older children treatment has focused on increasing their independence, and also helping them to appreciate and modify their social abnormalities.

THE USE OF INTRUSIVE TECHNIQUES TO INCREASE SOCIAL INTERACTION

Although a number of authors such as Tinbergen and Tinbergen (1983) have suggested that autistic withdrawal may become worse if deliberate attempts are made to foster interaction, it is clear from both clinical and experimental studies that this is not the case. Instead, it is when autistic children are *not* required to cooperate in social or constructive activities of any kind that stereotyped and ritualistic activities increase and social responsiveness declines (Volkmar and Cohen, 1982).

Techniques using deliberate intrusion into the child's solitary behaviours may be required in order to structure interactions to ensure that the autistic child becomes actively involved in social activities. If these interactions are to become meaningful and pleasurable to the child, his own special interests need to be harnessed. Accordingly, parents were taught how to engineer solitary play situations so that their involvement was needed if the child was to be able to finish lining up his toys, building towers, or playing with jigsaw puzzles. This could be done by ensuring that not all the material required by the child was immediately available to him. Thus, parents might withhold a piece of puzzle or particular building block or a toy needed by the child. In order to complete the activity in which he was involved the child would then need to make some sort of response to the adults, e.g. making eye contact, reaching out to them or verbalizing his needs in some way. By means of such structured interference the child can be helped to recognize the value and necessity of social interactions. Obviously, parental intervention should not stop at this point and once the child has made some initial contact, the adults can go on to become more involved in his activities. In this way the child comes to learn that social interaction is not only useful but can also be pleasurable for him. The introduction of physical contacts such as tickling, jumping and other action games may also serve the same purpose.

As acceptance of adult involvement increases, the tendency to spend time in solitary, obsessional activities often begins to decline. The frequency and quality of social interactions improves and the complexity of the child's social play can then be steadily increased.

Stevie's mother, for example, was able to use intrusive techniques effectively to modify her son's perennial collecting habits. When our intervention started he was obsessed with collecting 'Ladybird' books. The content of these was immaterial to him, but he insisted on having each new book in the series as it came out. Previously, in order to keep the peace whilst out shopping, his mother had brought him every new book that he wanted and allowed him to add it to his collection. In the early stages of intervention she continued to buy him the books he requested. However, instead of immediately handing these over to him, new books were withheld until mother had read a little out loud to Stevie, and he, in his turn, had read to her. This interference, although greatly resented at first, was gradually accepted by Stevie as inevitable. As time went on he began to enjoy his mother's reading of the books, and would enter into simple conversations with her about the theme of each one. In this way, what had been an essentially unsociable, ritualistic activity was turned into a mutually enjoyable experience for mother and child.

It is important to be aware that improvements in social interaction are beneficial, not only for the child, but also for his parents. Abnormal eye gaze, lack of reciprocity, and the failure to respond to parents' social overtures, may have an extremely adverse affect on parents' reactions to their children over time. The quality of parental interaction will be greatly influenced by the children's behaviour and, in the case of very unresponsive autistic children, it takes an unusually persistent parent to keep on playing and talking to the child with the same energy, interest and enthusiasm that characterize normal parent-child interactions. Without help, many parents of autistic children are likely to lose some of their involvement with a child who seems to care very little whether they interact with him or not. Parents need to learn how to intrude effectively into solitary activities. If this intrusion is successful and is also enjoyed by the child, he is likely to become more responsive, thereby reinforcing and encouraging more social initiation on the part of parents. In this way, very simple, and to begin with rather artificial, ways of interacting may become the basis of much more sociable and pleasurable activities for both children and parents.

The Encouragement of Play with Brothers and Sisters

Even when relationships with adults improve, most autistic children continue to show very abnormal peer relationships, and may well avoid contact with other children altogether. However, by carefully structuring the child's environment so as to ensure that other children are involved in playing activities, it is possible to increase peer group activities and interactions with brothers and sisters.

Thomas's social interaction with his younger sister, for example, was systematically increased over time by the careful restructuring of his play. To begin with, he rarely initiated social contact and although he would occasionally seek out his parents he avoided other children almost completely. Instead he spent hours alone, totally absorbed in highly complex constructional activities. He was extremely intolerant if his sister intruded upon these in any way, and her attempts to do so generally led to fights and disruption. Again, a combination of prompting, fading and reinforcement techniques was used to encourage more pro-social behaviour. At first, he was reinforced for allowing his little sister to sit close to him while he was involved in his solitary play activities. Gradually closer and closer proximity to his sister was rewarded, until he would allow her to sit next to him without protest.

His mother then began to intrude on Thomas's solitary activities. These generally involved extremely complicated puzzles, matching tasks and a variety of constructional games. His mother would deliberately divide the pieces required to finish the game between the two children. Each child was then dependent on the other's move for the activity to progress. To begin with, physical guidance was needed in order to ensure that the children placed their particular pieces in turn. Physical guidance was rapidly faded, however, as they learned to complete tasks together quickly and harmoniously. Thomas's rewards came from being able to complete the game. His sister was rewarded by praise from her mother and also by being allowed to join in games from which she had previously been excluded.

Over time further joint activities were introduced. These were somewhat less structured than the original tasks and included musical games, bubble blowing games and simple card games. Thomas's mother then began to introduce his *older* sister into the situation, which meant that the children now had to wait for two or three turns before being allowed to continue play themselves. Thomas rapidly began to show enjoyment in group activities of this kind (such as lotto, jigsaws, cards and ball games), and by the end of the summer holidays during which the programme had started, he was involved in a wide range of activities with both his sisters. Throughout this period his solitary play was interrupted whenever possible, making access to toys contingent upon a social approach towards an adult or one of his sisters. As he came to derive greater and greater enjoyment from group activities, his attempts to spend time in solitary play steadily decreased.

Developing Imaginative Play Activities

The ability of autistic children to interact with their peers is restricted, not only by their lack of social initiation, but also by their inability to take part in the imaginative games that constitute such a major part of normal children's play. Once more, the basic procedures of reinforcement, shaping and prompting were used to teach very simple play activities.

For example, although Matthew systematically collected every teddy bear he found, he did not use these in any imaginative way. He was deliberately taught, therefore, how to involve them in more complex activities such as dressing and undressing them, putting them to bed or offering them pretend cups of tea.

Patrick showed a considerable interest in cars, but his 'play' with them was limited either to spinning their wheels or lining them up in endless rows. In his case, as well as intruding into these ritualistic activities, his parents deliberately prompted more complex play with the cars. Thus, he was encouraged to drive the car to a garage, or to collect another passenger in it, or simply to crash into his parents' toy car.

Stevie, too, showed little capacity for imaginative play, although his command of spoken language was excellent. He was taught, using modelling and reinforcement techniques, to imitate and then carry out simple pretend acts —e.g. 'Show me how you laugh', 'Show me how you cry', 'Show me how you go to sleep'. Later, prompts were faded and more complex activities introduced— such as 'Be a car', 'Be a horse', 'Be a frog'. Later still he was given toy dolls and animals and taught to carry out such activities as 'Put dolly to bed', 'Give teddy his supper'. Play in the bath or sandpit was also used to encourage him to 'cook' pretend meals or to make cups of tea and offer them around.

Eventually, he began to enjoy such activities and to carry them out spontaneously. He also began to create his own 'dolls' out of small scraps of material and would play for quite long periods with these. Admittedly, his play, like that of most of the children, remained at a simple level and retained a number of obsessional features. He would, for example, create complicated 'family trees' for his cloth dolls and would impress visitors with the genealogy of his 'family'—such as 'Miss Red and White Gingham is a second cousin twice removed to Mr Blue Rag who is getting married to Miss Pink Silk'. Nevertheless, such activities could keep him occupied for prolonged periods of time and did involve him in the imaginative use of objects other than conventional toys.

Although these activities meant little to most children at first, the use of such techniques resulted in a steady increase in simple imaginative skills. As independent play activities increased, these could then be incorporated into joint play with other children.

For older children imaginative abilities could be developed in other ways. Simon, for example, by the age of 13, had made many improvements both verbally and socially, but still showed very little imaginative capability. Involving him in childish toy games would not have been appropriate. However, since he enjoyed card games, simplified versions of games involving some element of imagination, such as Monopoly or Cluedo, were introduced. He was also encouraged to take part in simple charade type games in which he had to act out specific roles—such as being a carpenter or a bus conductor or a train driver. These were played with his two younger brothers and gave them all much enjoyment. As time went on Simon became very adept at such games and their complexity steadily increased. Indeed, recently he has begun to write scripts for simple plays to be performed by himself and other members of the family. In his case, as with many other children, improvements in imaginative skills have not only resulted in increased abilities to play with other children but also have led to improved family relationships generally. Moreover, as imaginative skills develop, obsessional and ritualistic activities tend to show a steady decline.

INCREASING SOCIAL SKILLS IN OLDER CHILDREN

Teaching Basic Rules of Behaviour

For several of the older children in the study it was not withdrawal from social contact that presented difficulties, but rather their naïve or indiscriminate attempts to initiate contact. Studies of normal peer relationships indicate that successful social interactions are dependent on children being able to adapt their social style according to the varying demands of social situations. Socially skilled children are also better able to interact in a 'to and fro' reciprocal fashion that is both reponsive and rewarding to the other person (La Greca, 1981). Unfortunately, autistic children are grossly impaired in their ability to use social rules flexibly or to adapt them to the changing requirements of social situations. They are also impaired in their ability to react to peers and to build chains of mutually responsive interchanges. Hence, the social skills training techniques that have proved successful with other groups of adolescents (such as those described by Spence, 1980) tend to have only minimal effects. Social interventions with the younger autistic children, therefore, were often of necessity quite limited in their goals. Treatment focused primarily on the teaching of simple, invariable rules, in order to help to avoid at least grosser social blunders. Children need to be taught not to talk to strangers and not to indulge in socially embarrassing activities in public (such as taking off clothes or masturbating) and not to discuss highly personal topics. Stevie, for example, had very little spontaneous speech when younger. Eventually, encouraged by his parents, he began to comment spontaneously on all he saw around him. This was all very well at first, but eventually it generalized to loud and spontaneous comments about the people as well as the objects in his environment. Consequently, he would tend to remark about someone's spotty face or peculiar style of dress in piercingly clear tones. His parents did not wish to curtail the spontaneity of his utterances too much and therefore decided, instead, to try to reduce the volume of his remarks. Because the general concept of whispering was difficult for him to grasp, he was instructed instead to 'talk like people in the library'. Since he was a good mimic, a very specific command of this nature proved more effective than general instructions to lower his voice. He continues to make personal remarks about the people he sees around him, but at least his more vituperative comments now tend to be delivered in a quieter tone of voice.

Teaching Appropriate Social Responses

In the case of a number of older children, social involvements with peers were limited by their inability even to commence social interactions appropriately. Although they might approach another child or group of children they were generally quite unable to introduce themselves or to make any sort of routine, socially acceptable initiation. Thus, they might simply hover awkwardly on the edge of a group, or resort to more inappropriate ways of getting other children's attention. For example, several children, on getting no response from their peers, would just walk up to them and hit them. This was not done for any aggressive motive, but rather because they lacked more adaptive ways of making their presence felt. Unfortunately, such nice distinctions tended to be lost on the normal children who, as might be predicted, responded by hitting them back.

Other children overcame the difficulties of initiating social contacts by indulging in obsessional question and answer routines. Strangers would be met with a barrage of questions about their marital status, numbers of children or date of birth, which would be repeated over and over again. Sometimes any response would be acceptable as long as the child's query was answered. For a number of children, however, only one *specific* response would be admissible, and if this was not forthcoming screams and tantrums would result. Obviously, the repetitive questioning of many autistic children results in part from their obsessional interests. However, in many cases it also appears to reflect their inability to formulate alternative topics of conversation. This is particularly the case with older children who are keen to make social contacts but who possess few of the skills necessary for doing so.

For such children the teaching of simple conversational gambits, such as 'Hello, I am . . .', 'What's your name?' and so forth, can prove useful in opening a conversation effectively. Appropriate responses to social questions such as 'How are you?' 'Where do you live?' and how and when to respond with 'Please' or 'Thank you' or with 'Yes' or 'No' answers to questions, can also help the child to appear socially more acceptable. Teaching the autistic child to make use of conversational 'rules' in this way is particularly important in order to foster more normal relationships with peers. Sympathetic adults tend naturally to structure their conversations in ways that make it easier for the autistic child to participate. Children, however, are less likely to show sensitivity to the autistic child's problems, and conversations with same age peers will rapidly flounder unless the autistic child can develop some ability to sustain these.

Independence Training

As they grew older, many of the autistic children needed help with activities that extended beyond the home environment. Teaching them to go to the shops, buy a newspaper, or ask for a bus or train ticket was important in increasing their level of independence, and again, prompting and fading procedures proved useful in developing such skills.

To begin with, 'make believe' sessions were carried out at home, where the child pretended to go to the shops or get on the bus, etc. Once these activities were well practised at home, the next stage was to carry them out in a real live setting. This required careful and gradual fading of parental support. For example, in teaching Graham to go to the local shop (which was small and friendly) his parents first took him into the shop to buy what he wanted and then gradually began to fade out their presence. First, they began to wait outside the shop until he had completed his purchase. Then they waited at the corner, then at the garden gate, until eventually he was able to carry out simple errands alone. Similar techniques also proved useful in teaching Graham road safety. He had always had a passionate interest in cars but had no sense of their danger. He loved to wander about the local streets, but would cross roads without looking and also had a dangerous tendency to walk along the middle of the road. Initially, therapy involved the use of *toy* cars and dolls. Graham was taught to say whether or not a car was approaching the doll and was also encouraged to make the doll perform the correct manoeuvres before crossing the road. Training sessions were then transferred to a quiet road in his local neighbourhood. Every time he came to a kerb he was prompted to halt, to say audibly to himself 'stop at kerb' and to indicate whether a car was coming or not. If a car was approaching, he was prompted to remain at the kerbside. If the road was clear, he was prompted to cross. To begin with he was allowed to cross roads only in the presence of his parents, but once he was doing this reliably he was encouraged to cross quiet roads in the neighbourhood whilst his parents moved further and further away. Another adult would be stationed nearby to act quickly in the case of emergency or to help prompt him to cross correctly if necessary. Over the course of 6 months the amount of prompting required was steadily faded, and by the end of this period his parents felt that it was safe to allow him out alone. His greater awareness of traffic also made it possible for him to ride his bicycle alone around the neighbourhood.

Increasing Environmental Structure

Although in the case of young children, it is generally necessary to encourage adults to impose greater environmental structure, older individuals may need help to structure their own environment. Helping to foster self-help and independence skills can be a considerable aid towards a higher degree of independence, and since the project has ended it has been possible to arrange accommodation, at least of a semi-sheltered kind, for a number of individuals.

However, in these cases help has usually been required to structure their daily or weekly routines, so that the necessary chores of washing and shopping, etc., are coped with adequately. Many of the older individuals have considerable problems in showing any initiative in organizing their own lives, and unless some help is given with this, they tend to become extremely disorganized. Nevertheless, it is important to be aware that too much structure may prove counterproductive, as some individuals will then become so rigid that no additional or novel activities can be accepted. Thus, some degree of flexibility also needs to be incorporated into programmes involving daily routines.

Adrian, for example, who was not involved in the experimental group because of his greater age had many difficulties in organizing his weekly routine when he first left home. In order to deal with this problem he was given a very detailed weekly timetable to follow, which included all necessary activities (such as when to wash his hair, when to go to the launderette, when to call his mother and what shopping to buy) as well as some pleasurable ones (such as going to concerts). This seemed to work well for a time, until, when asked to visit the therapist concerned in order to discuss the success of the programme, he replied that he couldn't possibly come because such a visit was not included in his timetable!

Increasing Self-Awareness of Social Difficulties

In a number of cases children's social acceptance was severely limited by their abnormal motor mannerisms. Twitching, grimacing or other involuntary movements often meant that the autistic individual appeared quite frightening to younger normal children, or even adults. Such mannerisms also greatly increased the likelihood of their being teased by other children.

Many of the autistic children were quite unaware of these mannerisms, as was the case with Simon, whose language and social skills were otherwise developing well. Unfortunately, he was considerably socially handicapped because of his facial grimacing and his habit of talking to himself, particularly when annoyed. Although he shared a number of common interests with his younger brother, such as cycling or going to the cinema, his mannerisms caused so much embarrassment to other family members that they were rarely willing to accompany him on outings. To help him become more aware of these involuntary behaviours, brief video recordings were made which could then be played back to him. This helped to demonstrate to him the oddity of some of his mannerisms. Then, as soon as he became aware of how odd these behaviours made him appear, it was possible to teach him strategies to inhibit or at least disguise these. For example, if he realized he was talking to himself he would pretend to clear his throat. If he had begun to grimace, he would disguise this by apparently brushing his hair out of his eyes. And, if travelling on a bus or train, he was encouraged always to carry a paper or magazine with him, both to give him something to attend to (his mannerisms were much more marked if he was unoccupied) and to hide behind if he became aware that he was pulling odd faces.

Video sessions provided valuable feedback for a number of other children and were generally much enjoyed. Additional, extrinsic reinforcers to improve social functioning proved unnecessary by this stage, since children's own awareness that they were acting acceptably was generally a powerful enough motivator for them to maintain progress.

Video recordings were also used to teach individuals to become more aware of the non-verbal social cues used by other people. Adrian, for example, was well aware that he had many problems of a social nature. In particular he began to complain that he 'could not read people's thoughts' in the way that other people apparently could. This seemingly odd complaint stemmed from the fact that he was unable to understand or respond to non-verbal cues and hence tended to act very literally on what people *said*. He was perceptive enough to recognize that this frequently led him into trouble and misunderstandings, but was nevertheless unable to respond to more subtle social messages. Video recordings of his own interactions with other people were valuable in teaching him to pay more attention to people's facial expression and tone of voice. Conversational skills were improved by teaching him how to wait for pauses in other people's speech before responding or asking his own questions. A combination of role play techniques and video feedback also proved valuable in teaching him the basic skills needed to initiate conversations at parties or in larger group meetings. At the time he belonged to a number of groups, mainly associated with railways or railway routes (this being his particular obsession), and frequently took an active role at meetings. However, since he was quite unable to pick up cues about when he should stop or start speaking, he was no doubt at times intensely irritating to those around him. Role play procedures and feedback on his own behaviour resulted in at least limited improvements in his perception of his own disabilities. Also, by making him more aware of other people's irritation, he became a little better in modifying his own behaviours more effectively.

Chapter 6

Treatment of Obsessive and Ritualistic Behaviours

For autistic children, the reduction of stereotyped behaviours is necessary not only because of the disruption they cause to families, but also because the presence of ritualistic activities is likely to interfere with the child's learning of other skills. Hence, finding effective ways to reduce such behaviours is important, both for family harmony and for the child's development in other areas. In the past, most treatments involved the use of aversive techniques, but although these led to short term reduction in stereotypies, general improvements in the child's behaviour were less often achieved. Punitive methods may be justified in extreme circumstances but they carry important disadvantages (as well as raising ethical concerns). Accordingly we developed a variety of other treatment approaches.

One of the primary aims of treatment was to increase the child's communicative and play abilities in such a way as to reduce the need for, or time to engage in, obsessional activities. In many cases, as play and language skills improved, ritualistic behaviours showed a spontaneous decline. For example, teaching the child how to play in a functional way with toys frequently resulted in a diminution of stereotyped manipulative behaviours such as spinning wheels, or of ritualistic activities such as lining toys up in straight lines. However, although teaching alternative, appropriate ways of relating to objects produced considerable improvement, other, more direct techniques were frequently required to reduce ritualistic behaviours to an acceptable level.

GRADED CHANGE TECHNIQUES

Obsessive behaviours in autistic children often begin as fairly mild problems in early childhood and, because the children have so few other abilities or interests, parents often make little attempt to stop them. However, as children get older, the rigidities in behaviour often become marked; routines and rituals spread to incorporate an increasing range of the child's (and family's) activities, and the entrenchment of stereotyped and repetitive patterns of behaviour becomes increasingly disruptive. Direct attempts to prohibit or suppress long standing routines, rituals and stereotyped patterns of behaviour are rarely effective. Instead, just as the ritualistic behaviours have grown gradually over the years, a progressively graded introduction of change seems to be the best approach. In some cases this involved restricting the child's opportunities to indulge in ritualistic behaviours; in others it involved systematic modification of the behaviours themselves (Marchant *et al.*, 1974; Hemsley *et al.*, 1978).

Stereotyped Repetitive Activities

Many children spent a great deal of their day involved in repetitive, stereotyped, apparently compulsive activities of one kind or another. These included the frequent touching of particular objects, or placing them in endless lines. Our primary aim was to reduce the adverse impact that such behaviours had on families by gradually reducing their severity or frequency. Stevie, for example, spent almost all his time lining up his foreign coin collection. Trails of coins filled the living room, the kitchen, went up the stairs into the bathroom and through the bedrooms. Attempts by his parents to remove these coins, or their accidental displacement if his parents tripped over them, resulted in extreme distress. To begin with, therefore, his parents attempted to restrict the amount of space in the house taken up by this activity. Initially he was allowed to carry on making his lines of coins in all the usual rooms except one. The particular room chosen in this case was the bathroom, because Stevie loved baths and was only allowed to have a bath if no coins were found in the bathroom. Further restrictions were then gradually introduced. Thus, if he was to be allowed to get into his parents' bed in the morning, no coins were placed in their room. Subsequently, if he wanted some of his favourite snack food, no coins were to be found in the kitchen. Eventually television, too, was restricted if any coins were found in the living room. In this way his freedom to line up coins was very gradually reduced, until the only places where this was allowed were the hallway and stairs (which were rather chilly, particularly in winter) and in his own bedroom. He continued to spend some time playing with his coin lines in his room, but as he also enjoyed the company of his mother and father the amount of time he spent alone in this way was always fairly brief.

Slight variations on this theme have been used with other children. One of Matthew's many obsessions was lining up cars. This was reduced by insisting that the number of cars in a line at any one time was gradually lowered. Instead of spending his time lining up 50 cars or more, the maximum allowed was reduced to 20. Then it was reduced further to 10; then to 5 and eventually to 2. Although this resulted in pairs of cars being dotted at intervals around the house, it greatly reduced the disruption that had formerly occurred if his lines were broken into in any way.

Duncan's stereotyped motor mannerisms were dealt with along similar lines. These had begun relatively simply as a nod of the head accompanied by rapid eye blinking, but at the time of intervention involved a complex sequence of facial grimaces accompanied by hand flapping. In his case, restrictions were imposed on the amount of *time* per day that he was allowed to indulge in these activities. First they were prevented at mealtimes which he much enjoyed. (This was achieved by removing his food as soon as he began to flap or grimace.) Next, such behaviours were forbidden in the bathroom, and he only got his bath, which he loved, if he did not exhibit any manneristic behaviours. Then the behaviours were discouraged at times when he was actively engaged with his parents, as in playing or reading stories. Still later, the behaviours were discouraged whilst he was watching television or listening to records. In this way, although the mannerisms did not disappear entirely, they did not occur at times when he was otherwise occupied.

Because parents could not be expected to spend the whole of their time in highly structured tasks with their child, and because of children's lack of spontaneous enjoyment in normal activities, it was felt inappropriate to restrict their enjoyment of more ritualistic activities entirely. Therefore, once these had been reduced to an acceptable level and did not interfere either with the rest of the family or with the child's own ability to take part in other activities, they were tolerated, especially at times when the child had to be left alone.

Verbal Routines

As well as an insistence on behavioural routines, many older more linguistically able children developed marked verbal routines. Peter was fairly typical in having a variety of daily ritualistic question and answer routines in which his mother was obliged to take part. These involved her asking him a specific set of different questions to which he replied in exactly the same way each day. If she varied, even in the minutest detail, the way in which she asked the question he would have a severe and prolonged tantrum. He was also extremely rigid in the constraints he imposed on the ways in which other people spoke. Thus, although he did not insist that strangers took part in his verbal routines, he would become distraught if people's speech was not entirely grammatical. If anyone committed errors such as using the wrong case of a pronoun, the wrong mood or tense of verbs, or any slang expression he would scream continuously until they produced the correct form. This disrupted not only his own conversations but also those of his parents and made it very difficult for them to take him out in public.

In his case, a two-fold approach to intervention was adopted. First, question and answer routines were continued by his mother but *only* if he had accepted other people's grammatical mistakes without screaming. Gradually his mother (who had been programmed to speak impeccable English over the years) deliberately increased her use of less grammatical speech forms and this was tolerated by Peter as long as his other verbal routines were continued. Once he had become more tolerant of other people's solecisms his mother began to introduce slight variations into the daily question and answer routines. As soon as slight modifications in these routines were accepted she began to reduce the frequency of the ritualistic question and answer sessions. Initially there had been about ten to fifteen such sessions each day. These occurred at irregular intervals, whenever Peter thought fit to initiate them. His mother, therefore, began to insist that they took place only at certain times of the day. To begin with there was a session before and after breakfast, one before and after lunch, one before and after supper, and one at bedtime. Gradually the sessions *before* meals were eliminated, and meals were not commenced unless Peter accepted this. Sessions following mealtimes were then systematically reduced, until eventually the only question and answer session took place at bedtime. As long as Peter knew that he would get one opportunity each day to indulge in his question and answer routines, he seemed perfectly happy, and his parents, too, were content to take part in this for a brief period daily.

Other parents have dealt with verbal routines using variations of this approach. Sometimes this has involved insisting that the child is only allowed to ask his obsessional questions at certain *times* of the day and then gradually reducing the number of these occasions. Other parents have dealt with the problem by insisting that the *number* of questions at any one time is reduced. Thus, they may agree to answer five questions in a row, but no more until an agreed period of time has elapsed. The number of questions answered at any one time can then be gradually reduced. Stevie, for example, was almost constantly asking questions about specific topics, most of which concerned directions, points of the compass and tube or train routes. Although his parents had tried to ignore his questions this had produced such unacceptable levels of distress and anxiety that eventually they had given in and begun to respond once more in the way he required. Rather than a total ban, therefore, limitations were set on the number of questions he was allowed to ask at any one time. It was then made clear that the questions would not be responded to again for a specific (and initially very brief) period of time. During this period parents refrained entirely from answering obsessive questions, and attempted instead to encourage him to talk about other topics. Gradually, the period during which 'forbidden' questions went unanswered was extended until they were limited to only one or two brief occasions a day. In this way, parents' irritation at having to answer the repetitive questions, and Stevie's anxiety if he was not responded to, were both kept to a minimum.

Resistance to Change

Resistance to change in their environment can also be dealt with using graded change techniques. Many children become very distressed by minor changes in their environment, such as a door left in a slightly different position, or an ashtray moved a few inches out of its normal place or any redecorating in the house.

A typical example of this was Stevie's distress when his parents removed a large fitted cabinet from the kitchen while he was away at school. On his return he screamed incessantly for two days, but finally, on the third night, much to his parents' relief, he settled quietly. Only on waking the next morning did they discover their new paintwork completely ruined by a life size drawing of the original cupboard in indelible ink on the kitchen wall!

In such cases of resistance to change, barely perceptible alterations in the positions of objects was generally the first stage in modifying the behaviour. Once toleration of minor change was established children could then be gradually encouraged to accept more and more obvious changes. Whenever possible, too, the changes made should be predictable for the child. In the case of several older children, once acceptance of minor changes was achieved, it was often possible to explain to them the changes that were expected to occur in the future. If alterations in routines were predicted in this way, subsequent changes were often tolerated more readily. Indeed, many of the children eventually began to enjoy these variations in their daily life.

Obsessional Collecting Behaviour

A number of children, instead of indulging in ritualistic activities with objects, such as placing them in endless lines, simply hoarded as many objects as they could. Stevie, for example, in addition to his vast coin collection, had the definitive collection of Matchbox toy cars, and also a complete collection of all the Ladybird books ever produced. For over a year Matthew had routinely collected every teddy bear he was able to get hold of. Some of these had been bought by parents, others 'borrowed' from unsuspecting children. At the time intervention began, the collection comprised eighteen bears which were kept in his father's armchair in the living room. Matthew was instatnly aware if any bear was taken away or even moved slightly in the chair. To begin with, therefore, his parents insisted on the removal of one very small bear. It was kept within sight of the other bears but Matthew was not allowed to replace it on the chair, and in fact was prevented from doing so by its being tied to another chair with a bit of string. Over the course of the next week the bear was gradually moved away and was finally taken to Matthew's bedroom. At this stage a second bear was removed from the armchair. Matthew was encouraged to play with these bears at other times of the day, and his parents made a considerable effort to engage him in pretend activities, such as washing or feeding the bears. Gradually, over a period of about five weeks, all the bears were removed from the chair, allowing his father to sit in it for the first time in over a year. Following the removal of the final bear, Matthew continued to be encouraged to involve his bears in constructive or pretend activities but simply collecting them was no longer allowed. A year later he remained fond of his bears and knew where each of them was, but he no longer collected them, nor did he insist that they remained in the same position in the house. (Table 6.1 gives a brief summary of the steps involved.)

Maladaptive Attachments of Objects

Strong attachments to 'security objects' such as blankets are common in normal children (Boniface and Graham, 1979; Mahalski, 1983; Werry et al., 1983). The attachments are to specific objects (one particular blanket, not any blanket) and

Table 6.1
Graded Change in The Reduction of Obsessional Collecting

BASELINE	
1–4 weeks	18 teddy bears permanently resident in best armchair
TREATMENT	
Weeks: 1	One bear removed short distance from chair
	Rewards given for alternative play activities
2	Second bear removed. First bear placed in child's bedroom
3–4	More bears removed and left around house. Used in 'Pretend' play
5	All bears removed. Father sits in chair
6	Imaginative play with bears developed. No further collecting allowed.

their presence brings comfort when the children are ill, tired, anxious or unsettled. Typically, it is important for the child to have his 'security object' at these times and he will become distressed if it is not available. The phenomenon is normal, adaptive and not a reason for intervention. When very young, some children carry their objects about with them continuously but is unusual for this to persist after the preschool years and it is even more infrequent for the attachment to interfere with or prevent other activities.

The attachments shown by autistic children are similar with respect to their selectivity and the distress associated with loss or removal of the object. However, they differ in several crucial respects: the attachments do not show the same tendency to wane as the children grow older, the objects are not primarily used as a source of comfort, it is common for the child to be reluctant to relinquish the object to engage in other activities and, as a consequence substantial interference with such activities is a frequent problem. The nature of the object also tends to be unusual; a blanket may be used as an object, but the item is just as likely to be a sink plunger, a doll's torso or a tin lid. Some parents deal with the problem by ensuring that large supplies of replacement objects are kept in stock so that the object is never entirely lost. Jamie's father, for example, routinely bought every blue sink plunger he saw, so that as one wore out another was ready to replace it. Other children will accept no substitute, and there is protest or distress if replacement is attempted. The need for intervention arises primarily, however, because the child's insistence on keeping hold of the object throughout the day disrupts play, work and social interactions.

A system of graded change can be used to deal with this problem (Marchant et al., 1974). The change may be introduced with respect to either the time the object is accessible to the child or the physical qualities of the object itself if its bulk plays a major role in the disruptive effect on other activities.

Patrick, a diminutive 5 year old, had been attached to his blanket since he was a few months old. It could not be removed for washing unless he was asleep and its size interfered with most of his other activities. Since he refused to give up the

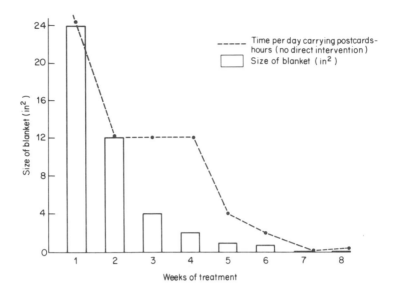

Figure 6.1 Reduction of object attachments using graded change techniques

blanket during the day it was decided to reduce the blanket in size at the only time when he would relinquish it—in his sleep. Gradually, night by night, a few inches were cut off by his mother. Patrick never seemed aware of the shrinkage taking place and was soon quite happy carrying a few threads around. Eventually, however, these were dropped so often that he began to lose interest in them. Of interest in Patrick's case, too, was the fact that he always carried around several postcards, at the same time as his blanket. As the blanket attachment was reduced the dependency on postcards also diminished, although this was never treated directly (See Figure 6.1).

Symptom Substitution

In almost every case when object attachment was successfully modified, some 'symptom substitution' did occur. That is, when the initial objects were finally relinquished, they tended to be replaced by other articles that the child carried around. 'Symptom substitution' sometimes carries a variety of theoretical connotations, usually of a psychoanalytical nature, but as used here it refers simply to the emergence of a new maladaptive behaviour in replacement of another which has been lost following treatment. There is no necessary connotation of an underlying disorder. The reasons for object attachments in autistic children are unknown. It is unclear, for example, whether such attachments serve the same role as in normal children. It is possible that marked and persistent object attachments occur because of the autistic child's inability to form normal social attachments. Marchant *et al.* (1974) also suggested that anxiety may be the underlying cause of some object attachments. The fact of 'symptom substitution' in the form of object replacement also suggests that the attachment has some purpose outside the specific object itself. Rather, it may be simply a strong *habit* of carrying anything. This hypothesis alone, however, is insufficient to explain why the attachment at any one point in time is to a *specific* object which is not replaceable by another.

Whatever the theoretical implications of object attachment may be, from a practical point of view the important finding seems to be that such attachments can be effectively treated by means of graded change. Substitutions are likely to occur but these are equally amenable to treatment. Indeed, subsequent attachments tend never to be as strong, and usually prove much easier for parents to modify.

For instance, after Patrick relinquished his blanket and postcards, he began to carry around a red plastic bus. To begin with, his parents dealt with this by splitting it into sections so that he could carry only a small piece around at any one time. Then, suddenly, they became aware of the potential value of this new interest. He had never before shown much attention to toys, but this interest in buses, and subsequently cars, was used to increase simple cooperative play which involved his pushing cars back and forth to his parents. His parents made sure that no particular car or bus dominated his attention and if a preference seemed about to develop they would quickly substitute a different vehicle. In this way, not only was the object attachment reduced to a manageable level, but it was also used to foster more social play activities. Thus, by the use of graded change methods it is generally possible to wean the child from attachments that interfere with other activities, or his ability to learn, but to do so with benefit to the child's overall development.

Feeding and Sleeping Problems

Although not conventionally viewed as obsessional problems, the feeding and sleeping difficulties shown by a number of children were clearly related to their general resistance to change.

Simon, for example, insisted on eating, not only at *exactly* the same time each day, but in the same position at the table and with the same cutlery and plates. The use of graded change techniques to alter, very slightly at first, the time of meals, or the layout of the table, rapidly proved effective, and soon it was possible to introduce considerable variability into mealtimes. Teaching him to cook also helped him to realize that cooking is not an exact science, and that foods are not necessarily ready at a specific time.

Graded change techniques also proved valuable in the treatment of other children whose feeding problems resulted from a resistance to change. A tiny amount of new, and hence 'unacceptable' food, would be mixed, unseen, into the child's habitual dish of (say) sausages and mashed potatoes. Once this was eaten without problem, the amount of novel food would be gradually increased. If the food could not be introduced without the child's knowledge a very small

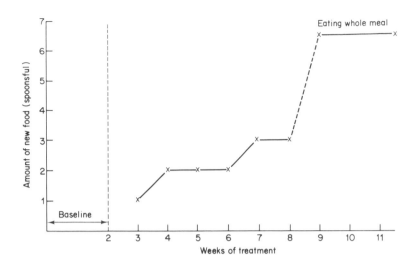

Figure 6.2 Graded change in the treatment of feeding problems

amount—such as a salt-spoonful—of the novel food would be given and the child reinforced for eating this with the rest of his favourite food. Once minute portions of new food were tolerated, increasingly greater quantities of new food were introduced daily until a relatively mixed diet was achieved. This approach was used in a number of cases, often with rapid success. In Patrick's case, new food was introduced very cautiously initially, but then, suddenly, as he came to accept this, he began to eat exactly the same meals as the rest of the family and the programme was terminated (see Figure 6.2).

In one extreme case, Gary aged 4 still ate only with his fingers and drank milk or diluted baby foods from a baby's bottle. Although prompting procedures were used successfully to teach him to use a spoon and fork to eat solid food, he remained extremely reluctant to relinquish his bottle and steadfastly refused to drink from anything else. Again, a graded change approach was adopted (see Figure 6.3), this time actually modifying the physical equipment used. The original bottle was changed for a smaller, squatter one, with a very wide mouth and teat. This was eventually substituted by a non-spillable plastic drinking cup which had a spout similar in shape to the teat of the bottle. The spout in the top of the drinking cup was gradually opened up, until a wide drinking hole was exposed. Finally, the top was removed from the cup and once this was accepted a variety of plastic mugs were then substituted in its place to ease generalization.

Sleeping problems, too, have been dealt with effectively by the use of graded change techniques. Wayne, for example, had gradually come to insist that his mother spent longer and longer with him each night when he went to bed, until eventually she was spending the whole night in his room. Her one attempt to ignore his protests when she left the room was rapidly abandoned following complaints from neighbours. For the 6 months prior to intervention she had

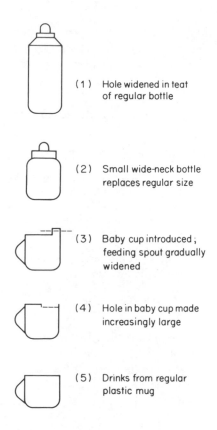

(1)   Hole widened in teat
         of regular bottle

(2)   Small wide-neck bottle
         replaces regular size

(3)   Baby cup introduced ;
         feeding spout gradually
         widened

(4)   Hole in baby cup made
         increasingly large

(5)   Drinks from regular
         plastic mug

Figure 6.3 Stages in reduction of
attachment to drinking bottle

been sleeping in Wayne's bed each night and, although her presence ensured that he was easily comforted when he awoke, she was suffering from a chronic lack of sleep and rarely had any opportunity to share a bed with her husband.

The graded change approach adopted here involved the systematic removal of the mother from the child's bedroom. To begin with, an inflatable mattress was introduced into Wayne's bedroom (which was too small to accommodate an additional bed). This was placed immediately next to his bed so that when he awoke mother could reach out and cuddle him as usual. Gradually the mattress was removed inch by inch from his bed. His mother could speak to and touch him when he awoke but could no longer cuddle him with the same ease. Night by night mother moved her mattress further away from the bed and closer to the door. If he awoke she was able to comfort him verbally but could no longer reach out and touch him. These changes were accepted quite readily by Wayne and by the second month of treatment his mother's mattress was placed in the hallway between his bedroom and her own. By the end of 2 months it was possible for the mother to return to her own bed and although Wayne did still wake occasionally this was easily dealt with by simply calling to him and encouraging him to go back to sleep. (The steps involved are summarized in Table 6.2).

Table 6.2 Graded Change in the Reduction of Sleeping Problems

BASELINE	
Weeks 1–4	Mother in child's bed each night
TREATMENT	
Weeks 5	Mother on inflatable mattress next to child
6	Mattress moved few inches from bed
7	Distance increased—Mother can still reach child
8	Mother no longer within child's reach
9	Mattress at door of child's room
10	Mattress in hallway
11	Mattress in doorway of parent's room
12	Mother in own bed
FOLLOW-UP	
Week 20	Child sleeping alone

Wayne has since made no effort to return to his parents' bed at night, and this change in his sleeping pattern has meant that parents not only sleep together, but can also go out together in the evening leaving him with a babysitter. They have also been to work successfully on a programme to deal with his bed wetting, which had not been possible before because of the other sleeping difficulties.

ROLE PLAY TECHNIQUES

Another method used to reduce obsessional behaviours in older autistic people involves the use of role play techniques. These can be extremely valuable in helping the individual to develop more appropriate ways of coping with obsessions. Adrian (who was not included in the project because he was much older) was very resistant to change of any kind, and also had very fixed ideas of how people should do their jobs. Although he enjoyed the company of other people he tended to have frequent problems in shops or pubs. Thus, he would become very argumentative if the shopkeeper or barman did not stock exactly what he thought they should, or if the price had changed since his last visit. He also became very upset if people 'did not do their jobs properly' and had a tendency to assault unsuspecting individuals with his umbrella if they did not live up to his expectations. So, there were frequent upsets at the local social security office when he went to collect his unemployment benefit and, invariably, found himself in the wrong queue. He would also become agitated and physically threatening over minor incidents, as when a cloakroom attendant gave him the wrong ticket. Helping him to rehearse these situations in a role play setting, and teaching him to cope with mistakes, confusion and rudeness in a more appropriate way proved valuable in helping him to deal with these difficulties. When similar problems arose subsequently he was very able to generalize the skills learned in the clinic to outside settings.

The flaw of this approach is that it tends to be successful only *after* particular problems have already occurred. It is quite possible, using role play techniques, to avoid future problems of a similar nature. However, it proves much more difficult to predict when different types of problems will arise or to provide the autistic person with adequate means of coping with these.

THE MODIFICATION OF OBSESSIONAL BEHAVIOURS

The persistence and pervasiveness of repetitive stereotyped behaviours of various kinds suggest that these are not secondary problems but in fact are fundamental deficits in autism. Almost all autistic individuals demonstrate some degree of rigidity and routine throughout their lives (DeMyer, 1979; Rutter, 1985c), and it is clear that behavioural techniques are not successful in eliminating these problems entirely. However, once they can be reduced to a level that does not interfere with other activities they may actually prove useful in themselves. First, obsessive interests can be used as reinforcers for more appropriate activities, and this approach is described in further detail in the next chapter. Second, they can be adapted in such a way as to form an inroad into more socially acceptable behaviours (Howlin, 1985). The use of attachment objects such as toy cars and buses to promote simple play has already been noted. Kanner, (1973), too, in his follow-up of older, autistic individuals, found that obsessional preoccupations and detailed knowledge of topics, such as music, mathematics, history, transport, foreign languages, could, eventually, lead to shared activities with groups of normal individuals who showed similar interests. Social intercourse may remain at a very superficial level; nevertheless, the ability to share hobbies and interests with others can greatly reduce feelings of isolation. Indeed, Kanner, found that the presence of some obsessional interest, potentially of a socially acceptable kind, was highly correlated with successful social adaptation. Thus, removing obsessional interests entirely, even if this were possible, may well be undesirable. The skill in developing successful treatment programmes lies in determining what behaviours are potentially useful, and how they may be modified to have the greatest effect, rather than attempting to remove them completely.

For example, Simon's early interest in distances and directions was encouraged by his parents in such a way as to foster his interest in geography. He accumulated a vast range of knowledge on this subject, and he also became interested in the languages spoken in other countries. Eventually his geographical knowledge and his smattering of a variety of languages proved very useful on family journeys abroad.

Peter's interest in aeroplanes was used by his parents to increase his general knowledge about different parts of the world. He remains an infallible source of information on the flights available from virtually any country to another.

Richard (who, like Adrian, was not included in the experimental group because of his age) showed an early interest in numbers that eventually led to a diploma in accountancy. He is able to do calculations considerably more rapidly than many calculators; can calculate the day of people's birthdays (useful for those who may have forgotten this) and also, if he has this information, can tell people their driving licence number (invaluable if they happen to have lost it).

Even younger children's obsessions can be modified to improve social interactions and this approach has been more fully developed with children seen after the cessation of the project. Robin's remarkable skill in spinning objects won him considerable status in the nursery school he attended and other children would fight to be accepted as his 'best friend'. William's interest in dice and numbers proved a useful basis for encouraging group games with other children, such as lotto, snakes and ladders. His early interest in electronic games has also been fostered to such an extent that now, at the age of 8, he has considerable skill with computers. Similarly, Carl's skill at spelling far outstripped that of the other children in the normal school he attended. Although his behaviour was odd in many ways, he achieved considerable acclaim for his spelling ability, and was promoted to 'spelling monitor' in the class, thereby reducing his isolation and increasing his self-esteem.

Interest in, or knowledge of, particular topics has also been useful in reducing the sense of isolation in older individuals. Several adolescents, for example, have expressed an overriding desire to be like their peers and to have girlfriends. Given their lack of empathy and social responsiveness it is usually evident that they will never be able to develop really close relationships of this kind. However, encouraging them to join groups of people with whom they share common interests, such as music or history or railways, has at least enabled them to develop a much wider range of social contacts. Being able to meet with and talk to girls of their own age is often enough to make them feel more socially accepted, and in this way the wish for a specific girlfriend can often be deflected.

Although it seems that ritualistic and obsessional behaviours are difficult to eliminate entirely, they can be successfully modified so as to cause less disruption to the child's own life and that of his family. With a little skill and ingenuity, they can be adapted in such a way as to improve the quality of life. The important element of treatment is to ensure that obsessional behaviours never entirely take over other aspects of the child's functioning. In general, the longer an obsessional behaviour has persisted, the longer the time required to modify it. For this reason, once initial problems have been modified, it is important for parents to be aware of other obsessional activities that might take the place of the original one, and to restrict these firmly, right from the start.

Chapter 7

Non-Specific Behavioural Problems

In addition to the characteristic handicaps of autistic children, many other problems occur. These include fears, disruptive behaviour, aggression, over-activity and difficulties with self-help skills. Although such problems are not specific to autism, and occur in both normal and other groups of handicapped children, they, too, require a multifaceted approach to treatment.

DESENSITIZATION TECHNIQUES IN THE TREATMENT OF PHOBIAS

The graded approach used in the treatment of obsessive behaviour (as described in the previous chapter) was also incorporated into procedures to alleviate the many irrational fears and phobias shown by autistic children. Unlike the normal child's fears of the dark or birds or dogs, autistic phobias tend to be of a more bizarre nature. A piece of pipe on a radiator, a certain corner of the garden, a particular neighbour or a lamp-post in the street may suddenly and inexplicably become a source of the utmost terror. Such fears may make it almost impossible for the child to be taken out, or may restrict his movement to a limited number of rooms in the house.

Desensitization techniques based on learning theory proved particularly useful in ameliorating such problems. Theoretically, desensitization works by the use of 'counter-conditioning'. In other words, the fear is removed by the simultaneous occurrence of an incompatible response (such as pleasure) that inhibits the expression of anxiety and reduces the fear. In adults and older children, relaxation techniques are generally used to counteract anxiety while subjects are gradually and systematically exposed to the feared objects, either in actuality or in their imagination. With very young or handicapped children, imaginal techniques are inappropriate, but the reduction of fear can be brought about in more practical ways.

In a now classic study of the reduction of phobias in children, Jones (1924) showed that a 3 year old's fears of rabbits and other furry objects could be successfully treated by presenting food simultaneously with the feared object. In the present study we used a combination of desensitization techniques (i.e. gradual exposure to the feared objects) and anxiety reducing procedures to overcome irrational fears.

This meant that the child would be systematically exposed to the feared object, but in a way that did not increase his anxiety. This was achieved either by presenting the object at a considerable distance from the child, or by showing him a facsimile or allowing the child to terminate contact with the object after a minimal period of exposure. In such a way the child learned to tolerate the feared object and could then gradually cope with ever increasing exposure to it. Anxiety was further reduced by having the parents constantly reassure and encourage the child, if necessary, by presenting him with something he particularly enjoyed, such as food, cuddles or a favourite toy. Gradually, exposure to the object was increased until the child was able to tolerate its presence without anxiety.

The following examples show how different types of phobias were treated using slight variations of desensitization techniques. Patrick had always been utterly terrified of baths and bathrooms and since infancy had always been bathed either in a baby's bath or the kitchen sink or simply sponged while lying on his bed. As he was 5 (and growing rapidly) when intervention began, keeping him clean was becoming increasingly difficult. However, the problem was reduced relatively quickly by taking advantage of structural alterations in the house at the time. The parents were having a new bath installed, and before it was placed in the bathroom Patrick was allowed to play in the bath and to store some of his toys in it. The novelty of this approach seemed to appeal to him, and by the time the bath was actually installed in the bathroom he had lost all fear of it. Whilst his toys remained in the bath, Patrick would also tolerate being washed in it, although he insisted on standing up all the time. Initially the bath plug was not inserted and he was washed in a stream of running water. This procedure continued for a week until eventually the plug was left in the bath. Gradually the level of water was increased each night. By the fifth week of treatment he would tolerate water up to mid calf level. His parents made no attempt to make him sit down but encouraged and played with him all the time that he remained in the bath. In the course of these games his parents would deliberately drop his toys in the water so that he had to crouch down to pick them up. After only 2 months of intervention Patrick's phobia of almost 5 years' duration was virtually gone. He still preferred to stand rather than sit in the bath but otherwise bathtimes presented few problems. It was also noticeable that, as his fear of bathing diminished, so too did his fear of having his hair washed, although at no time was this worked on directly.

The reduction of fears, not previously thought to be associated with the primary problem, has been noted in other studies (Morris and Kratochwill, 1983b) although the mechanism is not fully understood. Other fears, however, needed more direct intervention. Patrick's other phobia, of going in the garden, did not diminish until a desensitization programme (involving a gradual increase of time spent in the garden) was specifically introduced to deal with this (see Figure 7.1).

The fear of balloons shown by Graham was generally a less pervasive problem. However, it did make it impossible for him to go to parties of any

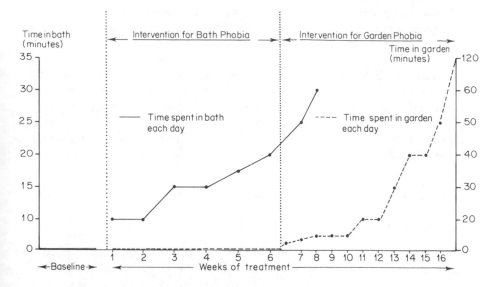

Figure 7.1 The reduction of phobias using desensitization techniques

kind, just as he had reached an age when he was beginning to develop better social competence and greater interest in his peers.

In his case, since exposure at any distance or to any sort of rubber balloon, whether inflated or not, gave rise to intense anxiety, a substitute material that produced non-banging plastic 'balloons' was used instead. Once he was able to blow up these without distress he was encouraged to blow up inflatable footballs which again he did without difficulty. Real balloons, which were gradually inflated more and more, were subsequently introduced, until eventually he would blow up and burst balloons by himself. Thereafter, to avoid the possibility of his fears incubating again once the Christmas party season was over, odd balloons were left up somewhere in the house throughout the remaining months of the year.

THE NEED FOR A FUNCTIONAL ANALYSIS: TREATMENT OF DISRUPTIVE BEHAVIOUR

The importance of a functional analysis in determining why and when difficulties occur has already been discussed. However, the need for a detailed analysis of possible causes and consequences is vital when dealing with disruptive behaviours. These may occur for many different reasons and treatment will need to be adapted accordingly. For example, if the child becomes angry and upset because of disruption to his rituals or routines, or as a response to a feared situation, the appropriate intervention would focus on the factors causing the child's outburst rather than directly on the outbursts themselves. If tantrums and aggression occur because the child has no other way of expressing his needs, the obvious solution is to provide him with such modes of expression.

Maladaptive behaviours may also be maintained by the attention the child receives for them, and in this case intervention needs to concentrate on building up alternative behaviours for which the child can obtain attention. It is also important to be aware of environmental factors, which, although not necessarily responsible for causing difficulties in the first place, may be modified in order to reduce existing problems.

Increasing Alternative Appropriate Skills

Improving Communication

In many cases, attempts to increase the child's communication skills resulted in a marked decrease in behavioural disturbance. Once the child was able to understand a little of what was going on around him, and was also able to affect his environment by more appropriate means, temper tantrums and aggressive outbursts frequently declined. In children with severely impaired language, disruptive behaviours often arise from the inability to communicate in more appropriate ways (Carr and Durand, 1985a, b). Tantrums or head banging, for example, may be the only means available to the child to express his confusion or dislike of a particular situation. If children can be taught alternative ways of expressing their needs, such as by simple signs or words, disruptive behaviours frequently decline. Carr and Durand found that if autistic children were able to terminate disliked activities by the use of signs, not only did this form of communication increase, but other maladaptive ways of avoiding the situation, such as screaming or head banging, showed a rapid decline.

Improving Other Skills

The autistic child's very limited repertoire of appropriate behaviours may also be responsible for maintaining a high level of disruptiveness. For example, if the child exhibits few skills that can earn him praise or attention, he will be most likely to elicit adult attention by inappropriate actions; it is invariably easier to get attention by kicking the television than it is by sitting quietly watching it. Moreover, if he lacks the skills required to occupy and amuse himself when left alone, he is more likely to indulge in repetitive stereotyped behaviours. It is of limited use suppressing aggression and disruption unless the child has other, positive, behaviours that can take their place. For this reason, therefore, rather than direct modification of the disruptive behaviours themselves, treatment may need to focus on increasing the range of adaptive responses.

In the development of language skills the use of shaping, prompting and fading techniques has already been discussed. Such procedures are also valuable for enhancing non-verbal activities. Again, the success of these procedures requires a careful analysis of the child's skills, deficits and patterns of response before intervention begins, and shaping the use of existing skills to develop more socially appropriate behaviours.

When the project began many of the children had simple constructional skills, but their utility was markedly limited by their repetitive stereotyped quality. Unless greater flexibility and complexity could be introduced, autistic children's early interests in jigsaw puzzles or building activities often tended to decline. Potentially useful skills sometimes came to be abandoned in this way. Although the eventual level of attainment will depend very much on the extent of the child's biological handicaps, even the simplest skills can be extended into more useful activities by the careful use of shaping procedures.

Patrick spent much of his day 'posting' virtually any object he found down the back of chairs or radiators. This 'skill', which was not particularly useful in itself, was successfully shaped into simple constructional activities with form boards. To begin with he was prompted both physically and verbally to complete a simple three-hole posting box by posting the appropriate shapes into place. Physical prompts were then faded until he could complete the posting box without help. A slightly more complex form board was then introduced and physical prompts faded as before. By the end of 6 weeks a ten piece insert board was introduced. Prompts were needed initially to help him complete this, but after only a few trials he was able to do this alone. By the end of 2 months he could complete a variety of form boards. Simple jigsaws were then introduced. Again prompts and fading of prompts were used in order to teach him how to complete these by himself. Then, once his skill at such tasks was well developed he was encouraged to use them in joint activities with his parents.

Shaping procedures were used to extend Thomas's simple picture matching skills into much more complex activities. The difficulty of these picture matching tasks was rapidly increased, and he was soon able to match pictures depicting quite complex scenes. Then, instead of matching pictures, cards requiring him to match geometric shapes were introduced. To begin with, shapes were large and simple, but these were rapidly increased in complexity (see Figure 7.2). He was soon able to match cards with groups of two and three items in different sequences, and by the end of 2 months could successfully match cards containing up to ten items. At this stage, the cards depicting objects began to be paired with cards showing the appropriate numeral. Visual and verbal cues were provided to ensure errorless learning at this stage, but were gradually faded. He was soon able to match cards containing one, two or three dots to the appropriate numerals, and by the end of 4 months was able to match the numbers one to ten to cards containing the appropriate number of items.

Thomas showed enormous enjoyment and satisfaction in these activities and progress thereafter was extremely rapid. By the end of 20 weeks it was possible to begin teaching him simple addition, and by 30 weeks he was able to do simple subtractions. By the end of a year he was able to complete multiplication problems and simple fractions. He still showed virtually no comphrension of

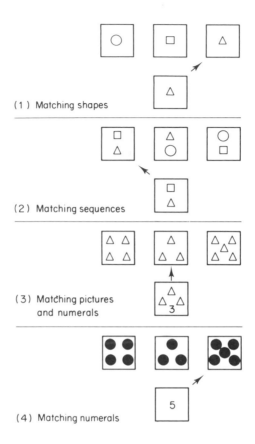

(1) Matching shapes

(2) Matching sequences

(3) Matching pictures and numerals

(4) Matching numerals

Figure 7.2 Stages in teaching simple number skills

spoken language, nor did he use any language himself. Hence the mental processes involved in his arithmetical computations remain something of a puzzle. However, so great was his enjoyment of these activities, that his parents eventually began to use them as reinforcement for other, more social activities and indeed sheets of multiplication tables are still one of the most powerful reinforcers they possess!

Altering Reinforcement Contingencies

Throughout our intervention with parents the emphasis was on the positive aspects of treatment and on the reinforcement of desirable behaviour. In many cases, as constructional and communication skills improved, disruptive behaviours steadily decreased. Nevertheless, problems were not always so easily solved, and it was often necessary to work more directly on the reduction of inappropriate behaviours.

Reducing Attention for Inappropriate Behaviour

It was common to find (from our functional analyses) that the children's disruptive behaviour was accompanied by a high level of parental attention. Although autistic children show impaired social reciprocity, this does not mean that they are unaffected by other people's interest and attention. Parental responses can serve as powerful forces for the maintenance of maladaptive behaviour, and since autistic children lack the appropriate social skills to gain adult attention, they tend to achieve this in less acceptable ways. For obvious reasons temper tantrums, aggression and destructiveness are likely to result in immediate adult attention. Sitting and playing quietly alone, on the other hand, is unlikely to achieve such prompt responses. Altering the distribution of parental attention according to the pattern of the child's behaviour is often one of the most successful ways of ameliorating behaviour problems.

The removal of attention, or whatever other reinforcements the child obtains for his disruptive activities, is a much used technique in behavioural programmes. *Extinction* procedures, for example, require that any attention or reinforcement that the child receives for inappropriate behaviours is removed until the behaviour ceases. Such techniques are particularly useful in dealing with relatively innocuous behaviours, as in the case of Sam's use of jargon utterances described in an earlier chapter. Obviously, parents need to be given support in order to help them persist during the early stages of the programme (ignoring behaviours is frequently much easier said than done), but if they can learn to be consistent in removing all attention for the behaviour this can prove extremely effective.

Unfortunately, the complete removal of parental interest or attention following disruptive behaviour has many practical difficulties. First, one *cannot* ignore a child's severely disruptive behaviours, such as smashing furniture or hitting his baby brother. Second, extinction, even if it is ultimately effective, frequently results in an immediate, short term increase in the disruptive behaviour. If parents respond to the child's behaviour during this particular phase, this will result in the child getting attention for even more disruptive behaviour. Rather than a progressive elimination of the disruption, there is a danger of an escalation. Finally, extinction procedures require a high degree of consistency to be effective. Even occasional attention to the disruptive behaviour will be enough to maintain it over a very long period. If maladaptive behaviours are attended to intermittently the child will be more likely to persist in his attempts to gain attention in this way. Ignoring behaviours may be relatively easy for parents who are feeling fit and well and who have had a good night's sleep. If they are worried, anxious or generally tired, however, it can be extremely difficult not to respond, at least intermittently, to the child's behaviours, with the result that all their earlier efforts are to no avail.

'Time Out' Procedures

An alternative approach, that serves the same end of reducing attention to inappropriate behaviour, is to ensure that any reinforcement the child receives for such behaviour is minimized. 'Time out from positive reinforcement' can be achieved in a number of ways. Either the child can be removed to a setting where he can no longer engage in the disruptive behaviour and where he will no longer receive social attention (because he will be on his own). Or, if it is safe for the child to remain where he is, the same objective may be met by the parents (or any other people present) leaving the room so that the child is left by himself. The procedure has come to be called 'time out' because it involves a time in which the child is without social reinforcement.

'Time out' from attention or any other sort of reinforcement in this way may prove very effective in reducing rates of disruptive activities. This does not necessarily imply that the behaviours were caused *in the first place* by adult attention—they may well have arisen for many other reasons,—but attention or other inadvertent rewards may well be responsible for maintaining them subsequently. For behaviours that are more irritating than dangerous, such as verbal routines, it may be enough for the adult who objects to the behaviour to leave the room, and not return until the behaviour ceases. Stevie's mother, for example, found it quite easy to deal with his spitting in this way, although she had not previously been able to ignore it as long as she remained in the room. For more disruptive behaviours the child himself may need to be removed to a place where he can do no harm, or can no longer indulge in the disruptive activity. It needs to be stressed to parents that time out is not meant to be an aversive procedure. The point is simply to remove social reinforcement from the child until the behaviour changes. Accordingly, time out periods should be brief and their termination timed to fit in with the child's change of behaviour. *As soon as* the child ceases screaming or swearing, etc., the time out period should cease.

Although time out procedures, like any other technique, need a considerable amount of thought as to how, where and when they may be best carried out, if well used they can be extremely effective in eliminating a wide range of behaviours. Obviously it is important to be aware that not all behaviour problems are eliminated by this procedure, and if disruptive behaviours do not terminate fairly quickly when time out is instituted, the implication is that this is not the best approach for this particular child or a particular behaviour. The next few examples, however, indicate the sorts of behaviour that *are* likely to respond to time out techniques.

Jamie's tantrums seemed to be maintained partly by the attention they aroused and partly by the fact that once he got into a rage it was almost impossible to interrupt the pattern. In his case, brief removal to the bathroom effectively reduced the amount of attention he received for such behaviours, and also seemed to break the rather set cycle of his tantrums. As can be seen from Figure 7.3, although there was an initial rise in tantrums when the programme

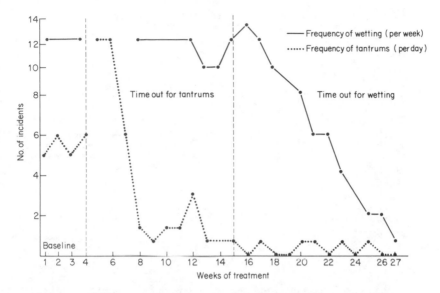

Figure 7.3 Reduction of tantrums and deliberate urination using time out

was first implemented, the frequency declined considerably after the first few weeks of treatment and has remained at a low level since.

Certain toileting problems may also be responsive to time out procedures. There are times when wetting or soiling is used deliberately to gain attention and Jamie, for example, although basically toilet trained, would deliberately wet when he was either angry or wanted attention. In the past his mother had resorted to smacking and shouting at him but this had little or no effect, except perhaps to make the problem worse. Therefore, following the successful programme to decrease the frequency of his tantrums, time out in the bathroom was used immediately following deliberate episodes of wetting. Since he could do little damage in there, and as the bathroom had a tiled floor, further urination caused no problems. Initially these procedures resulted in a small increase in the incidents of wetting, but eventually the rate dropped to about one or two occasions per week as Figure 7.3 indicates.

Eating problems can also be dealt with by time out procedures, but here the solution may involve the removal of food rather than simply adult attention. At the age of 6 Matthew refused to eat at the dining table at all and would simply grab food and run around the house until it was devoured. Because of the disruptive nature of this behaviour he had to be fed at a separate time from the rest of the family. Initially, his parents had tried to deal with the problem by physically restraining him and making him sit at the table, but this was becoming increasingly difficult. Instead, therefore, food was made available only as long as he sat quietly. As soon as he attempted to get up from the table his food was removed and not replaced until he was returned. Once he was eating appropriately while alone, the use of similar techniques was transferred to

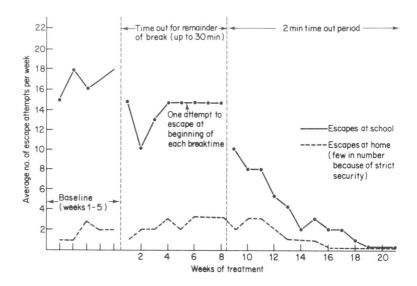

Figure 7.4 Effects of various lengths of time out on attempts to escape

the family dining table. Instant removal of food for getting up, grabbing other people's plates or other disruptive behaviours rapidly proved effective and he was soon able to take part in regular family mealtimes.

Mild self-injurious behaviour may also be dealt with very effectively by parents deliberately removing their attention. Self-injury, although often a problem in profoundly retarded children, is rarely of serious concern in children of higher IQ, such as the ones involved in this study. When it did occur it was usually in response to frustration or used as a means for the child to get his own way. In none of the children in this study was it used in any self-stimulatory way and hence it proved fairly easy to control. Once parents were assured that the child was extremely *unlikely* to do himself any harm, they could be persuaded to try not to respond to the head banging or hand biting or whatever self-injurious behaviour the child showed. Often, with the support of the therapist, they rapidly became aware of the manipulative quality of their child's behaviour. Alex, for example, could be clearly observed to stop his head banging and peer out from under the table to make sure that he was being observed before he continued. Once the parents recognized this, they were able to leave the room without anxiety and to respond to more appropriate ways of gaining attention at other times, with the result that the head banging rapidly ceased.

It should be noted, however, that injury of a self-stimulatory kind, especially in severely retarded groups, may be much more difficult to control and time out procedures here will not necessarily be effective. Possible forms of alternative treatment for such cases are described by Murphy and Wilson (1985).

How Long should Time Out be?

Time Out procedures, if carried out efficiently, should not prove time consuming and research evidence indicates that the optimum period for excluding a child is the order of a few minutes only. If excluded for longer periods, the programme is likely to be *less* successful. Indeed, as Figure 7.4 shows, the period of time spent in time out may be crucial to the success of a programme. Wayne was an inverterate escaper, and as both his home and school were on major roads such behaviour was a potentially lethal problem. His attempts to escape at school occurred mainly at breaktimes and time out procedures (i.e. bringing him inside into the school office) were used to deal with the problem each time it occurred. To begin with, this exclusion from the playground for the remainder of playtime seemed to be successful. However, as winter drew on and the weather became colder, Wayne gradually appeared to enjoy spending more and more of his playtime sitting in the headmistress's office. This resulted in his attempting to escape *immediately* playtime started. Consequently each breaktime was spent cosily indoors. Reducing the time out period to only a few minutes and then returning him to the playground resulted in a much more rapid reduction in this behaviour.

Where should Time Out be Conducted?

If it is necessary to remove the child to an alternative situation in order to prevent the occurrence of inappropriate behaviours, thought needs to be given to *where* the time out period should be conducted. Again this will depend entirely on the individual child and his family, and the layout of the house. Some knowledge of the home is necessary to ensure the family is given appropriate advice.

In the early stage of the intervention project, for example, the therapists had recommended that Martin be removed to the hallway in an attempt to control his aggressive outbursts, without realizing that this was full of valuable antiques. For another child, however, removal to the hallway was a very effective procedure. For Jamie, as already noted, the bathroom was used very successfully, and for Stevie the garage (which was an integral part of the house) was used effectively for time out. In several cases the child's own bedroom, if this was a room where he could do little damage, was used. None of the rooms used for time out was, in itself, aversive for the child and all the children were happy to spend time in these places either alone or in adult company at other times of the day. The only aversive element was the child's removal from adult attention or other forms of reinforcement to a place where this was no longer available. As soon as the disruptive behaviour ceased he would be removed from this setting and allowed to take part in family activities once more.

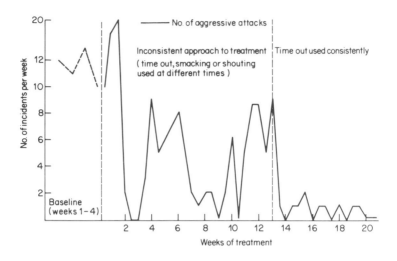

Figure 7.5 Effects of consistency in the use of time out procedures

The Importance of Consistency

Although time out procedures can be adapted to deal with a wide variety of problems and a wide range of children, consistency is essential for its success. Progress is only likely to be achieved if the behaviour is dealt with appropriately *every* time it occurs. Jamie's mother, for example, had successfully used time out to eliminate tantrums and other behaviour problems. However, she coped far less well with his aggressive outbursts and his attacks on adults. Although she would remove him quietly to his bedroom on some occasions, at other times she tended to scream and smack him for such behaviours, thereby ensuring he received a considerable amount of attention for them. Only when she began to implement time out *consistently* following each attack did the behaviour begin to decline. Figure 7.5 traces the effectiveness of this programme over time.

One of the problems with time out or extinction techniques is that although parents may learn to ignore inappropriate responses, other relatives in the family, or strangers in shops or on buses, are likely to continue to give the child attention. Intermittent attention of this kind is particularly effective in maintaining undesirable behaviours and parents may need to evolve additional techniques to cope when away from home. Sometimes, relatives can be persuaded to cooperate with the parents in ignoring the undesirable responses. However, this cannot always be achieved. At one time, for example, Stevie acquired an extremely choice vocabulary of swear words. Although time out procedures kept these to a minimum at home, the frequency of swearing rose rapidly when he was in the presence of strangers, or some of his more shockable elderly relatives. For a time, therefore, parents were asked to place a limitation on visits away from home. Stevie would be allowed to go on brief outings with them but these would be terminated *immediately* if swearing occurred. Once he learned that swearing resulted in the rapid termination of his favourite walks, there was a marked reduction in this behaviour and gradually longer and longer outings became possible without disruption.

The Importance of Attention at Other Times

The rationale of time out depends on a change in the *pattern* of social reinforcement and it is important that the overall level of parental attention should *not* be reduced. The aim is to alter the contingencies so that the disruptive behaviour is immediately followed by cessation of attention, whereas adaptive behaviour results in parental interest, attention and encouragement. As noted, this means that the parents need to be alert to the need to end the time out period *as soon as* the disruptive behaviour stops. Time out is not a punishment, nor is it 'out of sight, out of mind'. Equally, the parents should be careful that the use of extinction and time out procedures do not lead to a habit of ignoring the child. Special efforts are sometimes needed to ensure that there is ample social attention and interaction at other times and it may be helpful to encourage parents to seek to increase their overall level of involvement with their autistic child while using these 'withdrawal of attention' procedures. Also, time out alone is unlikely to have long lasting benefits. In order to be successful, time out or extinction procedures must always be used in conjunction with other programmes aimed at developing more positive skills.

Encouraging Alternative Behaviours; The Use of Differential Reinforcement Techniques

Differential reinforcement techniques may be effectively used to encourage adaptive behaviours when seeking to reduce a particular deviant behaviour, it is useful to focus on the encouragement of some alternative behaviour that is incompatible with the behaviour to be eliminated. For example, Wayne's habit of smashing objects when he was angry was initially dealt with quite effectively by time out. However, it was soon evident that his 'smashing' was not maintained solely by adult attention, but also by the considerable enjoyment he received from seeing and hearing the objects smash. Although time out resulted in an initial decrease in this behaviour the rates of smashing rapidly began to increase again. Only when additional reinforcement for playing and handling objects *without breaking* them was introduced did the problem behaviour fall to an acceptable level (see Figue 7.6).

Differential reinforcement of incompatible behaviours proved useful in the reduction of stereotyped behaviours and motor mannerisms. Matthew's parents ignored his stereotyped flicking of objects (if they tried to stop this directly it rapidly got worse) but gave him a lot of attention, both verbal and physical, if his hands were more gainfully employed, e.g. doing a jigsaw or turning over the pages of a book. The spinning of plates and other objects was also reduced by differential attention for more appropriate or physically incompatible ways of handling objects.

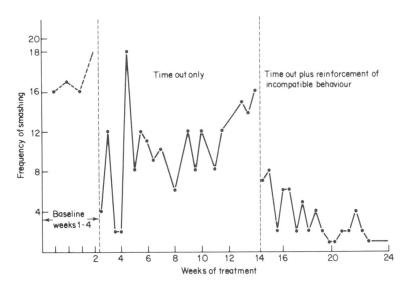

Figure 7.6 The comparative effects of time out and differential reinforcement techniques in modifying destructive behaviour

Differential reinforcement techniques were useful, too, in the management of developmental problems. A number of children showed occasional problems of wetting or soiling and these difficulties were dealt with effectively by ignoring the child's 'accidents' whilst reinforcing him for periods of dryness or cleanliness. These procedures were particularly effective when dealing with problems of daytime wetting. To begin with, rewards would be given for very brief periods of dryness, but non-social rewards were gradually reduced so that although the children were frequently praised for being clean, more tangible reinforcers were given only after several days, or eventually a week's cleanliness. 'Star Charts' recording the number of dry days were useful with older, more verbal children and Stevie, for example, very much enjoyed seeing the 'dry stars' on his chart. He also looked forward to collecting enough of these each week to enable him to win another Matchbox toy to add to his collection—another instance of how obsesssional activities can be used as differential reinforcers for more appropriate behaviours.

Environmental Modifications to Promote Change

The value of environmental restructuring has already been discussed with regard to increasing the child's language and social skills. Modifications of the child's physical environment can also be used to reduce behaviour problems.

Mechanical Aids to Understanding

For the majority of children excessive overactivity was dealt with relatively easily by increasing the range of the child's constructional activities. As these

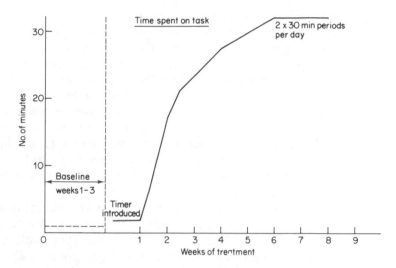

Figure 7.7 Increasing time spent on task using mechanical timer

increased in frequency, and the child actually had something of interest to do when he was sitting down, restlessness frequently declined.

In Graham's case, however, it proved very difficult to stop his habitual wanderings around the neighbourhood and to persuade him to sit still for even the briefest period of time. He became extremely distressed if his freedom to wander was restricted in any way, and his poor verbal comphrension meant that it was impossible to convey to him that his cooperation would be required for only very brief periods. To overcome this problem, his parents made use of a kitchen timer, which was set initially for a very short period (30 seconds) but which allowed him to see for exactly how long he was required to sit. Then, as soon as the timer rang, he was allowed off on his excursions again. At first some physical restraint proved necessary, but praise for sitting, together with the introduction of a task that interested him, and his instant release when the bell rang, made it possible to reduce this rapidly. The length of these 'on task' sessions was then steadily increased from 30 seconds to a minute, to several minutes and so on, until he was eventually sitting with his parents for two half hour periods a day. This made it possible for his parents to work on many different activities with him (see Figure 7.7). As skills in other areas increased, his aimless wandering began to decline.

The Use of Protective Devices and other Physical aids

In recommending time out or extinction procedures to parents, it was necessary for them to be able to ignore the undesirable behaviours without anxiety and without danger to the child. In certain cases, additional aids were necessary in order to achieve this.

Mild injurious behaviours, for example, tended to be reduced more effectively if some sort of simple protective device was utilized. Self-injurious behaviours, whatever their original cause, can become almost a habit with some children and may occur whenever they are upset or frustrated. This may eventually lead to physical damage, as in the case of 4 year old Peter. The original reasons for his hand biting were unclear, although there did seem to have been an attention seeking component at some time. However, as he grew older he began to bite whenever upset or angry so that his hands were permanently calloused. A half mitten covering the area usually bitten enabled his parents to ignore the behaviour, and this, together with their deliberate attempts to occupy his hands in another way (by giving him books or 'lego'), quickly reduced the amount of biting and the extent of his callouses.

The use of physical aids also proved useful in establishing other appropriate skills. Messiness at mealtimes, for instances, was often partly due to poor physical control. This can be helped by providing the child with eating equipment that is better adapted to his needs. Plates that cannot be easily upset or which adhere to the table; non-spillable cups, spoons and forks with large rubber handles that are easy to grip, can all be acquired cheaply and are often an important first step in establishing more acceptable eating habits. Physical prompting can then be used to teach the child how to feed himself appropriately with a spoon, or knife and fork.

Cots or beds with removable bars or sides are often useful when dealing with sleeping problems. Thus, when the child has learned to remain in a cot with bars these can be gradually removed until he is able to sleep alone in a normal bed. Simple aids to dressing—such as Velcro straps rather than laces on shoes, or pull-on stretch tops rather than button-up shirts—can also prove of considerable benefit in ensuring the success of behavioural programmes. The value of commercially available materials as a potential adjunct to therapy should not be overlooked.

The Use of Mild Restraints

Although restraint was not usually recommended, it was used once or twice in dealing with chronic sleeping problems. It is apparent that lack of sleep can cause considerable distress to parents and a great deal of disturbance to the family as a whole (DeMyer, 1979). So, on the few occasions when other methods had not worked, simple restraining devices were used in an attempt to ameliorate the problem. Patrick refused to stay in his bedroom alone and persisted in returning downstairs whenever he had the opportunity. Although his parents returned him to bed each time, this became so frequent that they were having to return upstairs with him up to ten or fifteen times each night. The house was a tall Victorian building on four floors and returning him to his bedroom took several minutes each time. It was difficult *not* to give him attention on the numerous trips back upstairs and parents' own time alone was being constantly disrupted. Eventually, they dealt with the problem by fixing a chain lock to his door. This prevented his leaving the room but at the same time enabled him partly to open the door and to look out and hear his parents downstairs. He showed no apparent anxiety at being shut in in this way and as soon as he realized that his shouts or attempts to remove the lock were unsuccessful he quickly gave up trying to escape. This rapidly resulted not only in his spending more time quietly in his bedroom, but also spending much more time asleep.

Other Environmental Modifications

Changes in the child's immediate environment also helped to decrease problems associated with resistance to going to bed or nocturnal wanderings about the house. Parents often complained that their children were not sleeping enough but it was uncommon for this to be a clinically significant problem. Children vary greatly in their need for sleep and usually children sleep the hours they need. Analysis of sleeping difficulties generally showed that the problems involved settling the child at night, a sleep–wake pattern that did not fit in with family routines, or a tendency to cause disruption when waking at times other family members are asleep. Accordingly, in most cases treatment was focused on night-time routines rather than on increasing the number of hours the child slept. Thus, the aim was to get the child to go to his bedroom at a reasonable time and to stay there without disruption until the morning.

The first step was to make the child's bedroom as pleasurable a place as possible, thereby encouraging him to remain in the bedroom throughout the night—if not actually in bed. Toys or objects that the child particularly liked were made readily available in the bedroom and no attempts were made to stop the child playing quietly with these. If the child left the room and came to his parents he would be firmly and quietly returned to his bedroom. If the child needed reassurance of his parent's presence, brief visits to the child would be made at fixed and gradually extended intervals. Parents were dissuaded from spending lengthy periods in the child's room—or from getting into bed with him (as some were inclined to do). These basic procedures resulted in a considerable reduction in sleeping problems although various modifications needed to be made to suit individual needs. Patrick, for example, was too small to climb back into his bed when he did eventually want to sleep, so a foam mattress was left on the floor in order that he could fall asleep where he was (for other possible ways of dealing with sleeping problems, see Douglas and Richman, 1984).

Environmental changes were also used as one way of dealing with feeding problems. Many mothers expressed anxiety about their child's limited diet and poor eating habits. Our initial approach stressed the need to keep detailed records of the child's eating behaviours. In none of the cases in the present study was it found that children were eating too little, and rarely was the child's diet as restricted as the parents feared. Once it was established that children were *not* in danger of suffering severe malnutrition, practical ways of dealing with the problems could be evolved. In many cases, the restriction of food *only* to

110

mealtimes and *only* if the child sat quietly at the dining table resulted in a rapid improvement in eating behaviours. Children were not given food except at regular mealtimes, although for one or two children 'meals' had to be made quite frequent during the day to begin with. Wayne, for example, demanded sweets and cakes throughout the day. To have limited his intake to only three times each day would have proved extremely difficult, both for him and his mother. To begin with, therefore, his mother designated six 'mealtimes' at regular intervals during the day. After a small amount of non-sweet food he would then be given something sweet, but other than at these times *no* food was provided. Gradually the number of 'mealtimes' per day was reduced to three, and the amount of non-sweet food he was required to eat before he received his dessert was extended considerably.

Mechanical Aids in the Treatment of Toileting Behaviours

Reinforcement techniques alone were enough to establish toilet-training in three of the four autistic children who had never acquired urinary continence during the daytime. Thomas, however, showed little response to this treatment and a modified version of the procedures described by Azrin and his colleagues (Azrin and Foxx, 1971; Azrin *et al.*, 1974) was implemented instead. This involved giving Thomas large and frequent amounts to drink and sitting him on the toilet every half hour. A 'potty alarm' was attached to his potty, so that a buzzer sounded when he urinated in it. An alarm, emitting a different sound, was also attached to his pants so that an adult could be quickly alerted if he began to wet himself. Although it may sound rather cumbersome, the combined use of these two alarms proved useful in helping the child gain greater awareness of, and hence greater control over, his bladder function. Because of the time consuming nature of this programme the two psychologists involved in the project stayed in

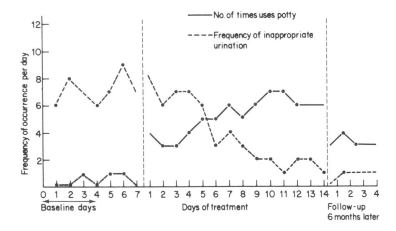

Figure 7.8 The use of an intensive toilet training programme with 4 year old Thomas

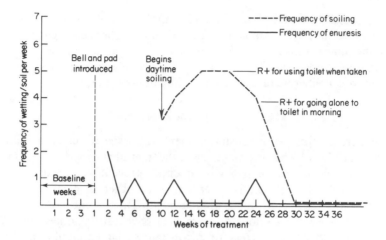

Figure 7.9 Techniques used in the reduction of nocturnal enuresis and diurnal soiling

the child's home each day for a week. At the end of this period Thomas was using his potty for urination approximately 80 per cent of the time (Figure 7.8). Although the 100 per cent success claimed for such treatment by Azrin *et al* (1974) was not achieved, his parents seemed quite satisfied with this level of achievement.

Enuresis Alarms

Various types of enuresis alarms that have proved effective with normal children (Shaffer, 1985) were recommended for children in whom night-time wetting was the main problem. Although the precise mechanisms differ somewhat from model to model the principle is that a pad containing two electrodes is placed under the bottom sheet of the child's bed or, in more sophisticated versions, attached to the child's pyjamas. When the sheet or pyjamas are made wet by the child starting to urinate, the moisture makes contact between the two electrodes; this completes an electric circuit so triggering an auditory signal (a bell or buzzer) which causes the child to wake up and stop urinating. The parents can then take the child to the toilet, change the bed clothing and reset the alarm. The precise learning process by which this leads to bladder control remains obscure (as success leads to the child sleeping through the night without wetting rather than to his waking to wet); nevertheless, whatever the explanation, the procedure is highly effective with most children.

As with normal children, 'cures' in the autistic group (as defined by fourteen continuous dry nights) were usually established around the second month of treatment. However, whereas in normal children the initial success is often followed by relapse, requiring further use of the alarm system at a later time, once dryness was established in the autistic children it was almost always lasting. Unfortunately, this did not mean that treatment was entirely effective. Ben, for example, ceased bed wetting quite rapidly after the introduction of an alarm device. Unfortunately, as can be seen from Figure 7.9, he then began to wet and soil in the house during the *day* and so it was necessary to reintroduce differential reinforcement techniques to encourage his correct use of the toilet, whilst ignoring deliberate or accidental soiling in other places.

MEDICAL INTERVENTIONS

Because there is no known medical treatment with a specific effect on autism or on its associated problems, the mainstay of the treatment programme comprised the various behavioural and environmental procedures discussed above. However, there were occasions when drugs or other medical interventions proved to be necessary adjuncts to treatment. Thus, some autistic children became more tense and anxious or more aggressive during adolescence. When this continued to cause distress or disturbance that could not be kept to manageable limits by behavioural means, one of the major tranquilizers was tried. Drug treatments were always carefully monitored for both benefits and side-effects, the drug being continued only if its use was associated with worthwhile gains. In a few cases, too, antidepressants have proved useful when older adolescents have shown clear indications of clinical depression. Severe overactivity in younger children has also occasionally warranted treatment with tranquilizers. However, as with severely retarded children, stimulants are *not* usually beneficial (in spite of their efficacy in non-autistic children of normal intelligence). Indeed, they can make matters worse by increasing stereotypies. Medical treatments may also be required for various physical complications. Thus, about a quarter of autistic children develop epileptic fits during adolescence (Rutter, 1979; Deykin and MacMahon, 1979) and, if these occur more than once, anticonvulsant medication is usually indicated. Soiling, too, may occasionally be associated with bowel disorders that require medical help.

Peter, aged 4, had suffered from severe chronic constipation associated with faecal incontinence since a baby. The anxiety and concern shown by his mother over this was obvious, and much of the child's day was spent in battles over going to the toilet. After appropriate investigation, Peter was found to show distention of the bowel accompanied by a partial blockage from the accumulated faeces. A short stay in hospital was required in order to carry out physical removal of the impacted faeces. Once this had been done, regular and frequent visits to the lavatory in a calm and unhurried atmosphere were instituted, with a 'softening' agent being used to ensure that constipation did not recur. His mother, relieved of the anxiety about his physical condition, was then able to carry out the programme herself at home. Complete training was achieved in about 3 months.

CONCLUSIONS

As discussed in this and the previous three chapters, although the treatment programme was based on sets of behavioural and developmental principles, their application required a careful individual assessment of each child's problems. The treatment methods were carefully adapted to the particular problems and family conditions prevailing at the time. Apparently similar problems, such as toileting or feeding, encompass a very wide range of difficulties each of which may need to be dealt with in a different way. Choosing the appropriate technique to be used with a particular behaviour required a detailed functional analysis of the problem—in terms of its component parts, its predisposition, circumstances, precipitants and consequences. The various possible techniques likely to be effective were discussed with the parents in order to work out a treatment plan. The parents' own wishes and skills were taken into account in deciding on a therapeutic strategy. The initial functional analysis provided the means for decisions on how to start treatment but systematic monitoring of effects was required in order to decide whether to persist or change tactics. When treatment approaches caused distress to the child or to his family, alternative methods of treatment had to be sought. To some extent effective treatment is an art rather than a science. There are, it is true, basic ground rules that will help in the choice of appropriate procedures. However, if such approaches are to be successful, their implementation requires imagination, ingenuity and sensitivity. In order to achieve optimal benefits it is necessary for art and science to combine forces.

Chapter 8

The Alleviation of Family Problems

Together with the goals of aiding the autistic child's development and reducing his level of disorder an equal priority must be given to the objective of alleviating *family* distress. The parents and siblings of handicapped children face many difficulties and this is particularly so in the case of families with autistic children, many of whom are unresponsive and unrewarding to be with, difficult to play and talk with, and demanding in their need for supervision, structuring and control.

Helping parents to develop effective management strategies and providing them with practical means of coping with their children's problems is, of course, central to treatment. The acquisition of effective coping mechanisms plays an important role in helping to reduce worries, anxieties and general feelings of inadequacy. However, it is important also that treatment should be sensitive to the needs of both parents as individuals, to their roles in their marital relationship, and to the needs of other children in the family. *What* parents are expected to do for their autistic child and *how* they are expected to do it must be adapted to the personal situation and characteristics of each family. But, also, the therapist must be alert to the irrational guilt felt by many parents, to their despair and depression when their child seems to make so little progress, to their anger and frustration aroused by difficulties in dealing with resistant problems, to their disappointment or hostility at the child's lack of affection and social response, and to their resentment over having a handicapped child at all. These are normal and understandable reactions experienced at some time by most parents of seriously handicapped children, but counselling and case work are needed to help parents realize that they are not alone in these feelings, that love and anger can coexist, and that there are ways of coming to terms with these troubling feelings and of channelling them in positive directions.

As well as providing specific help related to the child's problems, our work with families focused on the provision of guidance and support over the more general issues associated with having a handicapped child. The possible effects on siblings and other family members were discussed and advice was given about the parents' involvement with their non-handicapped children. Marital and other emotional problems were encountered fairly frequently, and our approach to these issues followed the same basic pattern of careful analysis, leading to whatever therapeutic strategy seemed most appropriate, as employed in the treatment of other areas of difficulty. Practical help in finding schooling or short term relief placements was given, there was advice about the future outlook for the autistic child and, if requested, genetic counselling was provided.

ESTABLISHING REALISTIC GOALS

Perhaps one of the most immediate aims of our intervention with families was to give parents a realistic notion of what their child was likely to be able to achieve, and also to sort out serious problems that needed intervention from those that were less important, or that were simply a part of the more normal process of growing up.

The Need for Information and Advice

Many parents had a tendency to blame all the problems shown by their child on the fact that he was autistic. Frequently, however, the problems were typical of those shown by young, normal children in the process of growing up. Providing parents with knowledge about normal developmental processes often proved useful in helping them to get the problems of the autistic child into a better perspective. Some parents, for example, became very distressed when children of around 5 or 6, who had just begun to develop more effective use of language, began to be more assertive or uncooperative at the same time. It was often valuable here to point to the similar difficulties shown by normal infants, admittedly at a younger age, in order to make parents aware of the normality of this particular stage in development. Advice about dealing with problems of eating, sleeping and toileting also made use of information about developmental processes. Parents often worried that their child was not getting enough sleep or food intake. Careful monitoring of the child's eating or sleeping habits usually indicated that he was in fact getting a good deal of sleep or food, although not necessarily in the way that best suited the family. Assuring parents that the child was getting enough food or sleep for his own particular needs was sometimes sufficient to remove the problem altogether. In other cases, advice of this kind, by effectively reducing parental anxiety, then helped them to implement more successful management programmes.

Sometimes, too, simply pointing out to families that the so called 'problems' shown by their child were characteristic of the family temperament or general pattern of interaction was helpful. Thomas's mother, for example, complained of self-absorption and the long periods of time he sat quietly by himself. However, this was also the way in which many of the other family members spent their time, and appeared very much to be a family trait. Jamie, in contrast, reacted histrionically to the tiniest upset. Pointing out, gently, to his mother that she tended to do much the same was not exactly well received, but it did seem to make her think a little more about her own styles of interaction.

Helping to Increase Independence from the Family

A handicapped child tends to generate feelings of protectiveness in adults; the tendency for parents to overprotect their child and to shield him from the normal pressures of life is particularly strong. At the start of treatment, for example, many children were entirely dressed and fed by their parents. Some had never looked after themselves in this way, whilst in other cases attempts had been made to teach them but because of the mess and frustration generated these attempts had been rapidly abandoned. Some children had acquired basic self-help skills, but did not use these in a particularly useful way. Thus, unlike other children in the family, they were not expected to carry out even simple household chores and played no role in the day to day running of the house. Realistic expectations of what the child should be doing at a particular developmental level can be helpful both in giving parents themselves more freedom and in increasing the child's own skills more effectively.

For some families advice based on detailed assessments of their child's developmental level and information about what is expected of normal children at this stage, may be enough to help them to encourage higher levels of maturity and self-help skills.

For other families more specific goals will need to be formulated and detailed advice may be required on how to attain these. Teaching self-feeding or dressing skills, for example, often involved a combination of behavioural techniques such as physical prompts, shaping, fading and reinforcement techniques. In this way the methods that parents had already used in the project in dealing with other problems could be adapted to increase the child's level of independence.

When it came to increasing independence in older children, a combination of emotional support and practical advice was often needed. After the close supervision necessary in the child's early years, 'letting go' was for many parents a difficult stage to face. Having taught the child skills such as road safety, how to buy tickets on trains or buses, how to go shopping, etc., the question of how far the child should be able to put these into practice on his own often gave rise to much heart searching. Even the best planned programme of fading prompts requires that, in the end, parents must reduce their supervision entirely. Some parents, particularly those living in the centre of towns, felt unable to do this, and always kept the child under some supervision, albeit at a distance. Others, living in less congested areas, were more willing to take risks. Although it was not for us to take the final decision for the parents, discussions about the level of the child's skills, and whether it was at least potentially safe for him to be out alone, sometimes helped them to make up their minds. Practical aids that might be useful in case of emergency were also recommended. These included having the child's name and address engraved on a bracelet, ensuring that he knew how to make a phone call home (and always had a couple of spare coins for a phone box), that he was familiar with local bus or train routes, and that he could tell strangers where he lived. Some parents supplied the child with an identity card, which also indicated that he was handicapped, although others felt there were disadvantages to this. Clearly we could never guarantee to parents that their child would come to no harm, but discussions about the risks involved did seem to help them make their own decisions. In fact, only one untoward event occurred, and that was in the case of Simon who got lost when riding his bicycle. However, heeding his parents' advice, he went to look for a police station and having given his name and address was driven home. Unfortunately, as is often the case with autistic children, the problem was not entirely solved. He so enjoyed the lift home that he repeated this escapade on another two occasions and it finally took a few firm words from the local sergeant to put a stop to his 'adventures'.

THE EFFECTS OF THE AUTISTIC CHILD ON THE FAMILY

Parents frequently expressed concern about the extent to which their other children might suffer from having an autistic child in the family. In dealing with these worries a combination of factual information, practical help and some direct intervention was required.

Effect on Siblings

There has been little study of the specific effects on children having an autistic brother or sister but there are some limited findings from research with other handicapped groups (Byrne and Cunningham, 1985). The conclusions are not entirely consistent but they provide some guidelines. Most children cope well with having a handicapped member of the family and there need be no expectation that necessarily they will suffer. Probably much depends on particular family circumstances. Nevertheless, siblings of handicapped children may show somewhat increased rates of disturbance and of problems of self-identity, and some also express considerable resentment. More physical demands may be placed on them by parents, and they may receive less time and attention from parents preoccupied by the needs and problems of the autistic child. Some children, too, feel that they need to overachieve in order to make up for the limitations of the handicapped child. However, there also appear to be benefits associated with being the sibling of a handicapped child. Some studies have reported greater maturity, responsibility and increased tolerance and altruistic concern. Simeonsson and McHale (1981) found that the handicapped child is generally loved and accepted by his siblings, with most problems resolvable. In Gath's (1974) study of Down's syndrome individuals, older sisters seemed more often adversely affected, possibly because of the demands put upon them to care for the handicapped child. If such demands can be reduced, and if parents themselves can be helped to share their time more evenly with all their children, any adverse effects should be kept to a minimum.

Overall, the aim of intervention was to help parents adapt their general management strategies in such a way as to help their autistic child to make progress and to keep behavioural problems to a minimum, but in a manner that did not impose undue stress either on the child or on the rest of the family. Developing the autistic children's self-help and occupational skills was important so that they could be left alone more frequently. Parents could then have greater opportunity to give *more* time to their *non*-autistic children. Parents were also given help to ensure that the restrictions and limitations imposed by the handicapped child on other siblings were reduced to a minimum. For example, we suggested minor modifications to the home, to enable the normal children to have a greater degree of privacy and a room or area of the house where they could play or work undisturbed.

Giving older children the opportunity to talk about their feelings for their siblings, and their worries and anxieties, was also considered important. Sometimes, this would be done through parents, by helping them to deal with the anxieties raised by their children. In other cases the child might ask for independent help and advice, and this would always be available if necessary.

Behavioural problems in siblings (such as demands for greater attention or disruptive behaviour) were dealt with by helping parents to generalize the management skills used with the autistic child to other children in the family. Parents' management of their non-autistic children was often very different from their handling of the autistic child and normal children frequently expressed some resentment that their autistic sibling 'got away with' many more bad behaviours than they did. Helping parents evolve consistent rules—not only for the autistic child but for other children, too—was useful, in reducing problems of this kind. Simple explanations of the autistic child's special needs were also provided if the autistic child clearly needed a very different approach to management and when 'fairness' could not be achieved.

Techniques such as time out or extinction were used, if necessary, to deal with problem behaviours but on the whole negative procedures such as these were avoided. It was generally felt that the siblings of the autistic children were at considerable disadvantage compared with other children and so the intervention focused as far as possible on the use of more positive approaches to dealing with their problems.

The Involvement of Siblings in Therapy

It was clear that the involvement of the whole family in treatment greatly improved rates of learning and the maintenance and generalization of new skills. Nevertheless, before involving siblings it was necessary to make sure that this would not impose further demands on them, thereby increasing rather than decreasing negative attitudes towards the autistic child. The successful use of siblings as co-therapists requires considerable sensitivity to their own needs and wishes, and should not be undertaken without careful preparation. It is important never to pressurize other children to become involved in treatment. Nevertheless, on the whole, those who did become involved in this way frequently proved to be remarkably good and consistent co-therapists. Such a role can also greatly help to improve siblings' feelings of self-esteem and many children expressed very positive feelings of achievement when involved in therapy in this way.

THE EFFECTS OF A HANDICAPPED CHILD ON PARENTS

The continuing sense of sorrow, loss and guilt experienced by parents of a severely handicapped child has often been noted. For families of autistic children, the additional feelings of rejection produced by having a child who shows little or no emotional attachment to them can make the burden even more difficult to bear. Helping parents to cope with the many conflicting emotions created by the presence of an autistic child is therefore an essential part of treatment. Again, a combined approach to therapy was necessary, involving factual information, emotional support, practical help and direct intervention.

The Need for Factual Information

Many parents had, in the past, been victims of outmoded and ill-founded beliefs that their lack of stimulation, or their inadequate parenting, had been the initial cause of the child's withdrawal. Simple but factual accounts based on existing evidence of what is known about the causes of autism were much appreciated by many families. It is clear that autism is related to organic brain dysfunction, and not to psychosocial deprivation (Rutter, 1985a). Although we could not give parents any clear guidance as to what had caused the brain disorder, we were able to reassure them that they had not in any way caused the autism.

It is important to be aware, whilst working within a behavioural framework, that such intervention, if insensitively applied, may actually reinforce parents' feelings of guilt and responsibility for their child's handicap. The very fact of suggesting to parents that they may be able to modify their child's behaviour may imply that they were initially responsible for the development of the problems. Such anxieties need to be dealt with in the very early stages of working with a family if therapists are to avoid increasing, rather than alleviating, existing feelings of guilt and inadequacy.

It was also felt important to provide families with a realistic appreciation of how far treatment can go in overcoming the child's problems. Many much publicized programmes, such as the techniques advocated by Doman and Delacato in America, have promised benefits only if parents give very extensive time to their child (often the bulk of waking hours!). Some behavioural psychologists, such as Lovaas (1978), whilst not promising cures, insist on substantial family sacrifice if therapy is to be effective. Parents must agree not to have another child during the intervention period and one parent may be required to give up their job. The evidence from follow-up studies, however, indicates that such extensive demands on a family's time and energy do not result in a markedly better outcome for the child. Indeed, such procedures may well disrupt family life more than ever.

The initial assessments of the child should enable the therapist to make at least tentative predictions about progress. Obviously, advice about prognosis can never be infallible, and it is always important to warn parents of this. Nevertheless, advice based on well conducted follow-up studies can help to give parents a clearer idea of what the future may hold in store for them and their child. This in turn will very much affect the goals of treatment, and can help parents to develop a more realistic expectation of the effects of therapy. It is important that therapists are sensitive to the potentially stressful effects of intervention, and that they strive to ensure that treatment results in fewer, not greater, demands on families. It is also crucial never to raise false hopes, and whilst encouraging parents to work effectively in developing their child's potential, the limitations of this potential should always be borne in mind.

Practical information of this kind can be of help in at least alleviating the many feelings of guilt experienced by parents of handicapped children. It is also important to make clear that it is neither necessary nor indeed advisable for them to devote all their time to their handicapped child. Helping parents to organize their day so that they are able to divide their time more effectively between the autistic child and other members of the family was, as already noted, an important aspect of treatment. But, since parents could not be actively engaged with their child all day long, it was also necessary to help them accept that there would be periods when no intervention would be possible and when stereotyped or obsessive activities might occur. As long as these are not disruptive and did not encroach on other activities, our advice to parents was to allow these, and even to accept them as being necessary for the autistic child. Learning to accept that both they and their child needed some time alone often brought considerable relief to parents, who previously had been led to believe that constant stimulation was the only answer.

Help with Practical Issues

Often, both physical and emotional distress arose from the practical restraints of being constantly tied to the house and the autistic child. It was crucial, therefore, to ensure that parents received as much physical relief as possible from the daily strains imposed upon them.

Liaison with Schools

Because few of the young children in the study were receiving any education when intervention first began, finding appropriate schooling was a task which faced us in much of our early work. In some cases, admission to a local unit or school specifically for autistic children was possible. For very young children admission to a nursery or playgroup was arranged; some catered for handicapped children and some for mixed groups with normal children. In the case of two children living close together in a small village, the local school was persuaded to make a classroom and a teacher available for them and for a few other local youngsters showing a variety of learning disorders. Establishing effective links with local schools required a considerable amount of liaison work with both the educational and social service teams involved, as well as with head teachers and their staff. If the child's difficulties were well understood *before* admission and if access to practical help and advice was readily available, many schools were willing to take on the challenge of accepting an autistic child. They also proved very willing to carry out teaching programmes that had already been established in the home, as well as to implement new programmes that were more specifically school oriented.

With children already established in schools or units before treatment began, the amount of cooperation between school and home was variable. Many units were only too pleased to cooperate, and were also appreciative of the help offered to parents. Only in one or two cases, where the teaching philosophy was very much opposed to behavioural methods, was liaison less successful. The failure of even quite well established skills, such as language, to show generalization to settings where these skills were not encouraged has already been discussed. Problem behaviours, too, tended to persist if they were not dealt with in all settings. Patrick, for example, whose attachments to objects was dealt with rapidly and efficiently at home, remained attached to specific objects at school (much to the detriment of his other attainments) because staff felt it 'cruel' to remove them.

This lack of cooperation obviously made learning more difficult for the child, and considerably increased the parents' task in gaining control over behavioural problems. Fortunately, however, the number of units in which such problems persisted were few. Many others, although initially opposed to the use of behavioural principles on the grounds that they were all 'Smackings and Smarties', could be persuaded to see the value of techniques once they were discussed in terms that were free from jargon; especially when it was pointed out that they already used many of the methods effectively anyway.

Helping parents and teachers collaborate on problems frequently improved relationships between home and school, and many parents who had previously felt isolated from, or even antagonistic to, the school became active participants in school activities.

Cooperation with District Education Teams was also essential in finding appropriate placements for children who were either in the wrong type of placement or receiving no schooling at all. Occasionally problems of 'demarcation' of responsibility arose, but with care and due consultation these could generally be avoided, and in fact very few practical problems were encountered in working together with local educational services.

Holidays

Holidays, or rather the lack of them, often produced considerable problems. Although some children could be taken to hotels or holiday camps without too much trouble, in many cases holidays in unfamiliar settings produced even greater strains on parents than if they remained at home. For other families, even contemplating taking the child away was totally out of the question. Thus school holidays, with all the children at home, were often a time when problems escalated dramatically. Organizing brief holidays for the autistic child with groups such as those run by 'Buckets and Spades', or 'Break' offered some relief. And, even if holidays could not be arranged at the peak of the season, it was often possible to organize a planned break for parents at other times of the year.

Help with Medical and Dental Problems

For children living at a distance from London good liaison with local medical teams was essential to ensure that, if the necessity arose, even a very handicapped autistic child could be treated in his nearest hospital. If admission for physical reasons was necessary, as it proved to be in a couple of cases, the psychologists involved with the family visited the hospital in order to discuss the child's difficulties with staff. We attempted to make the transition from home to hospital proceed as smoothly as possible.

Dental treatment was required by a number of children, and helping families to find a sympathetic dentist was clearly important. Unfortunately, many practitioners took little heed of parents' warnings about their child's difficulties until it was too late. Kevin's mother, for example, had specifically requested that her appointment in a large dental teaching hospital be kept promptly as he became 'upset' if required to wait. Kevin's particular way of expressing his upset involved banging his head against hard surfaces. When no dentist appeared on time, Kevin attacked the only flat object available, an extremely large tank of tropical fish. Faced with the inevitable, and with dying fish all around him, the dentist finally admitted that perhaps he should have listened to mother's advice!

Although, fortunately, this was an isolated incident, many children were extremely fearful of visits to the dentist, having already had one or two bad experiences. In these cases the use of role play, 'graded change' and desensitization techniques to reintroduce them to the feared situation often proved very valuable (as indeed it also did in the case of a large number of children who were fearful of visiting hairdressers). The implementation of these methods required a skilled and sympathetic practitioner, but once such individuals were found they were usually very willing to cooperate in treatment.

Links with Other Services

Finally, for many parents encouraging them to join the National Autistic Society proved immensely valuable. The society provides a useful selection of literature for the parents of autistic children, it is able to offer a good deal in the way of practical help and can put parents in touch with other families with similar problems. Following their initial contact with the national society, many parents set up their own local groups—which usually included parents of non-autistic handicapped children as well—and these frequently evolved into highly effective self-help groups.

Links with social services also proved important in arranging short term relief for families. Wherever possible, close liaison with social services was developed and was used to arrange brief planned breaks at regular intervals in children's homes or special hostels. The opportunity of having the odd free weekend often enabled parents, who might otherwise have requested residential placement, to keep their child at home. The provision of planned, occasional placements also meant that if, for illness or some other reason, the child had to be cared for away from home, this could be done in a familiar environment.

Before intervention began, most families had had very little contact with social services. Developing links with local services proved important not only in finding short term care, but also in helping to make families aware of their entitlements to various discretionary awards, such as attendance allowances, and helping them to claim these.

Help with baby-sitting was arranged if possible. Adequate baby-sitting arrangements could be very important in maintaining good family relationships. Obviously, in order to leave the child with a baby-sitter, existing sleeping or behavioural problems needed to be dealt with first. Once this had been achieved, parents were encouraged to go out together as much as possible, and advice about finding sitters through local charitable organizations or schools or colleges was appreciated by several families.

Marital and Psychiatric Problems

The strains on a marriage, and on family relationships generally, of having a handicapped child are bound to be considerable. However, they do not result in as many personal or interpersonal problems as perhaps might be expected. Whilst a number of studies report a higher incidence of mental breakdown or severe marital disharmony amongst the parents of mentally handicapped children, some parents report a strengthening of the marital relationship as the result of having a handicapped child (Gath, 1974). DeMyer (1979) also reported that although there were more strains in the marriages of parents of autistic children than of controls, few of the differences between autistic and non-autistic families were significant. Ratings of psychiatric problems, too, indicated that although the incidence of reactive depression was higher in mothers of autistic children, other problems were not significantly more frequent. Although having a handicapped child can impose severe marital and emotional strains on a family, this is not always the case and therapists need to avoid seeing problems where none exist. Clearly, however, within the context of a therapeutic programme it is always necessary to be sensitive to the possible risk of marital or psychiatric problems. Giving parents the opportunity to discuss their feelings of guilt, anger, resentment and confusion is important, but listening is not necessarily enough. Parents may need to be provided with more effective ways of dealing with or ameliorating these difficulties. This will sometimes involve a counselling approach and sometimes more direct behavioural advice.

The marital relationship of Alex's mother and father, for example, was under considerable strain both sexually and emotionally. His mother was given considerable support in dealing with her feelings of guilt and sorrow and anger at having an autistic child. She was also given practical help to deal with his problems during the day, so that she was less exhausted when her husband came home in the evening. Finally, and perhaps most importantly, the parents were encouraged to work together on a programme to ensure that their night-times were not disturbed by the children. When discussing their sexual difficulties, it had emerged that the parents shared a bed, not only with the autistic child, but also with his younger sister. Mother's way of coping with this problem was to leave her own bed and go and sleep in one of the children's. This resulted in disturbed sleep for all the family and little opportunity for the parents to be alone together. A simple programme to encourage both children to sleep in their own beds at night was soon successful, and although still under strain the marital relationship improved considerably thereafter.

This combination of behavioural strategies and some less directive counselling proved valuable in dealing with many of the emotional and marital problems raised by parents. There were times, however, when it became clear that more intensive psychotherapeutic help was needed. When it became apparent during the course of therapy that parents needed more help than could be offered by the psychologists undertaking the behavioural programme, they were seen by one of the psychiatrists or social workers who were part of the overall therapeutic team. During the course of the study two parents required a combination of counselling and medication for depressive disorders.

DEALING WITH WORRIES ABOUT THE FUTURE

The Outlook for Adult Life

As well as dealing with the day to day problems of childhood and early adolescence, many parents were already concerned and anxious about the problems to come as their children reached adulthood. Follow-up findings show that about three-fifths of autistic individuals remain severely handicapped, with only about one in six likely to make a sufficiently good social adjustment to live independently (Kanner, 1971; Lotter, 1974; Rutter, 1970). However, even those with a good adjustment tend to have continuing difficulties with both social relationships and obsessional behaviours. Generally, outcome is best for those with IQ's above 70 who have developed useful language skills by the age of 5 years, but even within this subgroup only about half show a good adjustment in later life. Even though the children in the present study were no more than mildly mentally handicapped, it was likely that many of them would be unable to lead an independent existence as they grew older.

Discussions about what is known of the expected outcome for autistic children were, for obvious reasons, painful for parents. However, although it was felt important not to shy away from the truth when asked about the future, our general strategy was to stress practical ways of approaching the problems of later life. Thus, it was important to ensure that behavioural difficulties were dealt with firmly whilst children were still young, so that effective management techniques were evolved before children became too big or too disruptive to handle. Emphasis was also placed on increasing communication and other social skills as much as possible.

In addition, families were persuaded to try to widen the child's range of social contacts. Older, less handicapped children were encouraged to join social groups such as the local Cubs or Scouts group, if these had a sympathetic leader. Youth clubs run by the Society for Mentally Handicapped Children were also useful in increasing the child's contact with less socially handicapped children. For some families, too, church organizations offered good opportunities for wider social contacts for their child.

Most autistic children will need to leave home at some stage in their lives. There is always a danger that sudden separation from the family will be associated with great distress and trauma (as when the death or severe illness of a parent necessitates admission to an unknown and possibly unsuitable residential institution). In order to avoid such disruption parents were encouraged to accept *planned* separations even when their children were young. Brief holidays breaks, run by charitable or professional organizations, and the occasional day or weekend spent in a local children's home were often much enjoyed by the children. To begin with, parents were often very reluctant to make use of such provision, but having got over their initial separation anxieties, they too usually came to appreciate the benefits that planned, short term relief could afford.

Because of problems in finding appropriate local schooling, a number of children had to attend boarding schools as they grew older, and this again helped them and their parents to cope with separations. Several parents have subsequently been instrumental in setting up communities for autistic adults, in the hope that their own child may eventually be able to live in such a community. In many cases, these efforts have proved extremely successful; although it was felt important for families with autistic children not to try to distance themselves too much from other groups of parents with handicapped children. Improving services for *all* the handicapped, not just specific groups, is an essential concern and for some families, particularly those with more severely handicapped children, it was felt important to help them recognize the extent of their child's disability. If their child was always likely to be considerably handicapped, it was important to help them to accept that eventually he would have to be placed with other, more obviously retarded individuals. It was for this reason that, at least for the less able children, we did not necessarily try to place them in autistic schools or units, but instead helped parents to find the school most suitable for the child's level of attainment—even if this was a school for more severely handicapped children.

Genetic Counselling

One of the most common questions posed by parents with one autistic child is, 'Can it happen again?' Concern about the risks of having another handicapped child or, in the case of families with older children, the risk that their *grandchildren* may be affected, was frequently raised by the families with whom we were involved. It was obviously important to share with them the current state of knowledge about inherited factors in autism.

For many years it was thought that genetic factors played a negligible role in the origins of infantile autism. This seemed to be a justifiable conclusion from the observation that it was quite rare for two children in the same family to suffer from autism and from the general lack of evidence that autism in any way 'ran in families'. Moreover, autism did not seem to be linked with any *other* form of adult psychiatric disorder, such as schizophrenia. These observations have stood the test of time but several recent studies have shown that certain inferences were incorrect and that, contrary to earlier suppositions, there *are* hereditary influences that do play a role in the causation of autism (Folstein and Rutter, 1987).

Obviously such findings are important in advising parents who are considering having other children. They are also likely to give cause for concern amongst families in the future, as their non-autistic children grow up, and they are faced with the question of the risks to their normal sons and daughters of giving birth to handicapped children.

The evidence for genetic factors in autism stems from two main sources (Folstein and Rutter, 1987). First, the twin study by Folstein and Rutter (1977), found that for monozygotic twin pairs, in which one twin was autistic, there was an 82 per cent chance that the other twin would be autistic or have some other form of language or cognitive disorder, often associated with social difficulties. In contrast the concordance rate in dizygotic twin pairs was only 10 per cent, suggesting that genetic factors played an important role in the origins of autism. However, the findings also indicated that it was not autism as such that was inherited but rather some broader predisposition to language and cognitive difficulties of which autism constitutes but one part.

A further study (August *et al.*, 1983) has shown that, compared with families of children with Down's syndrome, the siblings of autistic children are much more likely to show some form of cognitive disability. Again the cognitive disability took several different forms, including delays in language development, specific learning disabilities and varying degrees of mental handicap, but the 15 per cent rate of such problems was over five times higher in the siblings of autistic children than in the siblings of Down's syndrome children.

These findings, together with the observation that the incidence of autism in siblings of autistic children is approximately one in fifty (i.e. some fifty times as great as that in the normal population), strongly suggest the implication of hereditary factors.

However, what is inherited and how the pattern of inheritance works is less clear cut. It may be that the genetic risk applies to only some cases of autism or it may apply to most. Also, in so far as genetic factors are involved, there may be just one main type of genetic mechanism or there may be several. Counselling of parents necessarily has to reflect the many uncertainties in our current knowledge.

At the present time, accurate predictions on risk are possible only in the small minority of cases with some detectable single gene disorder, such as the fragile X anomaly (see Folstein and Rutter, 1987). In these cases the risk is linked with that for the medical disorder with which the autism is associated. Referral to a medical geneticist is indicated in such instances in order to carry out the investigations on other family members needed for an accurate appraisal of risk, and to provide the knowledge needed for skilled genetic counselling.

In the cases where autism is associated with a clear history of severe perinatal or postnatal trauma giving rise to neurological complications at the time, and where there is no family history of autism or cognitive disabilities, it may be inferred that the recurrence or risk is likely to be very low.

The usual circumstance, however, is that the autism is not associated with either a single gene medical disorder or any known environmental cause. In these cases the recurrence risk for autism is generally said to be about 1 to 3 per cent and that for cognitive disabilities (including both persistent mental retardation and transient language handicaps) about 10 to 15 per cent. However, these figures are most uncertain because they are based on a variety of samples with varying IQ distributions and diagnostic criteria. We know that autism is aetiologically heterogeneous and that it is highly likely that a few families have a high risk for recurrence, whereas others have a negligible one. Unfortunately, we do not as yet know how to tell which is which. As a very rough and ready general guide it may be supposed that the risk is likely to be greater than average if there is a high family loading for either autism or cognitive disabilities and less than average if there is no such history. But that is as far as one can go, and even that is based on no more than common sense extrapolations.

Obviously these figures on recurrence have been expressed in terms of the risk of things going 'wrong'. When families are considering whether or not to have children, it may be more helpful to put things the other way round in terms of the chances of everything being alright—that is of their having a healthy, normal child. Put this way, it is evident that when parents have given birth to one autistic child, the chances of their next one being fully normal are about 5 out of 6, and of being non-autistic are 49 out of 50 on average. If parents really want another child, that may well seem an acceptable risk to take. For the brothers and sisters of an autistic child the chances are very much better in that (probably) their children have on average some 249 chances out of 250 of not being autistic and some 29 chances out of 30 of being normal. A risk as low as that is not likely to put many people off starting a family if that is what they wish to do.

Another situation in which questions on genetic risk may arise is when someone is thinking of marrying into a family with an autistic child (e.g. marrying a normal brother or sister). However, since *most* families carry genes for some type of handicapping condition the presence of a very slightly increased risk for one particular disorder is not unusual—it is just that in the case of autism it is rather more obvious. Few putative parents are likely to be discouraged by the 1 in 250 risk but obviously it is right that they should know that this may be present. Of course, the risks would be rather greater if *both* the marriage partners had an autistic brother or sister, but that must be quite a rare occurrence.

It is important to emphasize that these figures are not only approximate but also they represent *averages* for the families of a large number of autistic children. Austim is a disability that stems from a variety of different causes. Accordingly, parents needed to be guided as to whether the risk in their particular case is likely to be higher or lower than these overall 'average' risks. This is not an easy question to answer as much information crucial to the issue is lacking.

In conclusion, the new evidence on genetic factors in autism is both theoretically and practically important. We still lack knowledge on the exact hereditary mechanisms involved and, until that knowledge is available, guidance on the risks of other autistic children being born into the family is necessarily rather imprecise. Nevertheless, it appears that the situation is the apparently paradoxical one, that hereditary influences are quite important in the development of autism but that, in most ordinary circumstances, the risks of a family having another autistic child are very low. However, several special factors need to be taken into account in estimating the precise risks for any particular family and full discussion of these should be available to any parent who is concerned about the risks to either themselves or other family members of having another autistic child.

Chapter 9

Short Term Effects of Treatment

As described in chapters 4 to 7, individual case studies had shown marked improvement in behavioural problems, language deficit and many other areas of disability. However, as single case studies do not provide evidence on the relative efficacy of different treatment approaches, group comparisons were also needed. In this chapter we examine the short term effects of therapy in terms of differences in 6 months' progress between children in the home based treatment programme and those in the control group.

In that our primary contact was with parents we first looked for overall changes in mothers' behaviour and in the nature of their interactions with their children. We examined the general quality of this interaction and assessed changes in particular facets of verbal interchange

Second, we monitored changes in children themselves. Overall changes in behaviour, language and social skills were analysed, using data from the parental interview. The quality of children's interactions with parents, and the frequency of appropriate or socialized activities, were measured by direct observations of mother and child at home. Particular attention was given to changes in language usage during the treatment period. And, in addition to overall group changes, individual differences in response to treatment were examined.

Finally, the efficiency of the general coping strategies used by parents and the effects of these on children's behaviour were assessed.

CHANGES IN MOTHERS' INTERACTION WITH THEIR CHILDREN

Time Budget Analysis

Before looking in closer detail at change in the ways parents interacted with their children, the time budget analysis was used to examine the amount of time they spent together during the day and the intensity of this interaction. The aim of the project was to ensure that the time parents and children were together was spent more effectively, rather than to increase its overall duration. At the end of the first 6 months of treatment, it was apparent that little change had in fact occurred in terms of the amount or frequency of interaction.

Initially, the patterns of interaction between mothers and children were very similar in both groups (see Figure 9.1) with between 40 and 50 per cent of

130

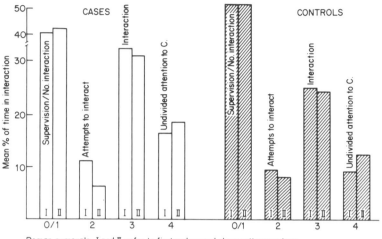

Roman numerals I and II refer to first and second observation sessions.
Arabic numerals 0 and 4 refer to levels of interaction.

Figure 9.1 Intensity of interaction with children: differences between cases
and controls

parental time used in getting on with their own activities or supervising the child
from a distance. Between 25 and 35 per cent of time was spent in direct
intervention with children. Highly intensive interactions, involving close physical
and verbal contact, occurred much less frequently (around 10 to 15 per cent).
Unsuccessful attempts to engage the child occurred somewhat less than 10 per
cent of the time. At follow-up, as Figure 9.1 makes clear, these proportions had
changed remarkably little in either group. No significant differences either
between groups or between occasions were found.

It was evident that although intensive intervention at home might have been
expected to increase the pressure on parents to spend more time with their
children, this had not, in fact, happened. Parents showed no marked changes in
the way in which they apportioned their time with their children and, in keeping
with the general aims of the project, neither the frequency nor the intensity of
their interaction had increased. Although there was no sign of increased
involvement, however, the important question was whether the *style* of this
interaction had changed and whether this had become more effective over time.

Observations of Mother–Child Interaction

In order to record in more detail the quality of parent–child interaction,
standardized observations were undertaken at home (see chapter 3). One and a
half hour recordings were made for both groups of children before the
programme commenced and again after 6 months.

Individual measures of many detailed aspects of mothers' behaviour were
obtained but, because of the rarity of many features, conceptually similar

categories were grouped together. Thus, mothers' behaviour was subdivided according to whether she had no involvement with the child (i.e. if she was ignoring him, getting on with a task of her own, or talking to someone else); whether she was paying attention to him; and whether she was physically involved with him at the time. In turn, physical contact was coded as being neutral, directing, positive or negative.

Mothers' speech was analyzed in a similar fashion. Speech was coded according to whether it was neutral (i.e. general statements to the child, explanations and so forth) or whether it conveyed information. The nature of this information was then coded as being positive, critical, confirmatory, correcting or directing.

Table 9.1
Changes in mothers' behaviour over 6 months

	Cases		Controls		Sig. of difference between cases and controls at follow-up
Assessment:	1 Mean (s.d.)	2 Mean (s.d.)	1 Mean (s.d.)	2 Mean (s.d.)	
Non-involvement	219.2 (180.0)	157.9 (144.2)	280.8 (159.4)	246.6 (206.3)	ns
Attention	62.3 (60.5)	47.3 (36.8)	19.1 (16.3)	36.1 (31.8)*	ns
Physical contact	25.8 (26.4)	25.7 (31.8)	59.5 (68.1)	48.6 (39.0)	0.05
Neutral	19.6 (22.4)	14.7 (28.3)	20.0 (27.5)	36.1 (34.2)	0.05
Direct	0.6 (1.0)	5.4 (6.5)**	7.1 (7.6)	4.2 (4.3)	ns
Negative	0.6 (0.9)	0.8 (1.1)	0.07 (0.25)	1.0 (2.5)	ns
Positive	5.1 (6.8)	5.1 (5.3)	8.5 (8.5)	7.2 (6.5)	ns

* = Significance of change over occasions   * = $P < 0.05$
** = $P < 0.01$
*** = $P < 0.001$

The overall pattern of mother–child interaction in both groups was broadly similar before the treatment programme began (see Table 9.1). Both sets of mothers spent much the same amount of time in activities *not* involving their child. But, whereas mothers in the control group spent more time in physical contact, mothers in the treatment group tended to spend more of their time simply watching the child. The amount of speech used was also slightly higher in the control group. However, apart from the difference in time spent in non-active supervision and in the amount of 'neutral' speech there were no significant differences between the two groups.

By follow-up, there were still few differences in the total amount of time spent in direct interaction with the children. Periods of *non*-involvement had fallen slightly in the controls, and rather more so in the treatment group, but in neither group was the difference significant. However, whereas parents in the treatment group spent less time simply supervising their children this had increased

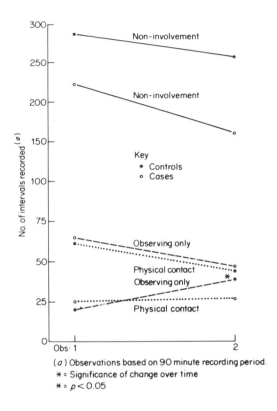

Figure 9.2 Changes in mothers' behaviour over
6 months

amongst the control parents. The amount of physical contact remained very constant over time and was higher in the control group on both occasions, but the quality of this interaction had changed in the treatment group. Neutral contacts, such as just touching or holding the child, had fallen amongst treatment mothers, whilst increasing in controls. In contrast, directing actions, designed to show the child what to do or where to go, or otherwise used as amplification of verbal instructions, had increased amongst the treatment mothers. Thus after 6 months of intervention at home, mothers who had been involved in the treatment programme seemed to have learned to show greater sensitivity to their children's needs. This was particularly evident in relation to the children's limited comprehension skills; mothers in the programme came to use frequent gestural and physical prompts in order to elaborate and clarify their interactions with the child. Negative contacts (smacks, pushes, etc.) remained at a constant low level in both groups, but although positive contact (hugs, kisses, etc.) did not increase in the mothers in treatment they had begun to decrease amongst the controls. (Figure 9.2 summarizes the pattern of changes in both groups over 6 months.)

Table 9.2
Changes in mothers' speech over 6 months

Assessment:	Cases		Controls		Sig. of difference between cases and controls at follow-up
	1 Mean (s.d.)	2 Mean (s.d.)	1 Mean (s.d.)	2 Mean (s.d.)	
Total	181.5 (79.0)	276.0 (61.9)***	253.8 (131.1)	223.9 (127.3)	ns
Neutral	83.4 (55.6)	125.8 (54.3)*	137.8 (85.6)	138.2 (96.1)	ns
Info. giving	98.5 (52.3)	150.2 (40.7)**	115.9 (73.4)	85.7 (49.6)	ns
Praise	15.1 (14.1)	32.5 (22.3)**	12.3 (13.7)	7.9 (5.7)	ns
Critic.	4.3 (4.3)	6.3 (4.9)	2.9 (5.2)	7.0 (5.7)	ns
Confirm	8.3 (8.9)	18.6 (12.7)**	22.6 (28.4)	18.2 (19.8)	ns
Correct.	5.7 (5.7)	17.8 (12.5)***	7.0 (7.2)	7.5 (8.0)	ns
Direct.	53.9 (30.3)	75.0 (22.6)*	71.0 (46.8)	45.1 (28.2)	ns

* = Significance of change over occasions   * = $P < 0.05$
** = $P < 0.01$
*** = $P < 0.001$

Changes in Verbal Interaction

Parents in the programme used their time with the children more effectively for communication after 6 months of treatment (see Table 9.2). They were talking significantly more with them than they had on the first occasion and general comments to the children were far more frequent. More importantly, however, the rates of information giving remarks had increased significantly and these were now considerably higher than in the control group (see Figure 9.3). The amount of praise given to the children had more than doubled and mothers in the treatment group were generally more responsive to their children's attempts to communicate. For example, they were more likely to confirm the appropriateness of their children's speech or actions, or to correct them when inappropriate. Directions, too, had increased, but whereas formerly instructions to the child had constituted by far the greatest proportion of the mothers' utterances, by follow-up these were less than half the total.

Amongst the untreated group of mothers there were few significant changes (apart from the fact that praise had fallen and criticism increased) and directions and commands remained the most common type of utterance used.

It seemed, therefore that, with help, mothers had learned to give much more feedback to their children and were less likely simply to tell them what to do than they had been formerly. In the absence of intervention, on the other hand, it was

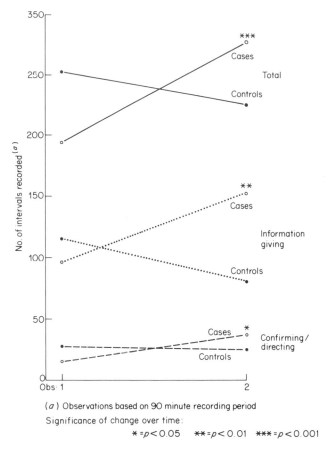

(a) Observations based on 90 minute recording period

Significance of change over time:

* =p<0.05   ** =p<0.01   *** =p<0.001

Figure 9.3 Changes in mothers' speech to children over 6 months

striking that parents showed remarkably little change. There were few differences in the amount of speech they used to their children, although if anything the quality of non-verbal interaction seemed to show some deterioration.

Analyses of Language Transcripts

The extent of the changes in verbal interaction became even more apparent when detailed assessments of language transcripts were analysed. Initially both groups of mothers had been very similar on most of the aspects of language studied. After 6 months of treatment, however, there were marked differences between them. As was the case with the direct observation of behaviour, the language of mothers in the control group remained very stable over time. In contrast, mothers in the intervention group showed large and significant changes, not only in the frequency of their verbal interaction with their child but also in the quality of this interaction. As compared with the pre-treatment measures, they were speaking far more to their children. From a mean of just over 50 utterances per half hour in the initial assessment the frequency of speech had risen to over 400 utterances in the same period of time 6 months later. In addition the proportion of language directed utterances almost doubled from an average of 25 per cent initially to 46 per cent at the subsequent assessment. In general the mothers who had received home intervention had become much more responsive to their children's speech and were using higher rates of reinforcements and corrections, thereby giving much greater feedback to the children. Prompts and questions, used deliberately to elicit more language from the children, also rose.

Affectionate and approving remarks increased whilst orders or directions, which tend to be associated with poorer language development in children (Cross, 1977) declined. As well as these specific increases in language directed utterances (see Figure 9.4), the speech of mothers in the treatment group generally became clearer and easier to understand and there was a marked decrease in the proportions of interjections and incomprehensible remarks.

As Table 9.3 indicates, whereas there were many significant changes in mothers in the treatment group there were very few changes in the control group over the same period. On the whole maternal speech styles remained much the same over time although, if anything, the amount of speech and the frequency of affectionate remarks declined slightly. The only significant change was a decrease in the rates of directions.

Table 9.3
Mother's Speech to child:
Case–Control Comparisons over the First 6 months of Treatment

Language assessment:	Cases		Controls		p value for significance difference between change scores (l-tailed t-test)
	Initial	6 months	Initial	6 months	
	Mean (s.d.)	Mean (s.d.)	Mean (s.d.)	Mean (s.d.)	
Total no. of utterances to child	253.6 (113.1)	407.6 (148.7)	309.6 (123.1)	286.8 (144.2)	.001
% language directed	25.8 (18.1)	45.7 (23.9)	32.8 (17.1)	36.6 (16.2)	.05
% non-language directed	64.9 (16.6)	48.1 (22.3)	56.4 (17.1)	49.7 (16.6)	NS
% interjections/ incomprehensible	9.2 (4.6)	6.2 (4.2)	10.8 (5.7)	13.6 (6.6)	.001

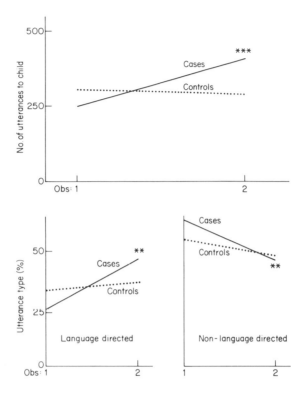

Figure 9.4 Mothers' speech over 6 months. Significance
of change over time *** = $p < 0.001$

It appears that, even after a relatively short period of intervention, considerable changes could be brought about in the quantity and *quality* of mothers' verbal interaction with their children. In the absence of intervention, on the other hand, the frequency and style of this interaction tended to remain constant.

The next question was whether these changes in parental behaviour would be paralleled by improvements in the children themselves. In order to provide answers to this question a combination of interview techniques and direct observational measures was used.

CHANGES IN CHILDREN'S BEHAVIOUR

The Parental Interview

Parental accounts provided our first measure of changes in children's behaviour (see Table 9.4). Of the sixteen behavioural and developmental areas assessed by interview over half showed no significant improvement. Parents felt that their children were somewhat more responsive to them and that their play and

Table 9.4
Parental perceptions of change over 6 months
(Experimental Group Only)

	Mean scores (s.d. in parenthesis)		Nos of children showing mild levels of difficulty only	
	Time 1	Time 2	Time 1	Time 2
Problem areas				
General behaviour problems				
At home	15.0 (5.4)	19.8 (6.1)*	3	7
Away from home	21.8 (7.6)	17.1 (7.1)*	1	5
Other behaviour problems				
Stereotypies	2.6 (1.8)	2.2 (1.8)	8	9
Activity level	3.8 (2.5)	3.5 (2.5)	6	6
Mood abnormalities	3.1 (2.6)	3.2 (2.7)	6	6
Autistic problems				
Obsessions and rituals	10.5 (4.2)	7.6 (2.4)*	1	5
Abnormal response to stimuli	14.3 (5.7)	10.1 (4.1)	2	1
Developmental areas				
Response to parents	6.3 (3.0)	3.8 (2.1)**	2	5
Response to other adults	8.2 (2.8)	7.0 (2.9)	3	5
Response to children	6.5 (1.5)	5.6 (1.6)	10	14
Level of play	26.1 (9.1)	19.0 (9.3)*	0	1
Reading, writing and arithmetic	14.0 (6.6)	12.3 (5.8)	3	5
Communication				
Language level	55.1 (23.1)	43.6 (29.6)	3	7
Abnormal use	46.7 (31.2)	38.1 (29.5)	3	6
Comprehension	11.0 (2.4)	8.5 (2.2)**	0	2
Non-verbal communication	10.6 (6.1)	9.1 (5.7)	5	8
			No change significant	

Note

On all items a low score = greater normality
* = P value for significance of change overtime

* = P < .05
** = P < .01
*** = P < 0.001

understanding of language were better than formerly, but the mean scores, although improved, still indicated many limitations. For example, verbal comprehension was limited to single instructions; there was little or no spontaneous *initiation* of verbal contact with parents, and improvements in play were related to the functional use of objects rather than to any greatly increased imaginative skills.

Behavioural items showed rather more change than developmental ratings, with four out of the seven global areas rated showing significant improvement. However, the level of behavioural disturbance recorded still indicated frequent difficulties at home and disruption if the child was taken out. Obsessional behaviours and rituals and abnormal responses to objects (such as touching, counting or staring at them) had declined, but they continued to cause disruption to family life as well as interrupting the child's own activities. Few children were felt to have made marked improvements and there were just small increases in the proportions showing mild problems only at the 6 month assessment.

Such results were disappointing. They suggested that, despite 6 months of intensive therapy during which mothers had shown many changes in their behaviour, the children had made relatively little improvement. However, it was also apparent that there were limitations to these data. First, they were based on subjective reports by parents. Second, at this stage of the intervention programme at least, there were no direct comparisons with untreated children. Thus, there was no way of knowing whether the relatively small changes that had occurred on these items were attributable to treatment or to the children's own growth in maturation. The next stage of the assessment, therefore, concentrated on an examination of group differences in children's behaviour as observed directly at home.

Observational Data

Children's Behaviour

The standardized measures of behaviour assessed whether the child was unoccupied; whether he was spending time in solitary play or in on-task activities; whether he was involved in play or task activities with his mother; whether he indulged in ritualistic and stereotyped behaviours (including object attachment), or whether his behaviour was non-cooperative and disruptive. Because speech was analysed in much greater detail from audio transcripts, the analysis of the observational data was confined to ratings of whether speech was communicative or non-communicative and stereotyped. The frequency of communicative words and utterances was also rated.

Observations made before intervention began revealed few differences in behaviour between treatment and control groups (see Table 9.5). Thus the amount of time they spent in on-task or play behaviours, either alone or with their mothers, was broadly similar. Although the untreated children spent rather more

Table 9.5
Direct observations of mother–child interaction: Changes in children's Behaviour over 6 months

Assessment:	Cases		Controls		Sig. of difference between groups at follow-up
	1 Mean (s.d.)	2 Mean (s.d.)	1 Mean (s.d.)	2 Mean (s.d.)	
Unoccupied	52.3 (33.5)	44.2 (35.5)	84.1 (61.0)	90.6 (70.7)	0.05
Task/play alone	93.7 (63.9)	57.2 (41.9) *	84.6 (62.0)	67.8 (70.3)	ns
Task/play with mum	125.2 (78.1)	185.1 (54.9)**	116.6 (87.2)	112.6 (87.3)	0.01
Rituals/ stereo typies	58.1 (83.3)	26.6 (30.9)	29.7 (28.6)	39.2 (44.9)	ns
Disruptive	8.9 (16.1)	5.2 (7.4)	5.6 (14.3)	14.0 (15.5)	0.05

* = Significance of change over occasions   * = $P < 0.05$
                                              ** = $P < 0.01$

time unoccupied and less time involved in ritualistic and disruptive behaviours, these differences were not significant.

By the end of the first 6 months' assessment, however, the *patterns* of behaviour shown by the two groups of children showed much less similarity. Solitary on task or play activities had fallen somewhat in both groups, but whereas amongst the untreated group these behaviours had tended to be replaced by longer periods of time spent *unoccupied*, in the treatment group they had been replaced by cooperative tasks or play activities with the mother. By follow-up, children in the treatment group were spending more time in joint activities with their mothers than in all other categories of behaviour put together. Amongst the untreated children the proportion of such behaviours had fallen with time, and there were highly significant differences between the groups on this variable.

Non-cooperative and disruptive behaviours also showed very different patterns of change. In neither group were such problems particularly marked initially, occurring on average five times a session in controls and nine times per session in the treatment group. By follow-up, the rates of such behaviours had increased almost three-fold in the controls (up to a mean of 14.0) whereas they had fallen in the group of children given home intervention. A similar pattern is shown in the figures for ritualistic and stereotyped behaviours and object attachments. Although, initially, these were somewhat higher in the treatment group, such behaviours had fallen to well below 50 per cent of their initial rate by the end of the 6 month treatment period. In contrast, untreated children showed a rise in such behaviours (see Figure 9.5). Overall, therefore, it seemed that even a relatively short intervention period resulted in quite marked behavioural changes. Cooperative on-task behaviours tended to increase significantly with

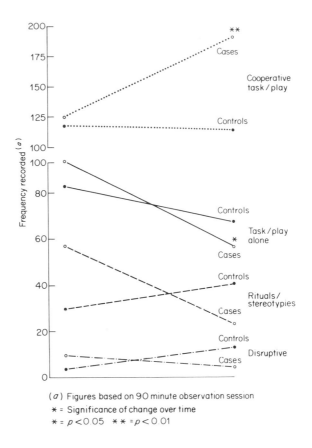

(a) Figures based on 90 minute observation session
* = Significance of change over time
* = p < 0.05 ** = p < 0.01

Figure 9.5 Changes in children's behaviour over 6
months

intervention, whilst disruptive and ritualistic behaviours were reduced. Moreover, it was not simply a case of the experimental children showing greater improvement than controls. Instead, it was evident that in the absence of intervention, some deviant behaviours tended to *increase* rather than to remain at baseline levels, whilst appropriate behaviours tended to reduce.

Change in Language Usage over 6 Months

In both groups, non-communicative verbalizations (i.e. echolalia, repetitive and stereotyped words or phrases, or non-verbal utterances) remained at much the same level throughout the 6 month period, with no differences between groups or occasions (see Table 9.6). However, although the rate of communicative utterances remained very stable in the control group, the rate almost doubled in the treatment group—from a mean of 57 initially to one of 102 by the second observation session. These improvements, however, tended to be related to an

Table 9.6
Direct observations of mother–child interaction: Changes in children's communication
over 6 months

Assessment:	Cases		Controls		Sig. of difference between groups at follow- up
	1 Mean (s.d.)	2 Mean (s.d.)	1 Mean (s.d.)	2 Mean (s.d.)	
Non-communicative utterances	49.2 (40.3)	47.9 (46.4)	49.3 (53.5)	48.3 (44.6)	ns
Communicative utterances	57.9 (69.5)	102.4 (76.8)*	81.8 (90.2)	87.3 (84.7)	ns
Words	15.6 (16.0)	44.3 (48.3)*	19.5 (26.8)	17.8 (16.7)	0.05
Phases	35.9 (60.3)	49.3 (67.8)	54.1 (73.2)	53.8 (77.7)	ns

* = Significance of change over occasions   * = P < 0.05
                                                ** = P < 0.01
                                              *** = P < 0.001

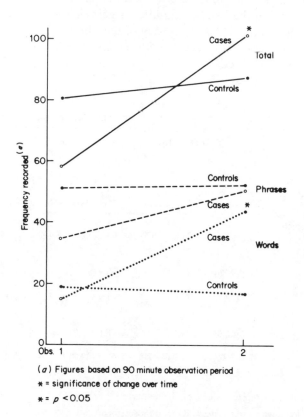

(a) Figures based on 90 minute observation period
* = significance of change over time
* = p < 0.05

Figure 9.6 Changes in children's communication over
6 months

increased use of single words to communicate. Simple, single word utterances more than doubled in frequency amongst the treatment children, whereas the use of phrase speech although showing a little improvement, increased much less.

Nevertheless, although changes in complex languages may have been limited, the increases in all aspects of communicative speech were much greater in treated than non-treated children, as is evident from Figure 9.6. Again, the most striking finding to emerge from these data is the stability of children who do not receive intervention.

Analysis of Spoken Language

Language changes were further assessed using more detailed audio transcripts of the children's speech during the same time period. These focused on the ways in which children used speech to communicate and on the complexity of their language. Initially, as the direct observational measures had indicated, there were no significant differences between the two groups of children but, after 6 months of treatment, major differences were apparent. By this time, children in the treatment group had shown significant gains on almost every measure of language usage analysed. The frequency of their utterances had increased significantly; the number of socialized utterances generally showed a marked increase and the quality of their communication had also improved (see Table 9.7).

Table 9.7

Children's Use of Speech: Changes in cases and short-term controls over 6 months[a]

Assessment:[a]	Cases (N = 16)		Controls (N = 14)		p value for difference between change scores (l-tailed t-test)
	Initial	6 months	Initial	6 months	
	Mean (s.d.)	Mean (s.d.)	Mean (s.d.)	Mean (s.d.)	
No. comprehensible utterances	72.7 (93.4)	154.8 (126.5)**	93.1 (127.5)	122.4 (157.5)	NS
% spontaneous socialized utterances	24.9 (25.6)	39.8 (33.8)	30.9 (33.4)	30.2 (28.7)	.05
% prompted responses	3.3 (5.6)	12.6 (15.6)*	1.9 (3.1)	1.9 (2.2)	.05
% echolalic autistic utterances	14.7 (16.0)	9.6 (12.3)	8.6 (13.8)	11.5 (6.5)	NS
% non-verbal utterances	57.1 (36.4)	37.9 (41.2)*	58.7 (42.2)	56.3 (37.4)	.05

Notes
[a] Figures based on ½ hour recordings of all children

Significance of change between first and second assessments.
* = $P < 0.05$
** = $P < 0.01$
*** = $P < 0.001$

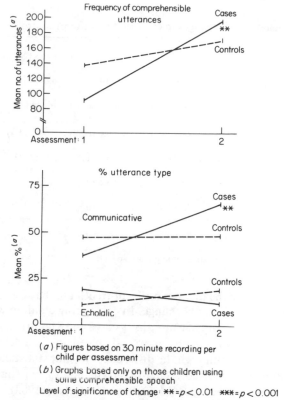

Figure 9.7 Change in cases and controls over 6 months

In particular, significant increases were found in their responsiveness to their mothers' speech, in their use of information giving remarks, and in the frequency of prompted utterances. Questions, answers and non-prompted speech also increased in frequency. Non-verbal and echolalic utterances on the other hand declined significantly.

In contrast to children in the treatment group whose speech showed both quantitative and qualitative improvements, very few changes occurred in the control group of children. Indeed, the changes that were recorded tended to reflect increases in more deviant aspects of language usage. Thus, whilst the frequency of socialized speech showed little change, rates of echolalic and autistic utterances increased slightly. Figure 9.7 illustrates the very different patterns of change in the treatment and control groups over this period.

Changes in Language Level

Although it was clear from both the observational assessments and the analysis of language transcripts, that children's functional linguistic skills

Table 9.8
Children's language level: changes in cases and short term controls over 6 months [a]

Assessment: Language	Cases (N = 9)		Controls (N = 8)		p value for change scores (l-tailed t-test)
	Initial Mean (s.d.)	6 months Mean (s.d.)	Initial Mean (s.d.)	6 months Mean (s.d.)	
No. of phrases	39.2 (69.7)	72.0 (75.4)*	60.6 (62.7)	77.0 (74.4)	NS
No. of morphemes	66.1 (126.8)	129.7 (118.4)*	123.5 (118.3)	129.5 (133.7)	.05
No. of transformations	34.1 (66.8)	67.0 (82.4)*	68.5 (70.9)	85.6 (96.6)	NS
Mean length of utterance	2.6 (0.7)	3.2 (1.9)	3.9 (0.8)	3.7 (1.0)	NS

* = Significance of change between first and second assessments
* = P < 0.05
(a) Figures based only on children using some phrase speech.

improved rapidly during the first 6 months of treatment, basic levels of language competence were slower to show change. In comparing children who were using some phrase speech by the end of 6 months (9 cases and 8 controls) it was apparent that control group to was slightly more advanced in their level of language development than cases, although the difference was not statistically significant. These initial differences were corrected for in the analysis of change as was the variability in change scores (see McCullagh & Nelder 1983). As Figure 9.8 indicates, both groups showed a steady increase in their use of phrase structure rules and there were no significant differences between the children at follow-up. Morpheme and transformational rules also improved in both groups, but the rate of acquisition was greater in the treatment group. This was particularly so in the case of simple morpheme rules; controls showed limited gains and the treated children made marked improvements. Additionally, whereas the mean length of utterance decreased slightly in the control group it rose a little in the treated group. Further details of these changes are presented in Table 9.8.

Thus, whilst changes in language usage seem to occur rapidly following the implementation of intervention procedures, changes in the complexity of language were less striking. Admittedly, children in the treatment group tended to make greater progress in these areas than controls, nevertheless steady improvements occurred in both groups over time. As compared with measures of language usage, the significance of changes in language level following treatment was much less.

In summary, it seemed that even a relatively brief, 6 month period of home intervention resulted in worthwhile changes between treated and untreated families. It was apparent that, in the absence of intervention, the ways in which parents interact with their children, both verbally and non-verbally, tend to remain stable. With the help of home intervention, changes occurred in both the frequency and style of parents' interactions with their children. In turn, these

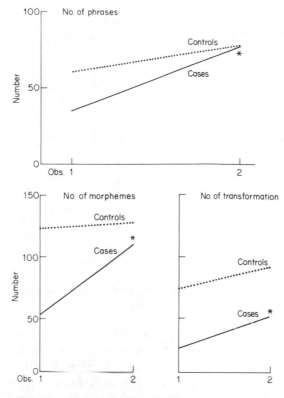

Figure 9.8 Change in language level over 6
months. * = $p < 0.05$

changes seemed to be reflected by improvements in children's behaviour. However, not all aspects of children's behaviour improved to the same degree. Treatment had differential effects according to the particular area of skill or disability being investigated. In keeping with the findings from the single case studies, intervention seemed to have most marked effects on behavioural problems. Ritualistic, solitary and disruptive behaviours all decreased markedly in the treatment group whereas control children either showed little change or a deterioration in these areas. Children in treatment also showed marked improvements in their constructional and cooperative behaviours, but again few differences over time were found in the control group.

Changes in language were somewhat more variable. Children in the treatment group appeared to make considerable gains in their use of functional language. Spontaneous, communicative utterances increased whereas they remained at much the same level in the controls. More detailed analyses of language changes, however, revealed that most of the significant increases were related to language usage. Furthermore, the major gains that did occur in the treatment group were related to simpler aspects of language, such as morpheme rules, rather than to more complex transformational structures. True, the children in treatment made steady gains in the overall complexity of their language, but the control children,

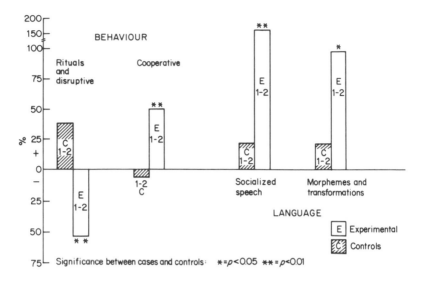

Figure 9.9 Percentage change in language and behaviour—cases and 6-month
controls

too, showed improvements in these areas. Hence, at the end of 6 months, there
were still few significant differences between groups on these measures.

Taken together, these findings indicated a differential response to treatment
effects. Behavioural difficulties, such as rituals, other solitary activities and
disruptive behaviours, proved most amenable to intervention. Language usage
could be improved, in that echolalic and stereotyped utterances fell following
treatment, while communicative speech steadily improved. Overall levels of
language complexity, however, showed relatively little change.

The contrast between cases and controls is perhaps best illustrated by
comparing the pattern of changes in different problem areas over time. As
Figure 9.9. indicates, there were significant differences in change scores on
behavioural items—such as rituals and disruptive behaviours—which increased
in controls but declined in the treatment group. Cooperative behaviours, too,
showed significant differences between groups, for while these declined slightly
in controls they increased considerably amongst children in treatment.

Language, however, showed a similar pattern of change in both groups.
Although the extent of improvement was significantly greater amongst treated
children, both groups made steady gains in language usage and language level.
These differential effects of treatment are explored more fully in the chapter
dealing with the longer term benefits of intervention.

INDIVIDUAL DIFFERENCES IN RESPONSE TO TREATMENT

Not only did treatment appear to have differential effects according to the nature
of the particular skill or disability studied, it also became apparent, particularly

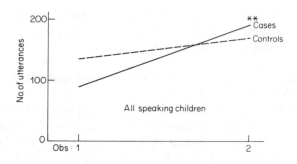

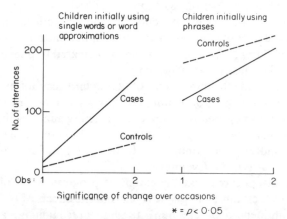

Significance of change over occasions

* = $p < 0.05$

Figure 9.10 Change in amount of speech according
to initial language level

in the analysis of language change, that there were marked individual differences between children in their response to treatment. Although group data are essential for comparative analyses of treatment results they may at times distort the findings for various subgroups of children. The treated and untreated children were matched at a group level but there was marked heterogeneity within both groups. The IQ range extended from 60 to over 100; language abilities from total lack of speech to grammatical sentence use; and age from 3 to teenage. These individual differences, as it turned out, had a considerable influence on subsequent outcome, particularly with regard to language development.

Whereas the treatment group as a whole showed a significant improvement in their use of language over time, the extent of change varied according to the initial level of the child. The greatest improvement in socialized speech occurred in children who were using single words or word approximations when treatment began. The subsequent rise in spontaneous language shown by these children was considerably greater than for the group as a whole. Less change was shown by the children who already had some phrase speech when treatment began. Figure 9.10 illustrates the rather different rates of improvement in the two groups as a whole: in children who were on the threshold of developing language when treatment began, and in those who already had well established language skills at the onset of treatment.

Although cases made relatively more improvement than controls, the pattern of change in both groups was very similar and was related to the initial language level of the children concerned.

Changes in the frequency of echolalic speech were also related to initial levels of communication. Thus, whereas overall the treatment children showed a decrease in echolalia some children actually became more echolalic over time. Again, these were the four children who were using some simple words or word approximations to begin with. Although they developed much more socialized speech over the 6 month period, as Figure 9.11 indicates, they also showed a greater increase in their rates of echolalic and egocentric utterances. This increase in echolalia would appear to reflect a similar pattern of development to that of normal children, who also tend to show increased frequencies of echolalic speech in the early stages of language learning.

These results indicate the importance of taking into account different patterns of change as well as overall group improvements when analysing results. Autistic children are not a homogeneous group and restricting analyses simply to change across groups may well disguise important differences between various subgroups of children. Such findings indicate, too, that intervention does not necessarily alter *patterns* of development.

In summary, it appeared that the extent of progress made by children was closely related to their initial language levels and the effects of treatment seemed to be directly influenced by children's fundamental language abilities. Mute, non-communicating school age children are unlikely to make rapid or significant improvements. The speech of children with relatively well developed language skills is also likely to be only moderately improved by treatment. On the other hand, children who are on the threshold of learning to use communicative speech seem to be most responsive to language intervention programmes. However, since these data were based on the results of a relatively brief intervention programme, it was possible that a longer period of therapy might produce greater gains in more fundamental aspects of language competence. A comparison of cases and controls after the full 18 month intervention period was needed to explore the longer term effects of treatment; the results of this investigation are reported in chapter 11.

THE EFFECTIVENESS OF PARENTAL COPING STRATEGIES

Measures of Coping

The final set of measures used in the short-term assessment of treatment focused on the efficiency and effects of the general coping strategies used by parents.

Information about coping strategies was collected, as described in chapter 3, by standardized interviews with parents. The quality of coping was assessed by

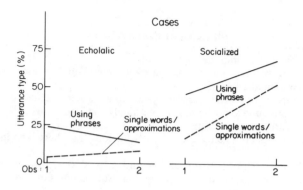

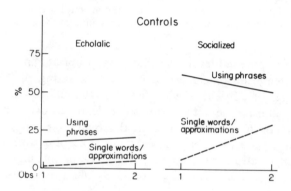

Figure 9.11 Change in type of speech according to
initial language level

independent raters who were blind to which group the children were in. Control families were interviewed 6 months after the initial visit to the home; experimental families 6 months after the cessation of treatment.

Three separate aspects of skill were considered to assess coping techniques. First, parents' ability to assess their child's level of developmental skills (i.e. communication, play and self-help), and to adapt their own behaviour appropriately to this, was monitored. Second, parents' skill in applying a suitable degree of pressure to achieve treatment goals was rated. Finally parents' skill in using generally sensible and efficient management techniques was assessed for the three main developmental areas noted above and also for disruptive behaviours (aggression, self-injury, destructiveness and tantrums); toileting problems, other non-specific behavioural problems (including hyperactivity, sleeping difficulties and phobias), and a group of specifically autistic difficulties (rituals, resistance to change) (see Table 9.9).

A three point scale was used to measure parents' ability to assess their child's developmental level and their skill in applying an appropriate degree of pressure. A rating of 1 indicated that parents' behaviour was consistently well matched to

Table 9.9
Efficiency of Parental Skills

(1)	Highly efficient and adaptive coping skills.
(2)	Generally sensible and appropriate parental behaviour but not fully meeting the criteria of maximal efficiency.
(3)	Parental approach to the problem behaviour rather inefficient and not well adapted to the child's needs but not definitely inappropriate and not associated with persistently adverse reactions.
(4)	No active attempts to change the child's behaviour (rate here if child is improving on his own).
(5)	Parental behaviour rather inappropriate and associated with some adverse effects.
(6)	Markedly inappropriate or manifestly harmful techniques which significantly exacerbate the initial problem.
(7)	Use of techniques so inappropriate that the inital problem is much exacerbated; or other marked problems arise as a result of parental actions; or there is a decrease in the child's level of functioning; or a general worsening of the situation.

their child's developmental level, and that an appropriate amount of pressure was used in attempting to change behaviours. A rating of 2 suggested an intermediate level of efficiency—with parental attempts to change behaviour being generally appropriate but showing some degree of over/underestimation of the child's level or the amount of pressure that ought to be applied. A rating of 3 indicated that the goals set were markedly out of keeping with the child's level (i.e. parental expectations were unrealistically low or too high), and that the amount of pressure used was inappropriately high or low—or extremely inconsistent.

Parental Response to Developmental Problems

As Table 9.10 indicates, parents in the treatment group were significantly more likely to achieve optimal scores than parents in the control group. In each area of skill assessed, parents in the treatment programme proved more successful than controls in assessing their child's developmental level and in matching their own behaviours to this appropriately. Only in the assessment of communication did this difference fail to reach significance.

The same pattern was shown for ratings of parents' sensitivity to the amount of pressure required to foster development. It was important that the amount of pressure placed on the child should be enough to ensure progress. It should not, however, be so excessive as to cause distress or disturbance to the child. Again, in each of the three developmental areas assessed, the parents in the experimental group showed a more sensitive use of strategies than controls.

Parental Coping Efficiency

Seven point ratings of parental efficiency were applied to a wide range of children's problems. A comparison of mean scores of cases and controls shows

Table 9.10

Coping strategies: frequency of cases and controls obtaining optimum rating scores

Parental coping ability:	Assessing level			Appropriate pressure		
	Cases	Controls	P	Cases	Controls	P
Child's behaviour						
Communication	*14/16*	*8/13*	ns	*14/16*	*6/13*	0.05
Self-help	*12/12*	*3/14*	0.01	*10/16*	*3/14*	0.05
Play	*7/15*	*1/13*	0.05	*7/15*	*0/13*	0.05

P = Fisher Exact Test.

Note

The numbers in each group vary slightly because inadequate information meant that ratings were not possible in every case.

that parents in the treatment programme were achieving consistently higher levels of efficiency in every aspect of behaviour.

Differences between groups were particularly marked in the areas of self-help skills, disruptive behaviour and 'autistic' problems (see Figure 9.12). The only

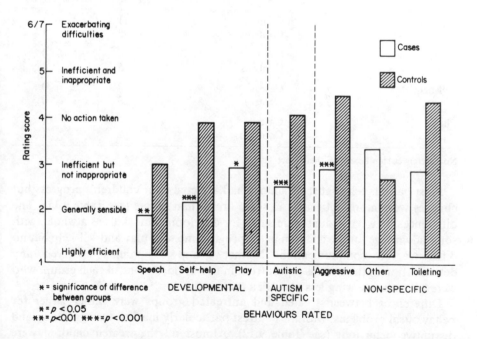

Figure 9.12 Coding strategies: mean efficiency ratings of case and control parents

areas where no significant differences were found were for toileting problems and non-specific problems such as fears, eating and sleeping. The mean scores of the control parents indicated that they were much more likely to use inefficient strategies than parents in the treated group or, alternatively, were likely to make no attempts at all to improve the behaviour. In addition, more control parents obtained extreme ratings of 5 or more, showing a much higher frequency of inappropriate responses to problems.

The effects of parental coping

Parents were questioned in detail in order to assess the effects on the children's behaviour of the coping strategies that they had adopted. These were examined in relation to three main groups of problems: developmental skills (communication, self-help and play); non-specific behavioural difficulties (aggressive and disruptive behaviour, difficulties in toileting, sleeping or eating and phobias); and a group of behaviours more specific to autism (such as rituals, routines and obsessions). Parents in both groups were asked whether they felt that the child had improved or deteriorated in each of these areas.

Table 9.11
Numbers of children showing improvements and deterioration over
time—developmental items

		Improvement	Deterioration
All developmental items	Cases	11	1
	Controls	8	1
Communication	Cases	6	0
	Controls	5	0
Self-help	Cases	8	0
	Controls	3	0
Play	Cases	7	1
	Controls	2	1

No differences significant—Fisher Exact Test

Most parents felt that their actions had affected their children's progress but changes were more noticeable in some areas than others (see Table 9.11). The differences between groups were small for developmental skills as a whole, with some advantage for the children in the programme with play and self-help but no difference on communication. Neither group of parents observed any deterioration in these areas (apart from in two children, one in each group, who were felt to be showing less play than previously).

Differences between treated and untreated groups were rather larger for behavioural problems, with the contrast particularly marked for aggression and disruptive behaviour (see Table 9.12). Almost all the treated children were considered to have made progress, whereas over a third of the untreated group

Table 9.12
Frequencies of children showing improvement or deterioration in problem behaviour

		No change	Improved	Deteriorated	Sig. level [a]
Aggressive and disruptive behaviour	Cases	2	14	0	0.05
	Controls	5	6	5	
Other non-specific problems	Cases	5	10	1	ns
	Controls	11	4	1	
Autism-specific behaviours	Cases	5	10	1	ns
	Controls	11	3	2	

Note
[a] χ^2 test for frequency of deterioration/improvement in cases and controls.

were felt to have deteriorated. Families in the treatment group also felt that there had been more improvement in both autism-specific behaviours and non-specific problems such as toileting, feeding and sleeping.

These patterns were also reflected in *changes* in the overall rating scores (see Figure 9.13). Again, no group differences were found for developmental skills, but there were significant differences on all the behavioural areas assessed.

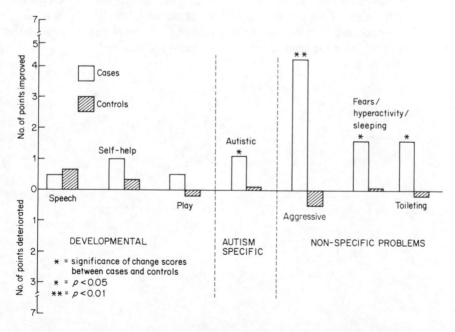

Figure 9.13 Amount of improvement/deterioration in children's behaviour: parental ratings

In parallel with the results from direct observational measures, the coping interview data suggested that changes in parental behaviour were accompanied by improvements in children's behaviour and that the treated families generally showed greater improvements than controls. There appeared to be a similar hierarchical pattern of change in behaviour with problems non-specific to autism showing most change; specifically autistic problems improving to a moderate extent; and developmental problems (such as language) showing less response to treatment.

Nevertheless in keeping with the findings from the parental interview, it was also apparent that parental *reports* of change are often less positive than the direct observations would seem to warrant. Despite the large and significant changes *observed* in children's language and behaviour, parental impressions of improvement, as assessed by both interview schedules, did not appear to reflect these.

This time lag between observed change and subjective reports of improvements has been noted in previous studies involving behavioural intervention procedures. Both self-reports by adults and reports by parents and teachers on children's behaviour tend to be much slower to reflect change than more objective measures of improvement (Wahler and Leske, 1973). This phenomenon was particularly marked in the first 6 months of treatment, and the mechanisms underlying it are obscure. However, without a longer term follow-up, it was unclear whether parental perceptions would always tend to be somewhat out of keeping with observed changes, or whether these discrepancies were only transient. This problem is further explored in the longer term case–control comparisons discussed in chapter 11, but first, the changes made by the treatment group over the second year of treatment are assessed.

Chapter 10

The Final Year of Treatment

The first 6 months of the treatment programme were necessarily rather intense, with at least weekly sessions in most cases. That was because many of the families were experiencing crises with their autistic children. It was necessary to work out *how* to intervene with a variety of coping skills and to teach a range of strategies by which normal development might be enhanced and by which maladaptive behaviour might be reduced. By the end of the first 6 months of intervention most families had gained such skills and strategies and were coping adequately. Because our aim was to enable parents to function effectively *on their own*, without dependence on professionals, we sought to reduce the frequency of home visits during the final year of treatment. The *pace* of that reduction was tailored to the needs of individual families; some continued to require weekly visits for a prolonged period, whereas others coped well with an early reduction to monthly contacts. With most families, however, the pattern was one of a gradual reduction from weekly visits to fortnightly sessions, to visits once every 3 or 4 weeks. In all cases we maintained the frequency of contact that was deemed clinically necessary. Our experience was that, in many cases, families continued to be more reliant on our help than we had anticipated at the outset. This was partly because it took a substantial amount of time for parental confidence to build up and partly because many parents experienced difficulty in applying general principles to new forms of problem behaviour. Thus, even though the underlying strategy required to deal with new problem behaviours relied on behavioural techniques already used by families, parents were often reluctant to act independently or to employ such methods without recourse to the therapists' advice. For this reason, in some cases against a background of reducing intensity of intervention, it was necessary temporarily to increase the frequency of visits to help parents tackle a fresh challenge or deal with a new crisis. In this chapter we consider how far the initial gains made in the first 6 months of intervention were consolidated during the second year of treatment.

First, there was the question of whether improvements in parents' behaviour were maintained as intervention was reduced. Second, changes in parental perceptions of the outcome of treatment were considered. Third, patterns of change in children's behaviour and communication were assessed. Finally, the meaning of the close association between changes in children and in their parents (particularly in the context of their verbal interactions) was examined.

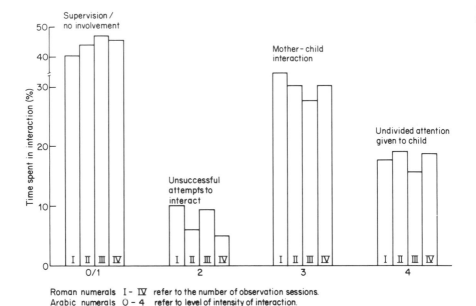

Roman numerals I - IV refer to the number of observation sessions.
Arabic numerals 0 - 4 refer to level of intensity of interaction.

Figure 10.1 Intensity of interaction change over 18 months

THE MAINTENANCE OF CHANGE IN MOTHERS' BEHAVIOUR

Frequency of Interaction

The *amount* of time parents and children spent together was measured, as in the short term assessments, using the time budget analyses. As is apparent from Figure 10.1, virtually no change occurred in either the frequency or the general style of interaction over the final year of treatment. The greater part of parents' time was still spent in getting on with their own tasks or keeping an eye on their

Table 10.1
Changes in mothers' behaviour over 18 months

Assessment	1 Mean (s.d.)	2 Mean (s.d.)	3 Mean (s.d.)	4 Mean (s.d.)
Non-involvement	219.2 (185.9)	157.9 (144.2)	131.6 (85.8)*	134.1 (105.5)*
Attention	62.3 (60.5)	47.3 (36.8)	37.1 (20.7)	32.9 (79.7)*
Physical contact	25.8 (26.4)	25.7 (31.8)	33.6 (31.6)	53.0 (54.8)
Neutral	19.6 (22.4)	14.7 (28.3)	9.7 (12.5)	18.3 (42.9)
Direct	0.6 (1.0)	5.4 (6.5)**	17.3 (18.5)***	28.9 (35.4)***
Negative	0.6 (0.9)	0.8 (1.1)	2.0 (5.8)	0.5 (0.8)
Positive	5.1 (6.8)	5.1 (5.3)	4.6 (5.8)	5.3 (9.5)

* = Significance of difference between first and subsequent occasions
* = P < 0.05
** = P < 0.01
*** = P < 0.001

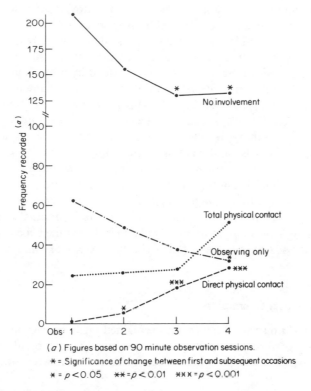

Figure 10.2 Changes in mothers' interaction with
children over 18 months

child from a distance. Approximately 30 per cent of their time involved some
interaction with the child and the amount of time spent in highly intensive
interaction remained at around 15 to 20 per cent.

Parents' unsuccessful attempts to engage their child (category 2) was the only
category to show significant change but the pattern of change was rather
unstable. Thus, as had been apparent in the earlier time budget analyses,
treatment did not result in parents' feeling obliged to spend more time with their
children. Indeed, the frequency of interactions, although showing individual
family differences, remained generally stable over the total 18 month treatment
period.

Direct Observations of Behaviour: Changes in Mothers' Interactions over 18 Months

Assessments of interactional *style*, in contrast with measures of interactional
frequency, indicated that the improvements recorded during the first 6 months
of treatment were well maintained over the subsequent year (see Figure 10.2). In
other words, the quality of the interaction could be successfully improved

without making undue demands on the amount of time parents were expected to devote to their children. A considerable proportion of mothers' time was still spent in other, non-child related activities, and there was only a small reduction in this over the second year of treatment. However, simple supervisory activities continued to fall with time, being replaced instead by a much greater degree of physical contact (almost twice as much at the end of treatment as at any time during the first 6 months—see Table 10.1). Again, the main increase here was in *directing* forms of contact, which gave the child additional information on what to do or how to do things or where to go. Thus, physical prompts and gestures showed a sharp increase and were used much more by mothers to clarify their instructions to the child, to gain his attention more effectively, or to give him greater feedback on the appropriateness of his own actions.

Figure 10.2 shows that changes in physical responsiveness were greater in the final year of treatment than they had been in the first 6 months. It is not just that prolonged intervention maintains early changes. For some behaviours, lengthier treatment periods may be required if the full extent of change is to become apparent.

Changes in Verbal Interaction

The *amount* of non-verbal interaction remained fairly consistent over time, but the frequency of verbal interaction showed a steady increase, although the rate of increase was less marked than it had been in the first 6 months (see Table 10.2).

The total amount of mothers' speech to children continued to rise, and there was a slight increase, too, in the extent to which mothers chatted away to their children whilst involved in other activities. Rates of specifically language directed utterances, such as corrections, were also maintained at a high level.

Table 10.2
Changes in mothers' communication over 18 months

Assessment	1 Mean (s.d.)	2 Mean (s.d.)	3 Mean (s.d.)	4 Mean (s.d.)
Total	181.5 (79.0)	276.0 (61.9) ***	324.8 (75.0)***	326.7 (73.7) ***
Neutral	83.4 (55.6)	125.8 (54.3) *	140.9 (64.9)**	157.0 (80.6)***
Info. giving	98.5 (52.5)	150.2 (40.7)***	183.9 (98.1)***	169.7 (98.1)**
Praise	15.1 (14.1)	32.5 (22.3)	26.1 (21.1)	21.9 (16.2)
Criticism	4.3 (4.3)	6.3 (4.9)	5.6 (5.1)	4.9 (5.5)
Confirmation	8.3 (8.9)	18.6 (12.7)**	22.3 (14.2) ***	22.6 (13.3) ***
Correction	5.7 (5.7)	17.8 (12.5)***	21.2 (17.7)***	15.9 (9.7) ***
Direction	53.9 (30.3)	75.0 (22.6)*	108.7 (45.5)***	104.4 (78.3)**

*   = Significance of difference between first and subsequent occasions
*   = P < 0.05
**   = P < 0.01
***   = P < 0.001

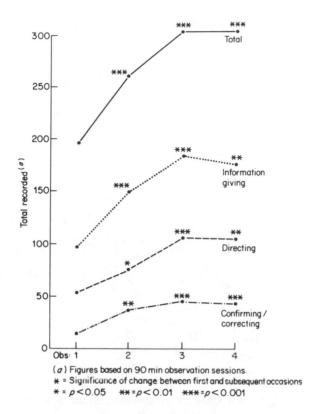

(*a*) Figures based on 90 min observation sessions.
* = Significance of change between first and subsequent occasions
* = $p < 0.05$ ** = $p < 0.01$ *** = $p < 0.001$

Figure 10.3 Changes in mothers' verbal interaction
over 18 months

Praise and reinforcement of the child's speech fell a little after the 6 month assessment but were still substantially higher than they had been initially. Both neutral and information giving remarks continued to show a small rise, but otherwise the pattern of change recorded in the second year of treatment was very similar to that recorded in the first 6 months (Table 10.2). Figure 10.3 illustrates the patterns of change found in the four major categories of speech assessed.

It appears, therefore, that relatively brief, but intensive, periods of intervention were highly successful in bringing about changes in parental behaviour. When such changes do occur they tend to do so quite quickly. Although physical contact required longer periods of intervention before significant changes were observed, most aspects of interaction showed the greatest change in the first 6 months of treatment. Such behaviours then tended to stabilize, with the earlier gains being well maintained (despite a reduction in therapist intervention) but with no further marked changes occurring. It was also apparent that substantial improvements in interaction style could be

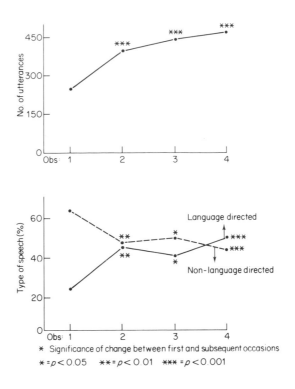

Figure 10.4 Changes in mothers' speech over 18 months

brought about without increasing demands for parents to spend significantly more time with their children.

More detailed assessments of mothers' speech, based on transcripts of half hour audio recordings, also indicated that improvements were maintained in many other aspects of their communication. Indeed, in several areas, mothers continued to show further improvements in the quality of their verbal interaction over the final year of intervention (see Figure 10.4). As the home observation data had indicated, mothers continued to show increases in the amount they talked with their chidren and the interactional style continued to facilitate their children's language usage. In particular, they used far more prompts to ensure that their children's speech was correct and appropriate. Indeed the frequency of prompts rose ten fold after the initial assessment. They used over twice as many questions as they had done initially in order to elicit responses from the child, and they themselves were much more responsive to the child's speech. Thus, imitations and corrections continued to increase and praise, too, was used far more frequently.

Non-language directed utterances showed a slight decrease over time but mothers still showed quite a high level of general *chattiness* towards their children and were just as likely to praise or correct their actions as they had done formerly.

In summary, the changes recorded in the first 6 months of treatment persisted and increased even after intensive home intervention was reduced. Change was less in the final year of treatment than it had been during the first 6 months, but by the second year of treatment most parents had already evolved highly effective ways of interacting with their children. By then, half their speech was directed towards improving their children's utterances whilst slightly less than half consisted of general, information giving comments and directions, or praise and criticisms of the children's actions.

Initially, the proportion of language directed utterances had made up only about 25 per cent of parents' speech. By the first follow-up, this had risen to a little under 50 per cent with modest gains only thereafter. However, it was not intended that all the parents' speech should focus on encouraging children's language usage. Talk between mothers and children is important for social reasons and natural styles of communication are desirable if both social and linguistic development is to be fostered. Although the level of language directed utterances achieved was higher than that reported for normal mother–child pairs (Cross, 1977; Nelson, 1977), the types of language eliciting remarks used were similar to those reported as having positive effects on normal child language development. Thus, as Table 10.3 indicates, imitations and expansions and reductions of children's utterances rose steadily over time but the greatest change was in the frequency of expansions, which Nelson (1983) has argued constitute one of the most important parental aids to children's language development.

Table 10.3
Imitations and expansions in mothers' speech

Assessment:	1 Mean (s.d.)	2 Mean (s.d.)	3 Mean (s.d.)	4 Mean (s.d.)
Expansions	5.7 (3.0)	16.2 (7.3)*	20.9 (8.6)*	19.6 (7.0)**
Exact imitation	3.4 (1.8)	10.9 (5.1)*	9.6 (4.0)*	12.7 (4.0)*
Reductions	1.0 (0.9)	2.4 (1.3)	2.4 (1.4)	3.1 (2.0)
Mitigated	0.1 (0.2)	0.3 (0.3)	0.4 (0.5)	0.2 (0.3)

* = Significance of change between first and subsequent occasions
* = $P < 0.05$
** = $P < 0.01$

The ways in which structures such as expansions and imitations were used were also very similar to those reported for mothers of normally developing children (Brown, 1973; Ling and Ling, 1974). That is, mothers tended to respond to the informational content of what their children said rather than to grammatical constructions. For example,

Child (pointing to a map he has drawn): 'That road go to Hamburg.'
Mother: 'Yes, that road goes to Hamburg'

Alternatively, responses were used by mothers to confirm that they had understood correctly what the child had said. For example,

Child: 'Draw Peter Rabbit.'
Mother: 'You want to draw Peter Rabbit do you?'
Child: 'Yes, draw Peter Rabbit.'

Expansions were often employed as a means of increasing the complexity of children's utterances. For example,

Mother: 'What is that?'
Child: 'A button.'
Mother: 'Yes, a little *pink* button.'

Occasionally, too, as with normal children, expansions or imitations were used as a form of implicit correction (see Table 10.4). As Cromer (1980) has indicated, mothers of normal children are much more likely to correct the truth of what the child has said than his articulation or his use of semantics or syntax. This was very much the case, initially at least, in the present study. Take, for example, the following recorded snatch of conversation:

Mother: 'Is Pat a man or a lady?'
Child: 'A man'.
Mother: 'Oh she is not, you fibber, you know she is a lady.'

Table 10.4
Corrections in mothers' speech

	Time 1 Mean (s.d.)	Time 2 Mean (s.d.)	Time 3 Mean (s.d.)	Time 4 Mean (s.d.)
Fact	2.7 (2.3)	8.5 (6.0)	9.8 (4.2)*	6.8 (5.1)
Articulation	0.6 (0.7)	5.3 (4.0)	9.2 (7.6)	6.7 (5.3)
Syntax	0.3 (0.2)	4.4 (1.2)*	3.7 (1.0)*	4.0 (1.2)*
Semantics	0.1 (0.3)	0.9 (1.0)	2.5 (0.5)*	6.0 (1.9)*

* = Significance of change between first and subsequent occasions
* = P < 0.05

As long as the statement made by the child was basically true, mothers frequently failed to correct errors in syntax or pronunciation. For example,

Mother: 'What did they do?'
Child: 'They stoled some fruit.'
Mother: 'Yes they did, clever boy.'

And if the mother understood what the child meant to say she tended to respond as if he had spoken correctly. For example,

Child: 'Won't let you down.' (Meaning: Don't you let me down.')
Mother: 'Oh all right, you can stay up there then.'

Errors of articulation or phonology tended to be corrected more frequently than syntactic errors although not always successfully. For example.

Child: 'How many reefs can you see?'
Mother: 'It is not reef, it is how many roofs can you see.'
Child: 'Yes, how many reeves can you see?'
Mother: 'Oh you do get me ever so muddled up.'

Semantic errors occurred relatively infrequently and the low rate of corrections for these represents the small number of such errors made by the children rather than parents' failure to correct them. Indeed, semantic errors, such as neologisms, when they did occur were usually corrected fairly consistently by mothers. For example,

Child: 'That's a sit on it.'
Mother: 'No, it's a *chair*.'

As Tables 10.3 and 10.4 indicate, rates of imitations and corrections increased considerably in the home treatment group. Among imitative utterances, expansions showed the greatest rate of improvement, an encouraging finding given the correlation between expansions and advanced language development in normal children. The style of corrections also showed some change. Corrections of fact or truth value remained higher than other forms but, by the final assessment, they were only slightly higher than corrections for articulation or semantic errors. Corrections of semantics and syntax showed significant changes over 18 months, whereas corrections of fact or articulation, although increasing, did not show significant improvements. The data indicate that mothers were paying increasing attention to the structure of their children's utterances and were less likely than they had been formerly to tolerate incorrect or inappropriate remarks.

All assessments of parental change were positive and encouraging. The short term effects of treatment had achieved far more than transient changes in amount or style of interaction. Not only were changes well maintained throughout the later stages of intervention, but many modest improvements continued to take place. The next question was whether these findings were reflected in the children's behaviour.

PARENTAL PERCEPTIONS OF CHANGE

In the short term, parents had been rather slow to acknowledge the improvements taking place in their children. This lag between observed behavioural improvements and subjective reporting of change has been noted in a number of intervention studies (Wahler and Leske, 1978; Yule, 1980). Clearly, there would be few advantages in bringing about changes in children's behaviour if parents continued to fail to recognize their existence. The next assessment therefore focused on parental perceptions of change and on whether or not their views had become more positive over the final year of treatment.

The areas assessed by parental interview covered non-specific behaviour problems both at home and away from home (these included tantrums, disruptive and destructive behaviours, aggression, phobias and difficulties with eating, sleeping, toileting, etc.); problems more specific to autism (rituals, object attachments and obsessions, etc.); communication skills; social relationships; and the development of play and simple academic attainments. Global ratings for each of these areas were made on the basis of codings for each individual category of that behaviour. Composite scores varied somewhat from variable to variable but for all behaviours a rating of 0 indicated normality or no problem. Changes in mean scores are illustrated in Figures 10.5, 10.6 and 10.7.

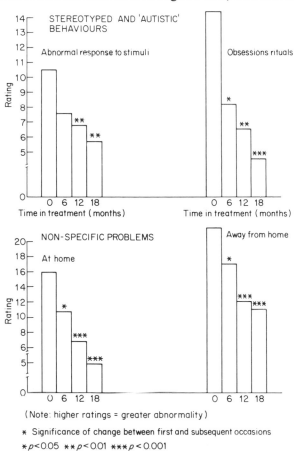

(Note: higher ratings = greater abnormality)

* Significance of change between first and subsequent occasions
*$p<0.05$ **$p<0.001$ ***$p<0.001$

Figure 10.5 Change in parental perceptions of behaviour problems over 18 months

Changes in Non-Specific Behaviours

Despite the fact that few behavioural changes had been reported by parents in the first 6 months of treatment, many more improvements were noted over the final year. Initial measures had indicated that most children were showing frequent difficulties in several behavioural areas. By the end of treatment mean rating scores had fallen considerably, indicating that both the number and severity of problems had been reduced (see Figure 10.5). As well as a marked decline in average scores, the numbers of individual children showing severe behavioural difficulties also fell steadily. Whereas thirteen children were reported as showing frequent difficulties in three or more problem areas at the start of treatment, by the end of intervention only two children were recorded as still having frequent difficulties. Moreover, even in these cases the severity of problems had decreased markedly.

Problem behaviours outside the home continued to be of some concern to parents. Such behaviours generally present more management problems in that parents have less control over their child's behaviour when they are out shopping or on the bus than at home. However, although some difficulties remained, they were much reduced in severity. Average ratings before treatment indicated that problems of this kind placed severe limitations on the extent to which children could be taken out. At follow-up, average ratings had improved markedly, indicating that although problems continued to occur occasionally, the frequency of outings had increased considerably and most parents no longer felt deterred from going out.

Problems related to activity level and mood showed little change. Few children had shown severe disturbances in these areas initially, although scores had dropped slightly by follow-up. Ratings at follow-up suggested that, so far as mood was concerned, children remained less than normally expressive, but that inappropriate affect or expression of emotion had decreased. Stereotyped and manneristic behaviours showed less change, but these had not constituted major problems at the outset. Only three children were reported as having severe stereotypies initially. In two cases they persisted to the extent that the children were quite conspicuous when taken out. The majority of children, however, showed only very mild to moderate mannerisms and there was relatively little change in these over the treatment period. Abnormal responses to stimuli (such as flicking, tapping, spinning, licking or smelling objects) showed a much greater decrease. Initially, these responses were reported as interfering considerably with the children's other activities. By follow-up, most children still demonstrated some abnormal response to objects but usually this was restricted to a single (rather than multiple) sensory modality and disruption of other activities was markedly less.

Problem Behaviours Specific to Autism

Quite marked improvements had occurred with rituals and abnormal object attachments (see Figure 10.5). Initially such problems had caused considerable disruption to family life, but by follow-up such behaviours were less frequent, less intense and much easier to control. However, such behaviours did not entirely disappear and all children continued to show at least some mild ritualized or compulsive activities.

Almost all children (fifteen out of sixteen) were reported as having moderate to severe ritualistic behaviours initially. By the end of treatment only one mother reported continuing disruption to family life because of rituals and routines (and even in this case the overall severity had fallen). Abnormal responses to stimuli continued to cause some problems but by follow-up this was generally much less than it had been formerly. At the outset parents had recorded such problems as occurring with much greater frequency, and as causing considerable disruption, especially when the child was taken out. This was no longer the case at follow-up.

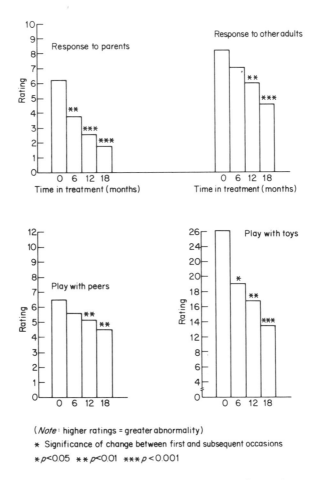

(*Note*: higher ratings = greater abnormality)

* Significance of change between first and subsequent occasions

*p<0.05 **p<0.01 ***p<0.001

Figure 10.6 Change in parental perceptions of behaviour over 18 months: social behaviour and play

Changes in Social Development

Social responsiveness was rated in a number of different ways. The child's responsiveness to parents was coded according to how much spontaneous and appropriate affection he showed. Responsiveness to other adults was rated on the basis of how well the child differentiated between his parents and other adults and how much interest he showed in them. Relationships with peers were rated on a continuum from 'withdrawal from other children' to 'spontaneous play' (i.e. joining in group games without direct intervention by adults).

It was apparent that the greatest improvements occurred in parent–child relationships (see Figure 10.6). To begin with, children were reported as showing little spontaneous demonstration of affection, although they did enjoy some physical contact such as tickling or cuddling. By follow-up they tended to be much more responsive in returning hugs and kisses, for example, but *initiation* of these activities still occurred only rarely. Play with peers also showed some improvement and children were said to be more willing to join in simple group activities. These still needed to be guided by adults, however, and spontaneous group play remained extremely limited. Social responses to adults improved to some extent over time, and the very disinhibited behaviours that had been reported initially had tended to decrease. Nevertheless, almost all children continued to show some embarrassing behaviours in public and these were generally related to a lack of inhibition and awareness in their dealings with strangers.

The Development of Play and Simple Academic Attainments

Although ratings in all these areas showed steady improvements over time, the ultimate levels reached tended to depend very much on the amount of environmental structure imposed. Thus, whereas many children showed an increase in simple arithmetic and reading skills, these activities were generally carried out only during structured teaching sessions with adults. None of the children read spontaneously for pleasure, and their understanding of number, although showing improvements in structured tasks, did not lead to much improvement in practical skills (such as using money in shops).

Play, too, improved, with many children showing increases in appropriate functional use of toys. However, as was the case with socialized play, these improvements were most apparent in structured sessions and under the guidance of an adult. Spontaneous play activity and levels of imaginative play in unstructured settings remained very restricted.

Changes in Communication Skills

Finally, changes in children's communication were assessed. These covered several different areas including comprehension, the use of gesture and other non-verbal cues, the level and frequency of communicative speech and abnormal language usage (see Figure 10.7).

168

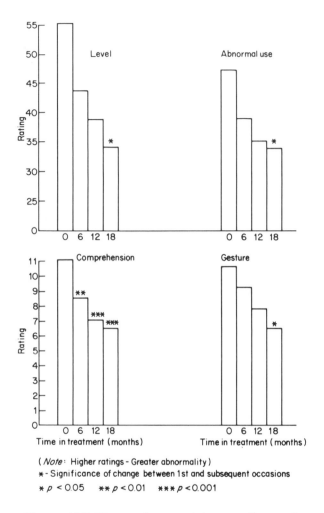

Figure 10.7 Change in parental perceptions of language over 18 months

Comprehension of speech was reported by parents as showing significant improvements. No children at the beginning of the study were considered to be able reliably to respond to instructions involving more than a single basic command, but by follow-up six children were reported to have reached this level.

Of the various areas of communication assessed, non-verbal expressiveness showed least change. The frequency of gestures and appropriate use of facial expressions had increased a little over time, but in general the communicative use of non-verbal skills remained restricted. Most children still showed very limited spontaneity in their use of gesture. Language level showed rather more improvements with significantly more children using phrase speech to communicate. Only three children were reported as using frequent phrase speech initially, whereas nine were doing so at follow-up. A further four children used simple words or phrases to communicate although this was limited in both range and frequency. Three children remained virtually non-communicating.

Mean scores suggested moderate improvements in language level, with children beginning to use more simple phrase speech. However, this still tended to be used relatively infrequently and was generally lacking in spontaneity.

In contrast, abnormal *use* of language showed greater change. By follow-up, over half the children were reported to be using mainly appropriate speech as compared to only three initially. Rating for abnormal language usage had also fallen. To begin with, children had used relatively little phrase speech and, when this did occur, much of it was echolalic. By follow-up, the majority of children still showed some echolalia, but its severity had reduced considerably.

DIRECT OBSERVATIONS OF CHILDREN'S BEHAVIOUR OVER THE FINAL YEAR OF TREATMENT

Assessments of improvement based on parental reports showed much greater change in the final year of treatment than during the first 6 months. The pattern of change in children's observed behaviours, however, was rather different. Here change was generally greatest in the first 6 months of treatment. Thereafter progress tended to occur at a rather slower rate. Nevertheless, the gains made during the first 6 months were well maintained throughout the following year despite a reduction in therapist intervention.

The amount of time spent unoccupied did not change during the intervention period. This was as anticipated, as the treatment goal had not been to keep the child fully occupied at all times. Indeed, some periods of inactivity and relaxation were considered to be necessary for the children. Parents had been actively encouraged to allow their child to have some time to himself, without

Table 10.5
Changes in children's behaviour over 18 months

Assessment:	1 Mean (s.d.)	2 Mean (s.d.)	3 Mean (s.d.)	4 Mean (s.d.)
Unoccupied	52.3 (33.5)	44.2 (35.5)	40.4 (30.0)	49.7 (41.6)
Task/play alone	93.7 (63.8)	57.2 (41.9)*	65.2 (37.9)*	52.0 (35.7)**
Task/play with mum	125.2 (78.1)	185.1 (54.9)**	186.0 (44.0)**	195.3 (36.2)***
Rituals/ stereotypies	58.1 (83.3)	26.6 (30.9)	24.2 (32.0)	23.7 (30.7)
Disruption	8.9 (16.1)	5.2 (7.4)	7.3 (11.6)	2.4 (4.0)

Note Figures refer to number of occurrences of each behaviour during the home observation sessions.

* = Significance of change between first and subsequent occasions   * = P < 0.05
** = P < 0.01
*** = P < 0.001

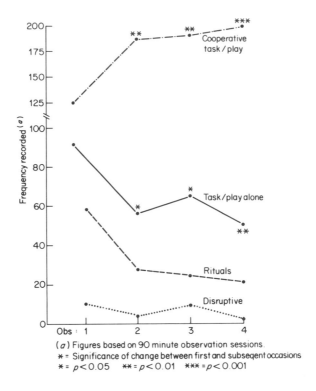

Figure 10.8 Changes in children's behaviour over 18
months

any additional pressures or 'stimulation' by adults. Instead, the nature of the child's on-task or play behaviours had changed, with a significant reduction in solitary activities and a concomitant rise in joint activities with the mother.

The greatest degree of change occurred in the first 6 months of intervention and there were only moderate changes in the final year of treatment (see Table 10.5). Although improvements continued, these were at a lower rate than during the first 6 months. A similar pattern occurred in the reduction of ritualistic and stereotyped activities. Disruptive behaviours, on the other hand, showed a rather different pattern of change, with a further reduction during the final 6 months. By the end of treatment, such behaviours were 75 per cent less frequent than initially, in spite of lack of change after the first 6 months of treatment. Figure 10.8 summarizes the pattern of these changes over 18 months.

Changes in Communication over the Final Year

Non-communicative utterances tended to occur at much the same rate throughout although, as a proportion of total utterances, they were considerably reduced (from approximately 50 per cent of recorded utterances initially, to

Table 10.6
Changes in children's communication over 18 months

Assessment:	1 Mean (s.d.)	2 Mean (s.d.)	3 Mean (s.d.)	4 Mean (s.d.)
Non-communicative utterances	49.2 (40.3)	47.9 (46.4)	36.2 (30.5)	48.1 (31.5)
Communicative utterances	57.9 (69.5)	102.4 (76.8)*	114.9 (80.2)*	133.5 (74.4)**
Words	15.6 (16.0)	44.3 (48.3)**	58.1 (61.1)**	52.4 (43.7)***
Phrases	35.9 (60.3)	49.3 (67.8)	40.7 (53.1)	64.0 (72.7)

Note Figures refer to number of occurrences of each behaviour during the home observation
session.
* = Significance of change between first and subsequent occasions
  * = P < 0.05
 ** = P < 0.01
*** = P < 0.001

approximately 25 per cent at the end of treatment (see Table 10.6). The use of
communicative speech rose rather more steadily than the changes recorded in
children's behaviour, presumably due to maturational as well as treatment
effects. Nevertheless, again, the greatest changes had occurred in the first 6

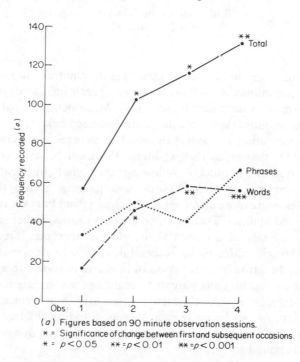

(*a*) Figures based on 90 minute observation sessions.
* = Significance of change between first and subsequent occasions.
* = $p < 0.05$ ** = $p < 0.01$ ** = $p < 0.001$

Figure 10.9 Changes in children's communicative
utterances over 18 months

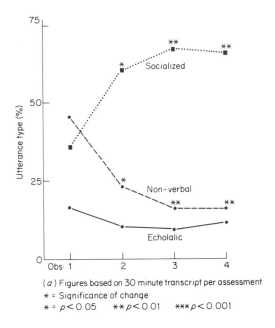

(*a*) Figures based on 30 minute transcript per assessment

∗ = Significance of change

∗ = $p < 0.05$ ∗∗$p < 0.01$ ∗∗∗$p < 0.001$

Figure 10.10 Changes in functional language
over 18 months(a)

months, with the most notable improvements in the children's use of single word utterances to communicate. Although phrase speech increased, it did so in a rather more erratic fashion (see Figure 10.9). More detailed analyses of these changes, based on audio tape recordings, are discussed below.

The home observation assessment showed that changes in maternal behaviour were mirrored by changes in their children. For most behaviours the greatest changes occurred very quickly following the onset of treatment, as if intervention were aiding both children and parents to use their existing behavioural repertoire more effectively and helping them to make the best use of inherent skills and abilities. Thereafter, behaviours showed rather more stability, but there was no loss of acquired skills, even as therapist intervention was withdrawn. Thus, in order to be successful, treatment does not have to be prolonged, and a relatively short period of intensive outside intervention seems to be adequate for encouraging parents to improve their management skills and for ensuring changes in their children. These early improvements cannot be expected to continue at the same rate, however, and as children and parents reach their own optimal levels of functioning, some slowing down in the rate of improvement is bound to occur.

Nevertheless, even when this stage is reached, regular, though much less frequent, intervention with families is successful is maintaining the earlier gains and ensuring that new ones are made at a steady, although usually slower, rate.

Table 10.7
Children's speech function change over 18 months [a]

	Time 1 Mean (s.d.)	Time 2 Mean (s.d.)	Time 3 Mean (s.d.)	Time 4 Mean (s.d.)
No. of comprehensible utterances	72.7 (93.4)	154.8 (126.5)**	162.5 (120.2)**	176.8 (127.2)**
% echolalic/autistic	14.7 (16.0)	9.6 (12.3)	9.1 (7.7)	10.9 (9.5)
% non-verbal incomprehensible[a]	57.1 (36.4)	37.9 (41.2)*	32.8 (38.2)**	33.1 (38.1)**
% prompted echoes	3.3 (5.6)	12.6 (15.6)*	12.8 (17.2)*	13.9 (22.0)*
% spontaneous utterances	24.9 (25.6)	39.8 (33.8)*	45.1 (30.3)**	42.4 (30.5)**

Notes
Length of recording = half hour at each assessment.
([a]) Figures based on all children.

* = Significance of change between first and subsequent observations
   * = $P < 0.05$
   ** = $P < 0.01$
   *** = $P < 0.001$

More detailed assessments of the children's language also showed that initial improvements were well maintained. The frequency of their utterances continued to rise and the average number of remarks to their mothers was well over twice what it had been originally. Moderate increases occurred, too, in the proportions of their socialized utterances. The proportion of utterances in response to prompts by their parents also continued to increase steadily.

There were no further dramatic changes over the final year of treatment in patterns of speech although initial gains were well maintained (see tables 10.7 and 10.8). The frequency of spontaneous utterances (i.e. remarks not in response to a prompt or question by mother) remained at twice the initial level.

Table 10.8
Children's speech function change over 18 months—individual categories[a]

	Time 1 Mean (s.d.)	Time 2 Mean (s.d.)	Time 3 Mean (s.d.)	Time 4 Mean (s.d.)
Types of utterances				
Total spontaneous	35.2 (52.1)	73.7 (75.0)*	73.2 (69.9)*	72.3 (60.5)*
No. of answers	12.0 (19.7)	41.4 (32.1)***	48.4 (36.5)***	56.9 (46.0)***
No. of commands	12.7 (19.4)	16.3 (29.5)	13.5 (16.5)	13.6 (15.0)
No. of questions	3.8 (8.9)	9.3 (19.2)*	7.9 (17.2)*	12.8 (20.2)*
No. of informative	18.8 (37.5)	47.5 (61.4)*	52.6 (61.7)*	45.8 (44.6)*

Notes
([a]) Figures based on half hour recordings, for the 13 children using some speech

* = Significance of change between initial and subsequent observations
   * = $P < 0.05$
   ** = $P < 0.01$
   *** = $P < 0.001$

Information giving remarks had more than doubled and spontaneous questions (although still at a relatively low level) were almost four times as frequent as they had been to begin with. The only category to remain at a fairly steady level was that of demands by the child. Before intervention much of the children's speech had been used for the fulfilment of their immediate needs. The frequency of such utterances remained fairly stable over time, but their proportional use had fallen considerably as other forms of communication increased. Thus, the *quality* as well as the frequency of children's language had improved over the 18 month period. Speech was less often used for the gratification of immediate needs and was more often employed for more general communication and conversation (see Figure 10.10).

Table 10.9
Changes in language level over 18 months[a]

	Time 1 Mean (s.d.)	Time 2 Mean (s.d.)	Time 3 Mean (s.d.)	Time 4 Mean (s.d.)
No. of correct phrases	32.1 (64.3)	58.9 (73.4)*	51.3 (48.4)*	65.0 (53.7)**
No. of correct sentences	14.7 (33.2)	23.9 (34.8)*	21.0 (26.6)	30.5 (40.5)*
Total morphemes	54.0 (116.5)	106.4 (117.8)*	90.7 (89.6)*	115.4 (90.8)*
Total transformations	27.9 (61.4)	54.8 (78.5)*	48.1 (67.9)*	61.4 (74.2)**
Mean length of all utterances	2.3	2.9	2.7	2.6

Notes

[a] Figures based on half hour recordings of the 11 children using some phrase speech at the end of treatment

* = Significance of change between first and subsequent observations

  * = $P < 0.05$

 ** = $P < 0.01$

*** = $P < 0.001$

The children's language level indicated a similar pattern of improvement. Rather more children (11 in all) were using phrase speech at the end of 18 months and as Table 10.9 indicates, the increase in the number of correct phrases and sentences used was maintained as was the increase in morphemes and transformational rules. The rate of change slowed down after the first 6 months; nevertheless, there were steady improvements over the final year of treatment (see Figure 10.11). Of the various individual aspects of linguistic complexity measured, those that showed greatest change over the final 12 months were noun and verb inflections, the use of articles and prepositions, the use of auxiliary verbs and transformations such as imperatives and questions.

To summarize, children's pattern of change mirrored that of their parents. Change was greatest in the first 6 months of treatment, but subsequent reduction

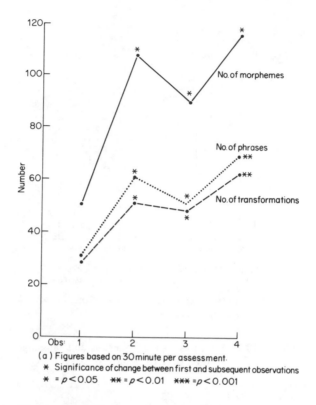

Figure 10.11 Changes in language level over 18 months[a]

in the intensity of intervention did not lead to any loss of skills. In almost every aspect of behaviour and communication studied, improvements were maintained at the same level or continued to increase.

Once parents achieve more efficient ways of interacting with their children, and as children themselves show improvements in their language and behaviour, direct intervention can be reduced without loss. Even so, although the effects of treatment were real and worthwhile, there were limitations in the extent to which more basic handicaps could be overcome.

Changes in Developmental Level

Although the initial improvements in language level were evidently well maintained, the growth in the complexity of communication skills was less marked than changes in children's *use* of language. Whereas on average the total number of utterances used had increased by over 120 (i.e. from a mean of 89 to a mean of 217 per half hour recording), as had their socialized responses, increases in language level were not so great.

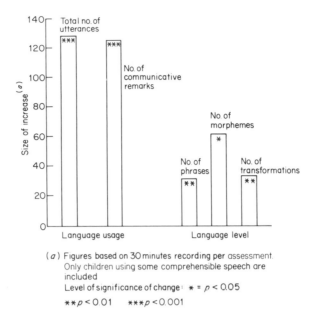

Figure 10.12 Increases in language use and language
level over 18 months

As Figure 10.12 indicates, although the average frequencies of morphemes and transformations increased steadily over time, the rise was less than expected on the basis of the large changes in the overall frequency of speech. Because the children were now much more communicative than formerly, one would have expected a much greater increase in their use of linguistic rules. Instead the average length and complexity of their utterances remained much the same, as measures of mean utterance length indicated. It seemed that, in contrast to language development in normal children, where the frequency of utterances is very much paralleled by rapid increases in language complexity (Klee and Fitzgerald, 1985), in autistic children improvements in communicative function do not necessarily result in improvements in the complexity or level of language used.

This failure to show marked improvements in linguistic skills was paralleled by a similar lack of change in the children's cognitive level. There were no significant changes in IQ scores over time (the mean IQ at initial assessment being 89.0 and at follow-up 85.6). The correlation between IQ scores before and after treatment was similar to that found in other studies of both normal and autistic children (rho = 0.52). Whereas the children showed improvements in a range of cognitive abilities, it seemed that the *level* of these skills relative to other children of the same age had not shown any marked change. Thus, although children continued to make progress in language and cognition their basic handicaps in these areas remained in spite of the benefits of the treatment programme.

The inference is that, while treatment successfully improves *performance*, the effects on basic levels of *competence* are less. In other words, treatment seems to be responsible for helping children to use their existing skills more effectively. It does not necessarily result in the increased complexity of these skills.

PARENTAL REPORTS AND OBSERVATIONAL MEASURES

The same hierarchy of change was apparent in both parental reports and observational measures, with the greatest improvements occurring in non-specific behavioural problems such as tantrums and disruptive behaviours, some worthwhile gains in the reduction of obsessions and rituals, and in the improvement of communication, but with least change in language capacity and cognitive skills.

General social responsiveness was not assessed by observational measures, except with respect to the child's interaction with his mother, so comparisons between parental reports and direct observations were not possible here. However, parental reports were very much in keeping with other observational studies of autistic children, such as those by Lord (1984). She found that interactions with peers and other adults (such as teachers) improved in highly structured settings. *Spontaneous* patterns of play with other children or relationships with adults, however, failed to show significant improvements. This seems to have been so for the children in the present study.

Although parental reports and observations agreed on the *patterns* of improvements across behaviours, parents were delayed in their recognition of changes already apparent in the observations. The greatest pace of change on the observational measures occurred in the first 6 months of intervention, whereas in most instances this did not occur until later on the parental reports.

Figures 10.13 (a) and 10.13 (b) compare changes in observed and reported behaviour on several variables assessed by both observation and parental reports. The scores are not directly comparable since the observational measures note the actual number of incidents recorded whereas the parental measures are based on global ratings (which sometimes used slightly different definitions). In most cases, observed changes were greatest in the first 6 months of treatment, with a slowing of change thereafter. By contrast, parental perceptions indicated slower but steadier improvements over time.

It is encouraging that over the full 18 month treatment period parents viewed their children as having achieved useful gains. However, the initial lag between parents' perceptions of change and those recorded by outside observers suggests that, although short term intervention may result in *objective* improvement, support for families may have to continue rather longer if they themselves are to fully appreciate the benefits that treatment can bring.

Autism is a chronically handicapping condition and the practical and emotional burdens on families are likely to remain in spite of objective

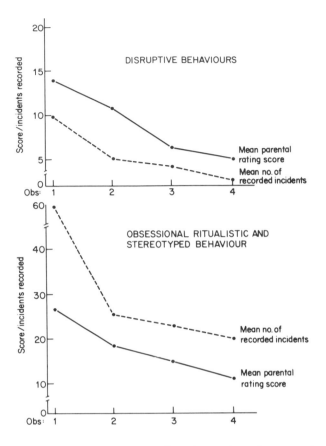

Figure 10.13(a) Changes in observed and reported behaviour over 18 months

improvements in the children's behaviour. Statistically significant gains are always gratifying for therapists and researchers involved in the evaluation of treatment. However, for parents, gradual improvements of this nature may seem relatively trivial in comparison with the lifelong problems with which they have to cope. Subjective perceptions of improvement will almost certainly be affected by the knowledge that the future will continue to bring many more difficulties. It is not surprising, therefore, that parental views are sometimes less optimistic than those of professionals, who ultimately are able to walk away from the problem. Properly controlled research data are, of course, essential in evaluation. However, if the real impact of therapy on family life is to be assessed, objective data collection needs to be combined with more subjective, longer term measures of parents' own views of treatment effectiveness. As the present findings indicate, if therapy is to have any real impact on family functioning, intervention may need to continue long after the first significant changes have been recorded.

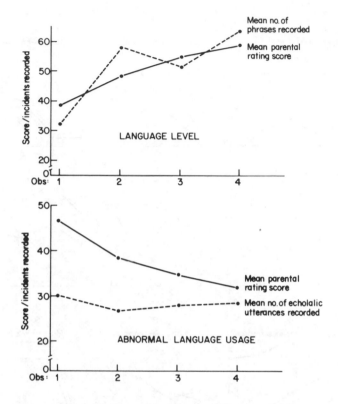

Figure 10.13(b) Changes in observed and reported language over 18 months

Individual Differences in Patterns of Mother–Child Interaction

Since change is rarely a one-way process, one of the purposes of the 18 month follow-up was to examine possible causal connection between changes in parents and improvements in children's behaviour (Howlin and Rutter, 1987). As already noted, there was a close association between the two at group level. It remains to be considered whether or not this was also the case at an individual level.

Not all children made improvements in their use of language, nor did all mothers substantially change their styles of communication over time. Nevertheless, mothers who increased their use of language directed utterances seemed more likely to have children with marked gains in communicative speech. This is evident, for example, in the parallels between changes in mothers' language directed speech and in their children's socialized speech within individual mother–child pairs (as shown in Figure 10.14). However, these changes appeared to be related to the initial language levels of the children.

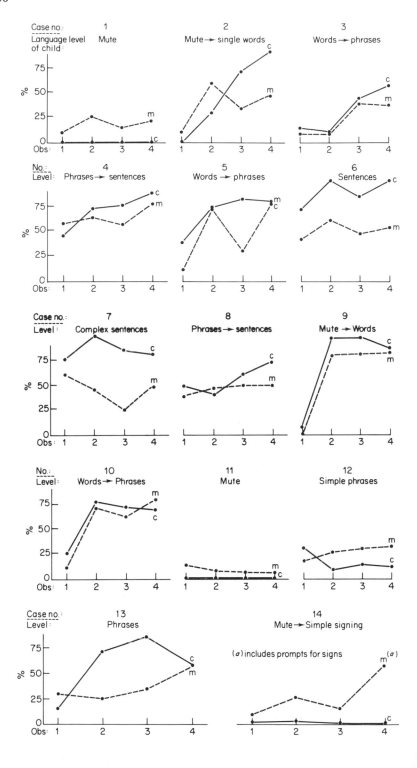

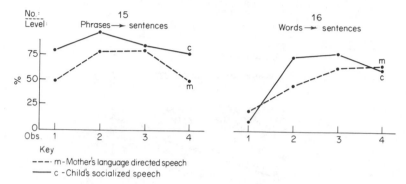

Figure 10.14 Relationships between changes in mothers' and children's speech

The experimental children in the study fell into three language groups: (1) those who were already using some phrase speech when treatment began; (2) those who were at the single word level (or who were at least using word approximations; and (3) those who were almost entirely non-communicating. The initial level of the child tended to predict, not only his own progress, but subsequent changes in his mother's speech as well (see Figure 10.15).

In order to study this relationship further, the treatment and control groups were compared. The pattern was similar in both. Children who were mute or making a few sounds only when treatment commenced had mothers who showed little overall change in their speech style. Mothers of such children in the treatment group increased their use of language directed utterances slightly, whilst the proportion fell somewhat in the controls. But, as can be seen in Figure 10.16, the difference between groups was very slight.

Mothers of children who were already using phrase speech at the start of treatment also showed relatively modest increases in the frequency of their language directed speech. Again as Figures 10.15 and 10.16 indicate, treated mothers and children in this subgroup increased their use of language directed and socialized speech respectively whilst control children showed a slight decrease. The *pattern* of change shown by treated and untreated families, however, was similar.

The most marked change occurred in mothers of children who were using occasional words or word approximations at the start of treatment. Children who were at this level in the treatment group showed much greater improvement than controls. But again, in both groups the rate of improvement was closely paralleled by increases in the language directed utterances used by mothers.

Correlational data also showed a significant association between mothers' language directed utterances and improvements in their children's speech. Although there was no relationship between the total amount of speech used by mothers and changes in their children, there were relationships according to the different styles of language used. Increases in the frequency of language directed speech, and in specific types of utterance, such as responses, echoes, corrections

182

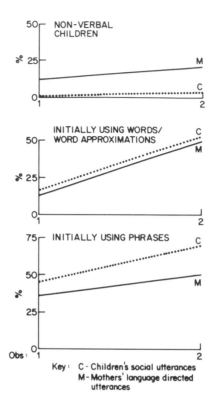

Figure 10.15 Relationship between
mothers' language directed utterances
and children's socialized speech—cases

and reinforcement, were all significantly related to improvements in children's
language. Non-language directed utterances, such as demands and statements,
tended to be negatively correlated with improvements in children's speech. Thus,
mothers who used these types of utterance most frequently had children who
showed least improvement. Other types of utterance showed no significant or
consistent relationships with changes in children's speech (see Table 10.10).

A similar trend was found in the relationship between changes in the language
of control mothers and children (see Table 10.11). However, the associations
here were generally weaker. Although the total frequency of language directed
utterances correlated with improvements in children's speech, individual speech
categories (with the exception of reinforcement) showed no significant relationships. Again, there was no association between the frequency of mothers'
utterances and the amount of appropriate speech used by children. Neither was
there any relationship between children's use of phrase speech and any aspects of
mothers' language. Indeed, for both cases and controls, virtually no relationship
was found between children's language *level* and mothers' speech, the only

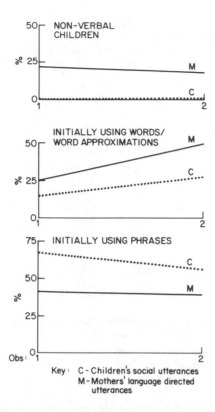

Figure 10.16 Relationship between
mothers' language directed utterances and
children's socialized speech—controls

exception to this was in the correlation between the rates of corrections used by
mothers in the treatment group and the frequency of phrase speech used by their
children.

Interpreting the Association Between Changes in Mothers' and Children's Speech

Although there was an association between changes in mothers' and children's
speech, it was necessary to ask whether this association reflected a causal
relationship and, if so, whether the changes in maternal language produced
changes in the children, or vice versa?

Since parents of mute children necessarily have much less scope for increasing
their rates of language directed utterances (there being no language to which
they can respond) it seems likely that this may represent an effect of the child on
the parents. Pooling the data for cases and controls, it was apparent that
mothers of mute children showed very little change in their use of language

Table 10.10
Correlations between changes in children's and in mothers' speech over time.
Cases: Change at 6 and 18 months

Changes in Mothers' speech	Changes in Children's speech					
	No utterances		% socialized		Correct phrase speech	
	6 m.	18 m.	6 m.	18 m.	6 m.	18 m.
No utterances	0.15	0.16	0.27	0.08	0.03	0.22
% language directed	0.71**	0.79**	0.67**	0.74**	0.05	0.27
Responses[a]	0.79**	0.46*	0.68**	0.65**	0.27	0.25
Echoes[b]	0.78**	0.46*	0.51*	0.65**	0.12	0.02
Corrections	0.82**	0.52*	0.65**	0.68**	0.44*	0.47*
Reinforcement	0.75**	0.46*	0.46*	0.74**	0.35	0.15
Non-language directed						
Demands	−0.06	0.09	−0.52*	−0.54*	−0.08	−0.19
Statements	−0.46*	−0.39	−0.26	−0.58*	0.34	0.22

Notes
(a) Includes answers, imitation, expansions, reductions, corrections and reinforcement.
(b) Includes exact echoes, expansions and reductions.

* = Correlations significant at $P < 0.05$ level
** = Correlations significant at $P < 0.01$ level

directed utterances over time. In contrast, mothers of speaking children showed increases in almost every type of language directed utterance used. These differences suggest that child effects are important in predicting the relative frequency with which mothers of mute and speaking children are likely to use language directed speech. They are also important in determining the amount of change that is likely to ensue following intervention.

It was apparent when change was assessed *separately* for untreated and treated families, that improvements were much greater in the mothers in the treatment programme. The mothers of non-speaking children who had not been involved in the intervention programme showed decreases in almost every aspect of their language directed speech over time. Mothers who had been involved in therapy made modest improvements in all areas. Similarly, for mothers of speaking children, overall improvements were only moderate in the untreated group, whereas the differences were much greater for mothers who had received intervention. Thus, although the extent of the child's language impairment seemed to place limitations on the amount of possible change, these differences between groups indicated that the changes recorded for the more verbal children were influenced, at least to some extent, by the changes occurring in maternal language.

That changes in the children and their mothers were correlated over time does not necessarily imply that the mothers' changed behaviour had a direct influence on changes in the child, for we would expect a mutual interaction of one upon

Table 10.11
Correlations between changes in mothers' and in children's speech. Controls: Change over 6 months

Changes in Mothers' speech	Changes in Children's speech		
	No. of utterances	socialized speech	Correct phrase speech
No utterances	0.49*	0.12	0.43
% language directed	0.52*	0.48*	0.13
Responses	0.34	0.05	0.18
Echoes	0.43	0.04	0.13
Corrections	0.05	0.43	0.26
Reinforcement	0.73**	0.04	0.44
Non-language directed			
Demands	0.28	−0.16	−0.12
Statements	0.33	0.03	0.44

* Correlations significant at P < 0.05 level
** Correlations significant at P < 0.01 level

the other. However, further analyses using regression techniques suggested that the influence of maternal changes were slightly greater on the child than vice-versa (Howlin & Rutter, 1987). Hence, variations in the children's language would appear to be attributable in part to the changes in the mothers' style of communication.

Mothers' opportunities for changing their speech styles will be severely restricted when their children are mute or near-mute and so producing little or no language for them to encourage or facilitate. At the other extreme, a high level of language competence in the child will also limit parental scope for change. A child who is just on the threshold of learning to use language, however, provides substantial opportunities for parents to increase and elaborate the ways in which they communicate. Not only is a child at this level more responsive to parents' efforts but he himself will also prove to be much more enjoyable and rewarding to parents. It seems that as parents become aware of improvements occurring in their child's speech they are more likely to encourage the child's attempts to talk.

Nevertheless, important as child effects are, the comparison between treated and untreated mothers also testifies to the influence of parental styles of communication. Regardless of initial language levels, intervention programmes can help parents to respond to and elicit their children's speech more effectively.

In summary, by focusing the analysis on the *relationship* between changes in children and parents, it became apparent that the association was bidirectional. Parental intervention can be successful in changing many different aspects of children's behaviour, but the extent to which this intervention is effective will depend very much on the abilities and handicaps of the individual child. The art of successful intervention would seem to lie in helping to encourage the most effective forms of parent–child interaction. Parents will then be better able to provide an optimal environment for the development of their child's inherent abilities. Nevertheless, it must be borne in mind that the level to which these abilities can be developed will depend, ultimately, on the extent of the child's handicap and limitations.

Chapter 11

Comparisons Between Cases and Long Term Controls

Evaluations of the efficacy of treatment programmes are nearly always based on the immediate responses to interventions or, at most, on very short term follow-ups. Studies of treatment for autism are no exception to that general rule. But autism is a chronic condition with handicaps persisting into and through adult life. This chronicity means that any adequate assessment of a treatment programme must include some form of longer term evaluation of outcome. It was for that reason that we included a detailed comparison with an individually matched control group of autistic children who were given only sporadic outpatient treatment because their distance from the clinic prohibited any more intensive involvement (see chapter 3 for details of sample and matching).

Because these cases and long term controls were well matched on crucial variables of prognostic importance, it could be anticipated that their outcome should be similar. Accordingly, it was a reasonable inference that any difference in outcome between the groups could be attributed to the effects of the treatment programme. Inevitably, however, the vagaries of varying patterns of clinic referral meant that, although the groups were well matched on individual· characteristics at the time of initial assessment, the duration of follow-up was not identical. In particular, the 'untreated' group had been followed for a longer time period and, as a consequence, were significantly older at the follow-up assessment. This difference was of little importance with regard to the outcome comparisons for behavioural disturbance because we found that the levels of such disturbance did not vary with age. However, for obvious reasons, it *did* matter with all the developmental functions (such as language level). Accordingly, when comparing cases and controls on language competence, regression equations were calculated to take into account the effects of age.

BEHAVIOURAL CHANGES IN CASES AND CONTROLS: INFORMATION FROM THE PARENTAL INTERVIEW

Because of limitations on resources, it was not possible to carry out direct observational assessments on the long term control children and their families in the same way as had been done for the treatment group. It was clear, however, that information from the parental interview provided reasonably good estimates of the skills and behavioural problems shown by children (although there was a tendency for parents to *underestimate* the amount of improvement). At follow-up therefore, this interview was one of the methods used to assess differences between children in the treatment group and their matched controls.

Parental Perceptions of Change

Parental ratings of behaviour disturbance were based on the frequency and severity of a range of specified individual problems shown at home and outside. These included sleeping, eating, toileting, destructiveness and tantrums. The extent to which these disrupted life, both at home and outside, was also assessed. A global rating of the severity of children's behaviour disturbance was then made on the basis of a combination of frequency, severity and social disruption. For every outcome variable, the *lower* the rating score the more 'normal' the behaviour (details of codings are provided in Appendix 3.5).

As Table 11.1 indicates, children in the treatment group were showing fewer problems than the controls on almost every behavioural variable. Children in the treatment programme usually showed only occasional problems at home in one or two main areas of difficulty. The control children, on the other hand, tended to have more frequent and more extensive behavioural problems. The difference between the groups for behaviour disturbance outside the home was much less and fell short of statistical significance. Nevertheless, parents in the treatment group were more likely to feel that they could take their child out with only occasional disruptions, whereas control families reported greater disturbance during outings.

Table 11.1
Ratings of cases and controls on parental interview at follow-up

	Cases	Controls	Significance of difference
	Mean (s.d.)	Mean (s.d.)	(P value)
General behaviour problems (tantrums, aggression, etc.)			
At home	4.8 (3.9)	10.8 (7.6)	0.01
Away from home	10.7 (6.8)	14.3 (7.6)	ns
Other behaviour problems			
Stereotypies	2.1 (1.7)	1.9 (1.2)	ns
Activity level (Hyper/hypo activity)	2.4 (1.9)	1.7 (1.2)	ns
Mood abnormalities	1.4 (1.2)	2.3 (1.9)	ns
Autistic problems			
Obsessions/rituals	4.6 (3.5)	10.6 (5.3)	0.01
Abnormal responses to objects (flicking, licking, smelling etc.)	4.8 (3.9)	7.3 (6.8)	ns

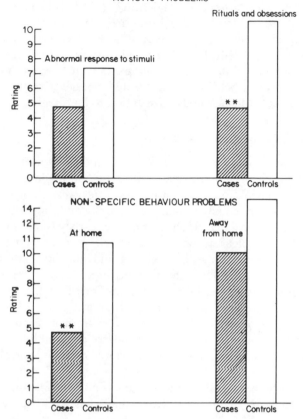

Figure 11.1 Parental ratings of behaviour at follow-up. ** = $p < 0.01$

There was no evidence of any effect of the therapeutic programme on other general behavioural characteristics, such as mood abnormalities or hyper-activity, although these did not constitute a major problem in the particular group of children studied.

This relative lack of effectiveness is broadly in keeping with the rather limited effects of behavioural treatments for hyperactivity in non-autistic groups (O'Leary, 1980) and for mood disturbances in adult life (Marks, 1975). Behavioural methods may be of value in reducing the negative *impact* of hyperactivity or of channeling it in more productive directions (Prior and Griffin, 1985) but they have little effect on activity levels as such. The same applies to disturbances of mood. Equally, treatment made little difference to abnormal responses to stimuli, such as smelling, flicking or tapping objects. Nor was there a marked reduction in motor stereotypies although, again, these were not a particularly troublesome feature in these children.

In sharp contrast, the treatment and control groups differed markedly in the severity and extent of 'obsessions' and rituals (see Figure 11.1). The average rating for untreated children indicated that problems resulting from obsessions or abnormal attachments to objects were still severe enough to disrupt family life, although other ritualistic behaviours and resistance to change were less of a problem. Whilst children in the treatment group continued to show some mild obsessional or ritualistic behaviours these were far easier to control, and were no longer felt by parents to cause undue disruption to family life.

Changes in Social Behaviour and Play

Although there were obvious limitations in the children's social behaviour at the end of treatment, children in the treatment group had made greater progress in these areas than controls, despite their being considerably younger at follow-up. They were much more socially responsive generally and, in particular, relations with their parents were much closer. For example, they were reported as being more likely to show pleasure upon seeing their parents, and more likely to reciprocate affectionate acts such as kissing and hugging, although they still failed to initiate these. Children in the control group were reported as being much less demonstrative and responsive. Reactions to other adults were also considered to be more appropriate and discriminating in the treatment group. Some treated children were still indiscriminatory in their response to strangers but they did not, in general, show the same degree of disinhibition (or in one or two cases severe withdrawal) that was characteristic of the control children (see Table 11.2).

Even in their peer relationships, an area that is notoriously difficult to change, treated children were significantly better than their controls, and showed a

Table 11.2
Ratings of cases and controls on parental interview at follow-up

	Cases Mean (s.d)	Controls Mean (s.d.)	Sig. of diff. (P value)
Social responsiveness			
Response to parents	1.8 (1.9)	4.8 (3.0)	0.01
Response to other adults	4.5 (2.9)	7.0 (3.5)	0.05
Response to peers	4.5 (1.1)	6.5 (1.8)	0.01
Play and other developmental skills			
Level of play	13.5 (8.6)	20.8 (10.9)	0.05
Reading, writing, etc.	8.1 (5.5)	8.25 (7.1)	ns
Communication			
Level of language	34.1 (33.0)	41.7 (33.0)	ns
Abnormal use of language	34.1 (32.4)	41.5 (34.1)	ns
Non-verbal communication	6.3 (5.3)	8.2 (6.1)	ns
Comprehension	6.5 (2.2)	7.6 (3.1)	ns

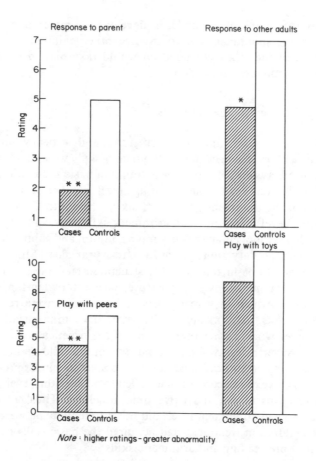

Figure 11.2 Parental ratings at follow-up: social behaviour and play. * = $p < 0.05$; ** = $p < 0.01$

greater tendency to join in games with other children. However, differences here related mainly to the frequency of *supervised* play.

Spontaneous, non-directive play remained limited in both groups. Only one child was reported as joining in any complex group activities (in his case, card games) without adult intervention, and no children were considered to have made any special friendships (see Figure 11.2).

Although all children remained limited in the sophistication of their play, children in the treatment group were consistently at a higher level than controls. One quarter of the untreated children were reported to use play objects *solely* for ritualistic purposes, whereas this was not true for any of the treatment children. Similarly, eight of the children in the treatment group were reported as showing simple pretend play with toys (such as putting dolls into bed, giving them food, etc.) as compared with only three of the control children. They also showed more appropriate functional use of objects, such as toy cars or furniture or cooking utensils. However, none of the children developed complex imaginative play, nor did they try, spontaneously, to involve other children in their games, although more of the treatment children would take part in group activities under the direct guidance of an adult.

Changes in Other Developmental Skills

In contrast to the encouraging improvements found in behavioural problems and social difficulties, changes in developmental skills were much less marked. Little difference between the groups was found in basic pre-reading or number skills and few children were achieving at age level in either of these areas. Only four children in the treatment group and six of the controls were reported as having achieved levels of reading and arithmetic skills that would be appropriate for normal infant school children (i.e. simple addition and subtraction skills and a limited sight vocabulary appropriate for 6 to 7 year olds). Moreover, skills in these areas tended to be linked to highly structured teaching sessions. None of the children read spontaneously for pleasure, except in two instances (one child in each group) in which they read parts of books that were related to their obsessional interests. Arithmetical skills referred to multiplication tables or sheets of number work, rather than to any of the practical skills required for shopping, etc. Nevertheless, whereas all but two of the children in the treatment group were considered to have made at least a start in simple pre-reading and arithmetic skills, five of the controls had failed to achieve this level, despite their advantages in terms of age and extra time at school. Thus, again, although overall differences in attainment levels did not differentiate between the groups, more of the children in treatment had acquired the basic skills needed for the development of pre-reading and arithmetic skills.

Changes in Language Development

Although many aspects of the speech used by children in treatment had improved steadily over time, without a comparison group there was no way of knowing whether these changes were a result of the intervention programme, or were simply a result of the children's increasing level of maturation. In the event, comparisons with the long term control group indicated that probably both factors were important. Parental interview measures showed gains in both groups (see Figure 11.3). At follow-up, although the treated children were reported as being slightly superior in their use of language, mean scores for both groups were very similar. The majority of children in both groups were using some simple phrase speech, but this remained limited both in frequency and spontaneity. Inappropriate use of language was reported as being somewhat less in the treatment children, but the differences again were small and insignificant. Language comprehension and the use of non-verbal skills were at a similar level for both groups of children.

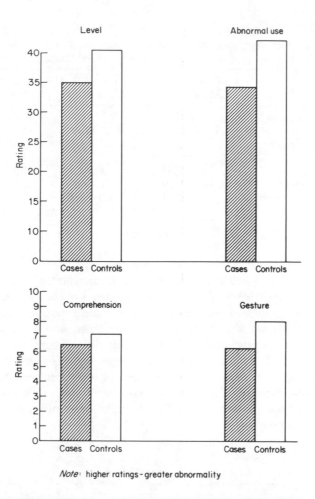

Figure 11.3 Parental ratings of language at follow-up

However, it must be remembered that as controls were older than children in the treatment group at this stage of the project this would be likely to bias the results in favour of the controls and hence minimize any real differences between the groups. Detailed analyses of language recordings, therefore, were used to supplement the data from parental reports, while the possible effects of age were taken into account using statistical regression techniques.

As might have been expected on the basis of other follow-up reports of children of this IQ level, it was apparent that the control children had made a considerable amount of progress since initial diagnosis. The majority of them were using some speech and over half were able to use at least some simple phrases. They had also shown a steady improvement in their language scores on formal tests. However, although many improvements had occurred these were less than expected on the basis of findings from the treatment group.

Table 11.3
Children's language usage: long term case–control comparison
(Scores based on qualitative analyses of audio taped language samples)[a]

	Cases Mean (s.d.)	Controls Mean (s.d.)	Sig. of diff. between groups
No. of comprehensible utterances	176.8 (127.2)	142.7 (127.2)	NS
% autistic/echolalic	10.9 (9.5)	8.5 (11.1)	NS
% non-verbal incomprehensible	33.1 (38.1)	46.8 (39.8)	NS
% prompted utterances	13.9 (22.0)	4.7 (7.2)	.05
% spontaneous utterances	42.4 (30.5)	40.0 (34.7)	NS

Notes
(a) Figures based on half hour recordings for all children

Even without taking age into account the children who had had help at home were found to be superior to controls in many aspects of their language function (see Table 11.3). Only two children in the treatment group, as compared with four of the controls, had remained entirely mute and uncommunicative. Amongst the remaining children, the general quality of verbal interaction was also better in the treatment group. They were using fewer non-verbal and incomprehensible utterances and the frequency of socialized speech was greater. They were using commands and instructions more frequently and effectively in order to control their environment and they were also more responsive to their

Table 11.4
Language level:
long term case–control comparison[a]

	Cases (N=11) Mean (s.d.)	Controls (N=9) Mean (s.d.)
Language recordings (half hour assessment)		
No. of correct phrases used	65.0 (53.7)	78.8 (79.5)
No. of sentences	30.5 (40.5)	33.0 (50.0)
Total morphemes	115.4 (90.8)	150.3 (118.6)
Total pronouns	31.6 (45.2)	51.6 (82.7)
Total transformations	61.4 (74.2)	54.6 (97.6)
Mean length phrases	3.6	3.9
Formal assessments		
Reynell Expressive Language Age	32.4 (21.2)	38.9 (27.6)
Reynell Comprehension Language Age	37.4 (18.7)	46.5 (21.3)

Notes
(a) Includes only children using some phrase speech.
No significant differences between groups

mothers' speech, in particular to direct prompts. They also used more spontaneous utterances such as information giving comments and questions.

Assessment of language level, however, revealed few differences in the major categories of language studied and, if anything, controls as a group remained generally superior to the children in treatment (see Table 11.4). However, although overall group differences were generally in favour of the older, untreated children, mainly because two or three children had attained particularly high levels of language competence, it is worth noting that, by follow-up, eleven of the treated children and only nine of the controls were using some inflected phrase speech. The treatment group were also somewhat better than controls in their use of a number of specific rules, such as the use of verb endings, plurals, articles, imperatives and questions. On the Reynell test, too, although control children were generally superior, this difference was less than expected on the basis of their age. Despite the fact that, on average, the control children were almost 3 years older than the treatment group, their expressive language scores were only 6 months higher.

When regression equations were calculated in order to take account of the possible effects of age, it was found that although group differences did not reach significance, the *rate* of improvement in language was invariably higher in the experimental group. That is, the language of children in the treatment programme was rather better than that of controls after taking into account the fact that they were substantially younger. Once again, though, the categories showing the greatest change in favour of the experimental children were those involving functional speech. Differences were most marked in categories such as the total number of utterances or the frequency of socialized speech. Measures of language complexity revealed few differences between the children.

A similar pattern of results was found when differences between individual case–control pairs were studied. Although differences between the groups failed to reach significance it was apparent that the treatment children were consistently superior to their matched controls on every measure of language usage assessed. Individual comparisons of treated children and controls (again using regression equations to take into account the affects of age) showed that on almost every measure the treatment children were superior. However, once more, the differences tended to be most marked in categories assessing the frequency and use of socialized speech. Children in treatment were generally using more speech than controls; a higher proportion of this speech was used for socialized, communicative purposes; and the proportion of incomprehensible and non-verbal utterances was less. In contrast, differences on the Reynell tests and in the children's use of phrase speech and morpheme rules were not significant. The greatest improvements in the treatment group were related to the quality of their functional language; changes in language complexity were less marked (see Table 11.5).

Finally, the use of inappropriate and echolalic remarks was examined in more detail. Single case studies of the children had seemed to indicate that echolalic

Table 11.5
Child by child comparisons on long term follow-up of language skills
(after partialling out effects of age)

Measures	Cases superior to matched long term controls	Cases inferior to matched long term controls	P value for sig. of diff. (X^2 test)
No. of comprehensible utterances	11	5	0.05
% socialized communicative utterances	12	4	0.01
% echolalic	9	7	ns
% non-verbal	11	5	0.05
No. of correct phrases	10	6	ns
No. of morphemes	10	6	ns
No. of transformations	13	3	0.01
Reynell Expressive Language	9	7	ns
Reynell Language Comprehension	9	7	ns

speech was very amenable to intervention, but in the long term few differences were found between the groups.

Closer perusal of the data suggested why this apparent discrepancy in findings should have occurred. Although differences in the total amount of inappropriate echolalia were non-significant at follow-up, there were differences in the *types* of echolalia used. Although the number of echolalic utterances remained fairly stable, overall rates of unprompted echolalia, as a proportion of the total speech used, declined steadily in the treatment group. *Prompted* echoes, however, showed a different pattern of change. At follow-up, they were considerably higher in the treatment group than in controls and also tended to be exact rather than partial repetitions. In that mothers in the programme were deliberately using prompted repetition as a form of teaching, this higher rate would seem to reflect the response of the children to intervention. Moreover, the fact that mothers in the treated group were more insistent on correct and *exact* imitations of their prompts, and were less likely to accept abbreviated responses, was also, no doubt, responsible for these findings (see Table 11.6 (a)).

The types of echolalic and repetitive speech used by cases and controls also tended to be generally less 'abnormal' than might have been predicted from previous studies. Although 'egocentric' utterances are reported as occurring frequently in the speech of autistic children (Kanner, 1973; Rutter, 1979), in fact the proportion of such remarks was quite small. Autistic and 'egocentric' utterances, such as 'thinking aloud' or 'metaphorical' speech, etc., never exceeded 3 or 4 per cent in either the treated or control children. Rates of immediate, non-communicative echolalia were somewhat higher but nevertheless were less than 10 per cent in almost every case (see Table 11.6 (b)).

Table 11.6 (a)

Mean number of prompted echoes per half hour recording

Assessment:	1	Cases 2	3	4	Controls	P value for sig. of diff. between cases and controls at follow-up
	Mean (s.d.)	Mean (s.d.)	Mean (s.d.)	Mean (s.d.)	Mean (s.d.)	
Total	2.8 (2.1)	31.8 (15.3)***	28.9 (15.5)***	34.7 (17.3)***	7.3 (4.5)	0.001
Exact Repetitions	2.0 (0.9)	18.7 (9.5)***	8.9 (9.7)**	25.4 (11.2)***	2.2 (1.3)	0.001
Reductions	1.4 (1.2)	11.6 (4.6)***	5.6 (3.2)***	6.8 (4.5)***	3.2 (1.8)	0.01
Expansions	0.2 (0.3)	1.5 (0.8)***	4.4 (3.0)***	2.5 (1.6)***	1.9 (1.8)	ns

* = Significance of difference between first and subsequent occasions

Figures based only on those children using some speech.

* = P < 0.05
** = P < 0.01
*** = P < 0.001

Table 11.6 (b)

Mean number of unprompted echoes per half hour recording

Assessment:	1	Cases 2	3	4	Controls	P value for sig. of diff. between groups
	Mean (s.d.)	Mean (s.d.)	Mean (s.d.)	Mean (s.d.)	Mean (s.d.)	
Total repetition of others	16.7 (8.6)	21.7 (14.2)	16.9 (8.4)	15.5 (10.3)	22.1 (6.2)	0.05
Exact repetitions	2.8 (1.4)	3.5 (2.8)	4.0 (2.9)	3.5 (2.8)	1.4 (1.0)	0.01
Reductions	2.7 (1.9)	3.7 (3.0)	6.1 (3.6)***	8.2 (5.7)***	5.7 (3.8)	ns
Expansions	0.2 (0.3)	0.0 (0.0)	0.7 (0.5)	0.2 (0.1)	0.0 (0.0)	ns
Repetition of self	11.0 (6.4)	14.5 (9.3)	6.1 (3.0)***	3.8 (2.4)***	15.0 (9.2)	0.001

* = Significance of difference between first and subsequent occasions

Figures based only on those children using some speech.

Of these non-communicative utterances, self-repetitions were found to be the most common form recorded. It has been suggested that such self-generated repetitions serve an important function in normal language acquisition and may well be important in the developing language of autistic children, (Charlop, 1983; Prizant and Duchan, 1981). Other types of echolalia, such as reductions or partial imitations of mothers' speech, also tended to occur with greater frequency than the more bizarre or 'metaphorical' types of utterance that are generally considered characteristic of autistic children. Again there is some evidence that such utterances may play an important role in early language development (Brown, 1973). Hence, their existence may reflect the children's acquisition of more normal language skills, rather than being taken as a sign of abnormal development. It is important to be aware that not all aspects of language development in autistic children reflect deviant patterns, and it is necessary that rates of 'abnormal' utterances are compared with normative data before judgements are made about the extent of the abnormality.

Cognitive and Other Developmental Changes

The final area assessed, both formally and on the basis of parental reports, concerned overall developmental levels. This was the area that showed least response to intervention. It was clear from parental reports that in areas of attainment, such as simple reading and arithmetic skills (or pre-number and pre-reading abilities), children in the treatment group had shown only limited gains although parental input here had been considerable. Moreover, at follow-up, there were virtually no between-group differences in the level of these abilities. The very modest results of treatment here, therefore, would not seem to reflect the large amount of parental time and effort put into developing such skills.

Cognitive assessments of the children, too, confirmed the fact that although progress continued to be made, overall IQ changes were minimal. At follow-up the mean scores for cases and controls remained very similar and correlations between initial and later IQ were also much the same in the two groups (see Table 11.7). Thus, suggestions that improvements in behaviour or social responsiveness may affect IQ scores would not seem to be borne out by the present results. Instead, in keeping with previous studies, IQ scores in autistic

Table 11.7
IQ scores of experimental and control children at follow-up

	Mean IQ score (s.d.)	Mean change score (s.d.)	Correlation between IQ at diagnosis and follow-up
Cases	85.56 (20.7)	–03.54 (24.3)	+0.52
Controls	83.60 (26.8)	–04.40 (25.1)	+0.48

Difference between groups non-significant

children tend to show a considerable degree of stability over time. Change cannot easily be brought about either by direct intervention, or indirectly, by improvements in other areas of functioning.

SCHOOLING AND LATER OCCUPATIONAL ATTAINMENTS

Outcome in the two groups was also compared on the basis of their placement at the present time. In general, few differences have been found. Of the children involved in the project, eleven in the experimental group and fifteen in the controls have now left school and the type of placement is essentially the same for both groups (see Table 11.8 and Appendix 11.1). Only one older child in the control group has gone on to get a permanent independent job although two further children, one in the treatment group and one control, have had occasional periods of temporary sheltered work. Generally, even the most verbally and socially responsive children remain in special day or residential units. In terms of both our and parents' expectations, the failure of the children to do better in their eventual placement is disappointing. The majority of children had developed useful, albeit simple speech, and their social relationships were much improved. Previous follow-up studies such as that by Kanner (1973) and clinical reports of other children who had attended the Maudsley Hospital in previous years had indicated that such children have a reasonably good chance of finding a job and achieving some sort of limited, independent existence. The failure of the children in the present study to find employment is probably due, in large part, to the current extremely high level of unemployment even for non-handicapped school leavers. Also, although all the children presently live at home or in residential units, it is possible that this situation may change and that a greater degree of independent living may be achieved as they grow older. Again, follow-up studies have shown that, especially amongst the more mildly handicapped autistic individuals, improvements in social functioning continue

Table 11.8
Present placement of cases and long term controls

	Cases	Controls
Normal school (private)	1	0
Autistic school	2	0
School for severely subnormal children	2	0
School for mixed handicaps	0	1
In regular employment/living at home	0	1
Sheltered employment/living at home	1	1
Adult training centre	1	0
Residential community—mixed handicaps	1	4
Residential community—autistic	6	3
Subnormality unit/hospital	2	4
At home—no special provision	0	1
Lost contact	0	1

well past school leaving age and that most who attain jobs do not do so until the mid 20s (Rutter, 1970). As the mean age of the children in treatment at the time of writing is still only 18 years (and that of the controls 21 years), there is still plenty of scope for maturational development. Hopefully, a greater degree of independent living may be achieved as the children grow older. Moreover, the finding that more of the experimental children have achieved placements in specialized residential units for autistic children (most of which demand fairly high levels of skill, a greater ability to work independently and more social competence) suggests that treatment may have resulted in their being able to use work related skills more appropriately and effectively. Whether or not ultimately this will lead to a greater level of autonomy and independence in adult life remains to be seen.

INDIVIDUAL RESPONSES TO TREATMENT

The overall results of the long term case–control comparisons indicated that in many ways direct intervention at home was more effective than similar advice given on the usual outpatient basis. However, as noted in the early chapters, group data may sometimes swamp individual findings of clinical or theoretical relevance. As well as looking at differences *between* groups, therefore, individual differences within groups were also examined. It was apparent that children did not respond to treatment in the same ways and that individual variation was greater in some areas than others.

Individual differences were least evident with respect to the modification of non-specific behavioural problems. Successful intervention here seemed to depend most on the skill of the parents and therapists in devising programmes tailored to the specific needs of each child and his family. As long as the various

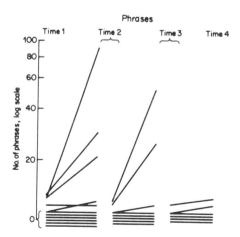

Figure 11.4 Improvement in children using less than ten phrase utterances at start of each observation period

stages in treatment were appropriately prepared, with progress at each level carefully monitored (so that procedures could be rapidly modified as necessary), treatment was usually effective in substantially reducing the levels or impact of deviant behaviour. In areas related to language development, however, individual characteristics of the children themselves had a much more direct effect on outcome. Of the sixteen children in the intervention group, four remained either non-communicating or using only single words whilst one used a few signs to communicate. Another eleven were using at least some spontaneous, if simple, phrase speech by the end of treatment. It was clear that language intervention had not been equally effective for all children, but what were the specific variables that seemed to predict outcome?

Although age and IQ levels had been associated with language development in previous studies (Browning, 1971; Rutter, 1970; Eisenberg, 1956), neither variable had much predictive value for the present groups of children. Group correlations between language and development, as measured on the Reynell scales at the end of treatment, and ages or IQ levels at initial diagnosis were small and insignificant (rho=+0.29 and +0.21 respectively). On the other hand, initial language scores (as measured by the Mecham scales) were significantly related to subsequent outcome (rho=+0.68).

The findings on the treatment group, where more longitudinal data are available, provide useful guidelines. Figure 11.4 shows the results of our measures of phrase structure for children with initially poor language skills (i.e. those who were mute or using less than 10 phrase utterances during the total recording period with the mother at home) at the beginning of each of the follow-up periods. Of the seven children with no measurable grammatical skills when we first saw them, six remained without such skills 6 months later. The pattern for changes in the second and third 6 month periods of follow-up were

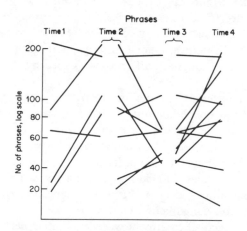

Figure 11.5 Improvement in children using more than ten phrase utterances at the start of each observation period

much the same. A few mute children made remarkable gains but on the whole they did very badly. On the other hand, *most* of those with just a little language made tremendous gains with treatment. This was the group for whom treatment seemed to have the most to offer. (It should be noted that the reason why improvements in the third follow-up period appear less than those in the first two periods is simply that by then there was only one child in this favourable prognostic group.)

Figure 11.5 shows the findings for the children who started with more language in each of the follow-up periods. Here the gains are less consistent. At all three time periods about half the children improved and about half remained the same (a few actually got slightly worse). However, over the 18 month period, all but one of these linguistically more advanced children made substantial progress in their use of phrase speech although the response to treatment seemed less direct. In addition, as the results from chapter 10 showed, although this group did not make such steady improvement in their use of syntax, the majority of them did improve considerably and consistently in their social use of language. Clearly, the initial level of language is of great prognostic importance and is a factor that must be borne in mind when assessing the potential usefulness, or otherwise, of a language training programme. Nevertheless, as we have seen, it is not an infallible measure. A few children who are still without speech at the age of 4 or 5 years do eventually go on to make considerable progress. On the other hand, not all children who are using some phrase speech initially will continue to show steady improvements. Graham, for example, used many simple phrases when we first began intervention and, although these were often used in a rather stereotyped way, they were nevertheless used largely for communicative purposes. However, there was little improvement in the proportion of non-stereotyped, socialized speech that he used over the course of treatment and, indeed, following the cessation of intensive intervention at home, his speech has tended to become progressively more stereotyped and echolalic and less socialized. In contrast, Stevie, whose language to begin with was at a very similar level to Graham's, made steady gains in both the complexity and functional quality of his language and today his speech is both communicative and informative.

Returning to the differential outcome for treated and untreated children of different levels of language ability, it is apparent that the children who were most likely to respond to intervention were those who were on the threshold of developing speech; who already had a few words or meaningful sounds when treatment began; who demonstrated at least limited verbal comprehension and showed some play activities, indicating the presence of internalized language. Four of the experimental children of this level progressed to using phrase speech whereas no comparable control children did so.

By contrast, the effects of treatment were less than expected in children who were already using some phrase speech, even if much of this was echolalic, when intervention began. Previous review studies such as that by Howlin (1979) had consistently indicated that treatment was most likely to be successful with this

Table 11.9

Initially non-communicating children who do or do not develop speech

Language outcome (N)	Age	Mean scores before treatment			
		Non-verbal IQ	Behaviour disturbance	Language age	Language ratio score
Remaining mute (5)	50.4 m.	101.8	32.6	5.8 m.	11.0
Single words/word approxs. (5)	58.2 m.	86.4	47.6	13.8 m.	24.6
Word combinations (2)	39.5 m.	102.5	33.0	14.0 m.	35.7

Language outcome (N)	Mean scores at follow-up			
	Language scores Reynell		Parental rating scores(a)	
	Expression	Comprehension	Social Responsiveness(b)	Imaginative play(c)
Remaining mute (5)	6.0 m.	19.2 m.	11.2	3.6
Single words/word approxs. (5)	14.0 m.	28.0 m.	12.8	3.6
Phrase speech (2)	32.5 m.	41.0 m.	5.0	0.5

Notes

(a) The lower the score the more normal the behaviour.

(b) A score of 11/12 indicates fair/good response to parents but poor response to other adults and children. A score of 5 indicates good response to parents and other adults (but not other children).

(c) A score of 3.6 indicates some simple imaginative play usually with adult supervision. A score of 0.5 indicates some imaginative play with other children (still with adult supervision).

group of children. Certainly in the present study, the majority of the initially echolalic children in the treatment group progressed to using good phrase speech. However, when untreated children of the same initial level were assessed at follow-up they, too, were found to have made good progress. Thus, the very fact that a child is echolalic is likely to be a positive prognostic indicator whether or not intervention takes place.

Overall, treatment was least effective for children who were still virtually non-communicating when treatment began. That is, at an average age of $5\frac{1}{2}$ years (with a range from 3 years 10 months to 7 years 4 months) they used neither words, word approximations, nor simple gestures (other than reaching out for objects) spontaneously to communicate their needs. At follow-up, most of these children remained linguistically very handicapped regardless of whether they had received special help. Nevertheless, as indicated above, there were suggestions even amongst this group of children that some could achieve useful language skills and prognosis was clearly not equally poor for all children. Because of the obvious clinical and therapeutic implications of these findings particular attention was paid to the differences between the initially non-communicating children who remained mute and those who developed some speech. In order to explore more thoroughly the factors associated with outcome, information on both treatment and control children was combined since the pattern was so similar for both groups.

Out of a total of twelve initially mute children two had a fairly extensive vocabulary, including word combinations, at follow-up. Four were using some words or word approximations and one was using simple gestures and some communicative sounds. Amongst the subgroup of children who remained non-communicative several variables related to outcome. The differences between children who did and those who did not attain useful levels of language competence are presented in Table 11.9. The numbers are small and tests of statistical significance are not really appropriate so the findings must be regarded as tentative suggestions rather than clear cut conclusions. However, certain variables appear of prognostic importance. Overall, levels of behavioural disturbance were not associated with subsequent language acquisition; the children who developed phrase speech and those who remained non-communicating had almost identical scores on parental rating scales at the beginning of the intervention project. IQ level also failed to differentiate between the children who made most and those who made the least progress. The mean non-verbal IQ of the children who developed phrase speech was 102.5, that of the children who remained mute, 101.8. Despite the fact that *low* IQ has been found in many studies to be a predictor of *poor* language function, a normal IQ is not, in itself, adequate to guarantee a good linguistic outcome.

The one factor that did seem to predict outcome was the overall severity of language handicap. Children who made least progress were found to have a mean language age of less than 6 months when intervention began. In contrast, all the children who developed some communicative speech had a language age of at least 1 year when initially diagnosed. However, because children's ages varied somewhat when the project began it was felt that a direct comparison of language ages might be inappropriate. A ratio language score was calculated for each child (i.e. language age divided by chronological age, multiplied by 100). Again, as can be seen in Table 11.9, this initial 'language quotient' showed a consistent relationship with subsequent outcome. Children with the lowest quotients (mean 11.0) made little linguistic progress. Those with an intermediate level (mean 24.6) showed some acquisition of simple language skills. Those who showed greatest improvement had a much higher language age in relation to their chronological age (mean language quotient = 35.7). Information from the parental interview also indicated that children who made most progress had shown some spontaneous imitation of sounds or gestures and more comprehension of spoken language even when younger. Amongst the children who remained mute, there was rarely any spontaneous imitation and both verbal and non-verbal comprehension had always been severely limited.

Obviously, caution must be taken in extrapolating too far from these data because they are based on such small numbers of children. However, the results do indicate that different subgroups, even amongst non-communicating autistic children, may have quite different prognoses. It appears, on the basis of previous findings, that at least amongst autistic children in the 4 to 7 year age group those most likely to make progress show relatively mild behavioural disturbance and are of normal non-verbal IQ. However, although this relationship between high IQ and later language outcome has also been noted in other studies of non-autistic but language delayed children (Paul and Cohen, 1984), it is clear that a normal IQ is *not* in itself sufficient as a prognostic indicator. Instead, children with the best outcome are those with an overall language age (on formal language tests) of above 1 year, and who have a higher level of comprehension and a greater use of spontaneous speech sounds when younger. Moreover, as Table 11.9 indicates, children who eventually acquire phrase speech are also likely to make the greatest progress in other areas. Thus, the severity of a child's language deficit may well predict not only later language acquisition but also development in other areas. Information from the parental interview indicated that the children who developed the most useful speech showed more appropriate responses within social situations, were more responsive to their parents, and had a higher level of cooperative and imaginative play at follow-up than the more linguistically handicapped children. They also communicated emotions and feelings more by gesture and facial expression. Children who remained limited in speech remained very limited in other domains too.

Unfortunately, although these findings suggest that it is not only language, but also development in other domains, such as play and social development, that are related to subsequent linguistic outcome, we do not possess enough information on the relative importance of these other skills. Play and social behaviours were not assessed objectively before treatment began and measures were based on rather global ratings made by parents. It may be that more detailed assessments of children's social and play behaviours, at much earlier stages of their development, may reveal other factors that will identify children who, despite having a relatively high level of non-verbal skill, are likely to remain profoundly handicapped in all areas of communication. Despite the small number of cases involved, these results strongly suggest that children respond in very different ways to treatment. It is to be hoped that future studies of language training will attempt to amass sufficient data on individual characteristics of children and across a variety of different domains for therapists and parents to be able to predict more successfully which children are likely to benefit from treatment.

Language training if carried out rigorously is an extremely arduous and time consuming process—for the child, for his parents and for the other therapists involved. If carried out inappropriately, it may cause frustration to the child and, if failure results, grave disappointment to parents. Only if evaluation in this area becomes more precise will progress be made in identifying those children who will be most likely to benefit from verbal language training programmes. Greater attention to individual differences in response to treatment is also required for the more accurate identification of children who are likely to benefit more from alternative forms of training, such as gestural, written or symbolic communication. Furthermore, it is clear that some children may never learn effectively to communicate by any means and for them the emphasis may have to be on developing comprehension skills, so that at least others can communicate with them, even if they themselves fail to develop spontaneous communication.

THE BENEFITS OF A CONTROL GROUP RESEARCH DESIGN

Although the main goal of the study, in comparing matched, untreated controls with a treated experimental group, was to evaluate the overall effectiveness of therapy, the findings also proved to be of substantial clinical relevance. First, it was clear that although children who are treated on a rather intermittent outpatient basis do continue to make progress and show improvements in their behaviour, this type of intervention is substantially less effective than help given directly to the parents at home. Home based intervention is better able to make effective use of the potentially successful strategies already employed by parents and to help them to modify their styles of interaction in ways that are best suited to the needs of their child. Only through direct observation of the child and his parents at home is a truly functional analysis of the child's problems likely to be achieved. And only with a detailed assessment of the causes and the factors maintaining problem behaviours are successful remedies likely to be achieved.

Secondly, as well as making clear the distinct advantages of home based treatment, the between-group comparisons were important in accentuating the findings concerning the hierarchical effects of treatment. Treatment benefits were most evident for the wide range of non-specific maladaptive behaviours that can cause considerable disruption to family life—such as temper tantrums, aggressiveness and difficulties with sleeping and toileting. Substantial gains were also achieved in reducing problems related more specifically to the autistic rituals and routines, and in improving autistic children's play and social behaviours (although severe limitations in these areas remained). Treatment improved children's communicative use of language but made less difference to language competence and no difference at all to their overall cognitive capacity. These findings from the longer term control group comparison, in replicating the results of the short term evaluation, lend considerable support to the hypothesis, noted in earlier chapters concerning the way in which treatment exerts its effects. Thus, direct intervention would seem to be most effective in reducing behavioural disturbance (in particular problems that are non-specific to autism) and in encouraging children to use existing skills more effectively. Direct intervention, even of a very intensive kind, has least effect on fundamental areas of deficit.

Third, the findings from this comparative study indicate how, in the absence of control groups, totally erroneous conclusions may be drawn about the value of intervention. This is particularly true for developmental skills, such as language. The longitudinal study of the children in the treatment group had indicated that language changes occurred steadily with time. Without a control group comparison it would have been all too easy to assume that these changes were directly attributable to treatment. Instead, monitoring of change in untreated as well as treated children indicated that, although there were certain areas in which treatment did seem to be effective (notably in increasing the use of socialized language skills), there were other areas in which intervention produced relatively few gains. Levels of language complexity, for example, showed little change in response to treatment. Moreover, there is evidence that certain children, particularly those who are already echolalic and are using a little phrase speech, are likely to make considerable progress over time whether or not they are involved in a direct intervention programme. Hence, claims such as those made by Lovaas (1977) that 'as a consequence of these procedures the children acquire strikingly complex language behaviour' would seem to be based on insufficient evidence. Instead, the very fact that the child is echolalic is likely to be a positive prognostic indicator, whether or not intervention takes place.

Finally, in addition to allowing an investigation of between-group differences, the combination of data for both untreated and treated children allowed a better evaluation of individual differences within groups. Again, the main findings of clinical relevance here were related to the outcome of language training programmes. It seemed clear that, although in certain cases these could prove very effective, for other children, notably those with the most profound degrees of language deficit, the results (at least with programmes designed to encourage spoken language) were far from encouraging.

In summary, the need for control group evaluation and for adequate descriptions of the children involved in treatment is not simply a nicety of experimental design. Only if adequate attention is paid to differences both between and within groups can reliable conclusions be drawn about which techniques are most effective, which behaviours are most likely to respond to treatment, and which children are most likely to benefit from intervention. If these basic research criteria are not met, not only are erroneous conclusions likely to be drawn about treatment effectiveness but, more importantly, children are likely to be exposed to treatment strategies that are neither appropriate nor beneficial for them and which indeed may have a detrimental effect on their families as a whole.

Chapter 12

Parents' Views on the Treatment Programme

Our approach to the treatment of autistic children deliberately differed from the modes of intervention that were usual at the time we started the study. We sought the extensive cooperation of parents in asking them to take the major role in treatment. This role was needed because autism is a pervasive, chronically handicapping condition that demands a consistent treatment approach designed to aid development throughout time (rather than focused interventions needed just for particular behaviours confined to specific situations and at specific times). Parents were in the best position to provide such an approach. Of course, inpatient care could also have enabled an around the clock treatment programme. However, it had been found that the gains achieved in hospital frequently fail to extend to the child's normal environment on leaving the residential unit (Koegel *et al.*, 1982; Lovaas *et al.*, 1973). Accordingly, it was necessary to work directly in the home where the problems presented and to invoke the help of parents. Both the multiplicity of autistic children's difficulties and the need to train parents in a wide range of therapeutic strategies and tactics meant that the treatment programme had to be fairly intense. For this reason, home visits during the first 6 months of the programme usually lasted a couple of hours and took place on a weekly basis. Our approach aimed to provide families with extensive support, practical advice on how to deal with particular problems, and sensitive counselling to help them deal with the many worries and concerns posed by the care of a handicapped child. As the results described in the last three chapters indicate, the approach was successful in bringing worthwhile benefits for the autistic children. In this chapter we consider the outcome in terms of the rather different criterion of the perspective of the parents. Were the gains for the child sufficient to enable parents to feel relieved of some of the burdens of rearing an unresponsive, uncommunicative autistic child? Were the coping skills acquired by parents beneficial in relieving the feelings of frustration and guilt so often engendered by the birth of a handicapped son or daughter? Or, alternatively, were the demands of involvement in an intensive therapeutic programme merely a source of additional burdens for parents already overwhelmed? These are the questions that we consider in this chapter.

THE ISSUES AS POSED BY PREVIOUS RESEARCH

At the outset, we were aware that there were potential dangers in asking parents to become, in effect, co-therapists. Critics of behavioural intervention with families of handicapped children have suggested that such methods may be insensitive to the amount of stress placed on families or parents (Mittler, 1979). In the past, there is no doubt that parents were too often *excluded* from treatment, but maybe now there is a danger of *too much* pressure to become involved (Mittler and Mittler, 1983). It is important to be aware that, for most children with severe developmental delays, their handicap will last throughout life. Although parents may be able to evolve better ways of managing problems, no intervention is going to produce a cure. Mittler argued that parents should be allowed to choose '*not* to be involved at the level of detailed collaboration that some professionals are now demanding'.

Zigler (1981) suggested that very intensive home programmes may result in damage to the whole family, and others, too, have questioned whether small improvements in a child, who will anyway always remain handicapped, are worthwhile in terms of cost to the family (Dornberg, 1978). Is it reasonable to expect people to combine the roles of parent and therapist?

Parents sometimes complain that "They [professionals] always tell us how well we are doing', but then go on to say, '*but* if you do this it will be more helpful" (Black, 1978). 'No sooner is one skill mastered than another skill is presented, clouding the simple sweetness of success' (Fulwood, 1981). Carr (1984) described the attitudes of a family who moved from a well-served area to one where little help was available. Instead of bemoaning the lack of local resources, 'their first reaction was one of relief at being free of all the professionals who had been overwhelming them'.

Fortunately, such complaints are voiced by a minority of parents and most welcome any interventions that enable them to help their own children more effectively (Baker *et al.*, 1980; Holland, 1981). However, it is important for therapists to be aware of the potentially stressful effects of their involvement. The ultimate goal of intervention is to benefit the whole family, and not to train specific skills at the family's expense. It was that concern that led us explicitly to limit the time parents were expected to spend with their autistic child, to pay attention to the needs of *all* members of the family, and to seek to be responsive to each family's resources and burdens. Were we effective in this, and did the parents involved in the project feel that the experience was worthwhile?

AN INDEPENDENT EVALUATION OF PARENTAL PERCEPTIONS

In order to consider these questions, we asked a group of researchers who had had no connection with the treatment programme to undertake an independent evaluation of parental perceptions of the project. We provided what help we could in designing measures and in contacting families but deliberately we kept ourselves quite separate from the interviewing and the ratings in order to avoid any inadvertent biasing of perceptions. As before, families in the treatment project were compared with the long-term control group. Some time after the cessation of the project, families were contacted by letter asking if they would be prepared to take part in a study of parents' views of treatment. Fourteen of the families in the experimental group and fourteen control families agreed to cooperate; details of the children are presented in Table 12.1. It was made clear to parents that this was an independent evaluation of treatment and that their views, both positive and critical, would be welcomed (Holmes *et al.*, 1982).

Table 12.1
Details of matching experimental group boys with comparison group boys[a]

Measures	Experimental group (N = 14) Mean (s.d.)	Comparison group (N = 14) Mean (s.d.)
Age at referral	59.8 m. (18.4)	62.8 m. (19.5)
Non-verbal IQ at referral	89 (17.9)	87 (19.3)
Meecham language score	24 (22.8)	19 (11.2)
Behaviour rating score	49.9 (12.1)	46.6 (12.2)
Social classes I and II	50.0%	64.3%
Social class III	14.3%	14.3%
Social classes IV to VI	35.7%	21.4%

Note
[a] No difference statistically significant

The follow-up interview was specially devised for the study and was semistructured in form since this type of format has been found to produce a greater wealth of information than can be obtained by the more restricted format of questionnaires (Richardson *et al.*, 1965). The interview began with an unstructured conversation in which parents were encouraged to talk generally about their problems with the child and about their contacts with helping agencies. This lasted from 5 to 20 minutes and was designed to put parents at their ease as well as to give them an opportunity to talk about issues that they considered particularly important. This was then followed by structured questions on the expectations parents had had about treatment, their ability to cope with the child, the family problems before treatment and their views concerning the effects of treatment. Parents were also asked about their feelings towards the therapist and her demands on them, and there was a general section at the end regarding improvement since treatment had finished.

As judged by retrospective data from the follow-up interviews, the experimental and control groups were broadly comparable before treatment began with respect to their expectations of treatment and to their perceptions of their ability to cope with their children's problems. There were no differences, either, between experimental and control group parents' views of family problems. Over half mentioned difficulties in arranging holidays and in their

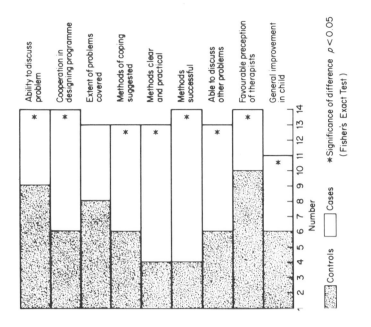

Figure 12.1 Frequency of case and control parents expressing satisfaction with treatment

social life generally. Half felt that the child had had a bad effect on their marriage, with frequent disagreements about how to deal with him. Two-thirds of those parents with other children in the family felt that the autistic child had affected his siblings badly. Two-thirds of all parents mentioned feelings of frustration with the child, and just under half admitted to feelings of guilt.

PERCEPTIONS OF TREATMENT

When questioned about their view of treatment, most experimental parents viewed the home based programme favourably. There were no complaints about being used as co-therapists, and most were grateful for the advice that they had received. The approach also seemed to have dealt successfully with many of the family problems encountered by parents with autistic children. Most of the parents in the treatment group felt that they had been able to discuss these with the therapists involved and had found this helpful. Very few of the comparison parents reported having had the opportunity to do this. Typical comments recorded by the 'co-therapist' mothers were remarks such as: 'The support was a great comfort', 'She was like a friend . . . very sensitive, concerned and involved'.

However, support alone is not enough, unless coupled with practical advice about alleviating problems. Significantly more treatment than control parents felt that direct methods of coping with the problems had been suggested to them and most of the mothers seemed to have an accurate impression of the treatment and its aims. As one mother said, 'They always offered something concrete about what action to take ... unlike the social workers who were just comforting.' Although no specific questions were asked on the topic of treatment, it was clear that all remembered general principles, such as the need to attend to good behaviour, or to ignore inappropriate behaviour where possible. For example, Ben's mother remembered, 'I saw their way of coping; for example, of withdrawing certain things. I saw it worked—and I saw Ben in a different light.' Most recalled elements of the language training programme and the advice to be consistent with the child. Some gave examples of how they had treated specific problems (e.g. using graded change techniques for treating abnormal attachments to objects) and others were particularly grateful for help when new problems arose. Wayne's mother, for example noted that if new difficulties arose 'I'd wait till they came—tell them and get advice—also I got better at thinking up my own solutions'. However, even though most parents reported that they found the methods clear, one or two did show misunderstandings. One mother claimed that she had been told to deal with bedwetting by ignoring it the first time, being cross the second time, and slapping the child the third time—although obviously this was entirely out of keeping with the therapeutic orientation. Another mother denied that any methods were suggested to her, despite having had weekly visits for 18 months.

Less than half of the control parents (six out of fourteen) said that they had received detailed advice on how to tackle their child's problems, whereas nearly all (thirteen out of fourteen) of the parents in the treatment group did so. The finding that the majority of parents in the control group felt that they had received little or no help during their outpatient attendances emphasizes the need for specific problem orientated advice. Significantly more parents in the programme (thirteen out of fourteen) also said that they were able to talk about general family stresses and strains during treatment; only four comparison parents felt able to do this, despite the obvious benefits to families. 'It helped an awful lot...' 'They were very sympathetic ... I could talk over any problems.' 'She was like a friend... it helped so much to say how you feel.' Figure 12.1 summarizes the major differences between treatment parents and controls with respect to their views about therapy and therapists.

FEELINGS ABOUT TREATMENT DEMANDS

Opinions varied on the demands on parents arising from the treatment programme. Some parents, such as the mothers of Simon and Stevie, were very positive: 'They showed me how to work out problems for myself—but they never took over.' 'They were very uncritical people—no outright criticism—but I altered my way of doing things gradually.' However, half the parents in the therapeutic programme found it an effort to use the methods suggested to them, although thirteen of the fourteen actually put them into practice. And, three or four mothers said they were not entirely convinced by behavioural principles and admitted that probably they did not apply the methods wholeheartedly. Two felt that their own methods were best. One mother commented that she had great problems in using effective reinforcement procedures with her son because he was unable to make the connection between his behaviour and the reward. Another parent said that she was very unhappy about using time out procedures.

Almost all the parents in the treatment group reported some difficulty in keeping daily charts and diaries, yet only three found it hard to give up their time to the workers. Many parents felt more positive towards their children as a result of intervention. As Peter's mother said, 'Not only did I realize there were different ways of treating him... it made me realize that it was *worth* working with Peter.' Nevertheless, over a third of the programme parents and three of the comparison parents felt that the therapists had had too high an expectation of what they could achieve with their child. This suggests that possibly for some parents therapists were making too many demands, or alternatively that what the workers saw as encouragement was perceived by parents as demands.

PARENTS' FEELING ABOUT THERAPISTS AND THEIR VIEWS ON THE SUCCESS OF TREATMENT

Significantly more parents in the programme were nervous at their first meeting with therapists than comparison parents, although on subsequent meetings there was no difference between the groups. Treatment group parents tended to report that they found it easier to get on with the workers than did control parents and, on the whole, as the quotations earlier in this chapter indicate, all parents felt very favourably inclined towards the therapists, seeing them as sensitive, easy to get on with, encouraging, understanding and 'on the same wavelength'.

In general, therefore, it seemed that most parents actively welcomed the visits by psychologists and did not find them intrusive. Although one or two parents felt a little uneasy about the workers coming to their homes and making tape recordings and observations, the predominant parental feeling seemed to be one of relief that someone was 'finally' doing something for their child. Indeed, in many cases the parents struck up a strong relationship with the therapists involved and viewed them as friends, and many of these relationships are still in existence almost 10 years later.

The finding that most parents did not view the programme as unduly demanding or intrusive would seem to reflect the care with which the home project was designed and carried out. First, mothers were asked to spend only brief periods each day in intensive interaction with their child, not all day, as in some other programmes (e.g. Lovaas, 1978). Second, the therapists began the treatment, in all cases, by concentrating on the problems of main concern to the parents themselves before attempting to cover other areas. Third, the therapists made every effort to ensure that treatment programmes were devised in close consultation with the parents, that they fitted in with the family routine, and could be carried out without imposing undue restrictions on family life. Therapists were careful not to concentrate just on the autistic child's problems but to recognize the needs of the family as a whole. They gave practical advice on schooling, baby-sitters, etc., as well as arranging periods of relief care if necessary. They also encouraged parents to spend time with their non-autistic children, and on recreational activities for their own benefit.

FEELINGS ABOUT THE LONGER TERM VALUE OF TREATMENT

All but three of the parents in the programme felt that the child's behaviour improved as a result of therapeutic intervention, whereas, as noted earlier, many comparison parents felt they had received virtually no treatment. The programme parents also found the specific techniques suggested for dealing with problems to be more successful than did the control parents who had been given similar advice. However, when parents were questioned about their views of the extent of improvement after intervention had ended, there was no difference between them in their perceptions of the child's behaviour, their own coping ability or levels of family stresses and strains. In the treatment group only eight of the mothers felt that the coping techniques helped them to deal with new problems and only five reported that they had helped them to teach the child new skills. Thus, although most of the mothers in the treatment group felt that their child had improved as a result of treatment, many of the beneficial effects appeared to have declined over time. Few parents reported that they were still using the techniques advised and in fact there were no differences between

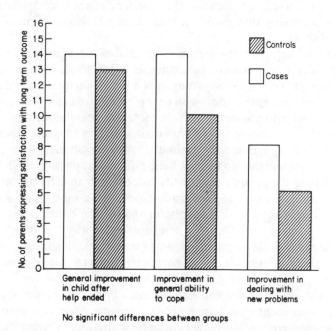

Figure 12.2 Parental views of therapy—long term effectiveness

the groups in their perceptions of general improvement after help had ended. Both groups felt that things had improved or stayed pretty much the same (see Figure 12.2 for summary of findings).

In general, therefore, the conclusions indicated that home intervention was welcomed by families; they did not find it intrusive or overdemanding and they appreciated specific advice about management. However, at the same time it was clear that the effects were neither as extensive, nor as long lasting, as had been hoped. Clearly, several of the parents in the programme were unable to generalize the techniques they had learned to new problems. On the other hand, half reported that the methods helped them to deal with new problem behaviours, and five reported that they were better able to teach their child new skills. Immediately after treatment it seemed that parents were demonstrating more flexible and efficient coping stragegies, but these effects persisted in only half the group, and few parents were able to generalize such skills to deal with difficulties that arose subsequently.

Although such results were disappointing given the large amount of time and effort expended on the project, it is important for professionals to bear in mind the fact that parents who are faced with the daily problems of having a handicapped child may *never* feel entirely competent in their approach to management—even if, objectively, their ways of handling their child improve considerably. A severe and pervasive disorder, such as autism, does not disappear, no matter how competent parents become at dealing with day to day problems. Faced with the realization that the handicap will always be with them, it is hardly surprising that many parents are less than confident in their own skills as therapists.

It also seems likely from the present findings that, once intensive intervention has ended, parents need something further, in order to maintain the gains made during treatment. This could be arranged as a follow-up meeting occurring, say, once every 6 months, both to deal with new problems and to re-establish parents' skills in using behavioural techniques. In fact, in the case of some of the parents in the original study, contacts have been maintained on a regular basis, although this has not been systematically evaluated. Another alternative is for parents themselves to get together to discuss their difficulties, possibly with an outside therapist visiting the group occasionally to deal with specific problems. Again several parents in the experimental group have set up semi-formal groups of this nature. These appear to be very successful and to offer considerable support to many other parents too. Clearly there are many ways in which follow-up treatment sessions could be arranged, and future research should direct itself to investigating how gains made during parent training can best be generalized and maintained.

Finally, the other important implication of the follow-up study is that intermittent outpatient care is not able to provide effective remedies for the problems encountered by the parents of autistic children. Many control parents did not simply complain of insufficient help; rather, they felt they had been given *no* support or advice at all. Few considered that their child's problems had been adequately assessed; nor had they been given help in coping with these or with more general family difficulties. Thus, although the parents in the programme may have found it hard to generalize the techniques they were taught, and although home based therapy was far from entirely successful, such treatment was seen as being far more satisfactory than the usual, less intensive outpatient help given to families.

Chapter 13

Treatment Implications

The results from our evaluation of the home based approach to the treatment of autistic children are clear cut in indicating the benefits that stemmed from the intervention programme. The individual case studies showed that it was possible to bring about major reductions in many forms of maladaptive or deviant behaviour and also that autistic children could be helped to make better use of their limited skills in language and social relationships. These, sometimes dramatic, improvements are very much in keeping with the single case studies and the uncontrolled group interventions previously reported in the literature. However, the research findings went beyond previous work in indicating that the therapeutic gains associated with the treatment programme were significantly superior to those obtained from more conventional forms of treatment. This was apparent in the systematic comparison of cases and controls followed longitudinally over the first 6 months. At the end of that time the children in the treatment progamme showed marked improvements, whereas there was no appreciable change in the control group, most of whom were receiving only sporadic outpatient treatment of the kind generally available in most hospital and community clinic facilities at the time. These results were very encouraging. However, it is important to be aware that autism is a chronically handicapping disorder and the more important test of the benefits of treatment is whether the children in the treatment programme had a better outcome in the long term. The findings at the 18 month follow-up once more showed significant and substantial benefits of treatment compared with that evident in the control group of children who had received broadly similar advice but on a much less intensive basis.

The programme, like that of Schopler and his colleagues (Short, 1984), made a point of involving parents in all elements of the treatment procedures and parents were engaged as co-therapists to a major extent. In effect, there was explicit recognition of the fact that autistic children are severely handicapped and that the main burden of caring for them falls on the families. Both our findings at the end of the project and the independent follow-up by Holmes and her colleagues (1982) indicated that this approach worked well. The parents gained in confidence and in practical coping skills. Concern has sometimes been expressed that asking parents to serve as co-therapists may possibly *increase* family tensions and burdens and also detract from the spontaneity of parental affection and playful interactions with their children. Neither concern was borne out by our findings. We went to considerable trouble to ensure that the burden on parents was kept to a minimum and we took explicit steps to help with the variety of worries and tensions that are inherent in caring for a handicapped child. The findings showed that parents appreciated this approach and that the practical gains served to reduce, rather than increase, family burdens. The fact that parents gained in their ability to cope with the manifold problems presented by an autistic child meant that the relief of tension helped them to be more relaxed in their parenting role. There is no need for the co-therapist role to interfere with normal parenting.

Because the treatment programme was very broad ranging in what it did, it is not possible to identify the specific elements that were crucial to its success. Nevertheless, the analyses of the associations between changes in parental behaviour and changes in the child's behaviour suggest that the parents had made an important contribution to their children's improvement. And, since positive changes occurred much more consistently in the treatment group than in either group of control families, it must be assumed that direct intervention at home was responsible for these changes in parents' behaviour. In the past, it has sometimes been felt that there were difficulties in the combination of counselling and behavioural approaches. Our findings indicate that the two can be combined successfully and that there are benefits in so doing. An exclusively behavioural focus on the child's problems may lead to a disregard of the needs and difficulties of parents. We sought to counter that tendency by making explicit the breadth of our therapeutic concerns and by asking systematically about different aspects of the family functioning. The findings indicated that the parents felt well able to raise these broader issues and felt helped by what was done. In summary, the findings from the evaluation were consistent in showing that the treatment programme had made a worthwhile difference and that the benefits were superior to those of other treatment aproaches. Accordingly, there is the strong implication that services of this kind should be made more generally available.

However, although the findings were indeed encouraging about the benefits of treatment, they were also explicit in indicating some of the very substantial limitations of intervention programmes with severely developmentally handicapped children. Both the short term and the long term evaluation agree in showing that the greatest effects were found in the therapeutic modification of the non-specific emotional and behavioural problems of autistic children. That is to say, there was considerable success in alleviating problems such as fears and phobias, sleep difficulties, temper tantrums, bed-wetting and eating difficulties. Of course, it was highly beneficial to both the children and their families that such problems could be relieved to such an extent. Nevertheless, these are not the abnormalities that are specific to autism, nor are they the ones associated with the most persistent handicaps. The treatment programme had some success in the reduction of the severity of various aspects of more specifically autistic abnormalities and, particularly, in reducing the impact of these behaviours on the children's everyday life. Still, for the most part, the children continued to show the characteristic pattern of deviance in use of language, in social relations, and in rigidities of behaviour. Treatment resulted in some slight increases in the children's developmental progress in language but the case–control differences were small (and short of statistical significance). The main effect was on the children's social utilization of such skills as they had, rather than on any long term increase in their basic level of competence.

A somewhat related finding is that the maximum progress was in the first 6 months with a rather slower rate of improvement thereafter. It seemed that, initially, treatment was able to do a good deal in enabling the children to use skills that had hitherto remained latent. The greater use of language and social skills shown by children in the therapeutic programme probably made some difference to their developmental progress in language and socialization. After all, such skills do not develop in a vacuum; practice and active use are important in facilitating development (Rutter, 1985b). Nevertheless, the findings suggest that, with a severely handicapping disorder like autism, treatment can have at best only a very modest impact on the growth of language and of cognition more generally.

A further reservation, about the success of treatment, concerns the rather limited impact of short term intervention programmes for families coping with lifelong handicaps. The study findings after the first 6 months of treatment showed that the parents had made significant gains in their general coping skills. Not only had the children's behaviour improved, but the parents' ability to deal with difficulties had also increased. When planning the study initially, we had hoped that these gains in parental coping might enable the professional input to be markedly reduced after the first few months so that parents would need only occasional help at times of particular difficulty. In the event, that proved too optimistic a view. To begin with, as data from the parental interviews have shown, parents may need quite prolonged periods of support before they are able to acknowledge the improvements that have occurred in their children's behaviour. And, even when this was achieved, while certainly it was possible to reduce the amount of time we spent with families, most parents continued to need to be seen at least once a month. The burdens on families of caring for autistic children are very considerable and to some extent these tend to increase as the children grow older. It is not that their behaviour is in any real sense worse. Rather the difficulty for families stems from several other considerations. First, the practical management of some sorts of problem behaviour becomes markedly greater when the children become physically larger. For example, when young children are aggressive and have severe temper tantrums parents can, if necessary, simply pick up the children and remove them from the situation. For obvious reasons, that is impractical with older teenagers who may be taller and heavier than their parents. Second, when autistic children are young many parents are willing to go to almost any lengths to help in the hope that, by so doing, they will enable the children to grow normally. When the young people have reached adolescence they may be very much less handicapped than when young; nevertheless, it is not surprising that many parents feel disappointed and disillusioned that the young people remain handicapped and still need considerable supervision and help (Wikler, 1978). Third, parents themselves have become older, perhaps less resilient psychologically, and probably physically less energetic and less strong. Short term intervention may help parents develop more effective strategies for coping with behavioural problems, but it would be naïve to expect a brief treatment programme to be able to solve longer term problems of either a practical or an emotional nature. If therapeutic intervention is to have any real benefit for families, help must continue to be available to support families through the various lifelong crises with which they must cope. Accordingly, it is not unexpected that the burden on families remained considerable as the children grew older and that support from the therapists involved could not be abruptly terminated once better coping strategies had been evolved. The families of children in the treatment programme and the families of children in the control group did not differ substantially in their use of boarding school provision and it is apparent that residential facilities are needed for some autistic children. The proportion requiring such facilities tends to rise as the children reach adolescence.

Another problem, and one common to other investigations of this kind, was the substantial degree of situation specificity in the therapeutic gains. Because we were concerned that this was likely to be the case, we went to some efforts to generalize the treatment programme to the various settings in which the children functioned. In particular, we sought to engage the cooperation of schools. For the most part, we were successful in this and it did much to reduce the problems of situation specificity. However, some schools had a philosophy that made them reluctant to fit in with the approaches employed by the parents. When this was the case, it was often found that the children's behavioural gains at home did not extend to the school situation.

Finally, the results underlined the marked individual variation in children's progress. Some children remained mute and highly dependent on others for all their daily needs in spite of strenuous therapeutic efforts by the families and by the professional therapists. Others gained very considerable autonomy. In the past, an unnecessary burden of guilt has been placed on parents by the implication that greater progress would have occurred if only they had tried harder, or had spent more time with the child, or had persisted more effectively. Some therapists, both behavioural and ethological as well as psychotherapeutic, have offered hopes for a cure or a near-cure. There is no adequate justification for placing such responsibility on parents and our results, like those of others, are clearcut in indicating that the children's progress in response to treatment is predictable on the basis of their initial level of handicap. In particular, the severity of the children's impairments in language and in general intelligence are the main determinants of outcome. With these considerations in mind, more detailed attention can be paid to some of the specific practical implications for treatment that follow from the research.

THERAPEUTIC AIMS

Autistic children show problems in many different areas and it is important that each of these be considered in planning treatment (Rutter, 1985c). First, autism always involves deviance, and usually marked delay, in the development of language, social relationships and general intelligence. It is necessary that treatment focus on facilitating the more normal development of these functions. That may involve direct teaching of skills in these areas, attention to the environment to ensure that it provides the optimal opportunities for developmental progress, concern to reduce the abnormal behaviours that interfere with developmental progress and the provision of alternative means of performing these functions. For example, some autistic children with severe handicaps in spoken language may be helped by the introduction of sign language or other alternative modes of communication.

Second, there needs to be a focus on the reduction of specifically autistic patterns of behavioural deviance. In the past, such patterns have often been conceptualized in terms of the oddities or peculiarities of autistic behaviour. Thus, attention has been focused on the stereotyped mannerisms and motor movements or the rituals and obsessive-like behaviours, and on the various peculiarities of language. However, probably, these behaviours are more appropriately conceptualized in terms of aspects of deviance and developmental progress than in terms of 'symptoms' of a mental illness. Thus, the features that seem to link various abnormalities are: (1) a lack of social responsiveness and reciprocity leading to diminished social involvement and social utilization of skills; (2) a lack of spontaneity, creativity and imagination that impedes language, social relationships, play and also work; and (3) a tendency rigidly to impose stereotyped structure and uniformity on patterns of life and on the environment generally. It appears that therapeutic efforts need to be focused on the reduction of these tendencies as much as on the reduction of the specifically abnormal behaviours that are associated with these tendencies.

Third, in addition to the various specifically autistic abnormalities, autistic children show a wide range of non-specific emotional and behavioural problems. Although not central to the disorder, these are often the difficulties that impinge most on families and cause most immediate disturbance. Accordingly, it is necessary that the treatment programme be organized to deal with these problems at least as much as those that are pathognomonic of autism. That is both because these behaviours are often those most immediately troublesome to parents and because it is in these areas that treatment has most to offer.

Fourth, it is important to appreciate that it is not enough to be concerned with the child's behaviour. Children are part of families and handicapped children present many difficulties for their parents. That is particularly so with a disorder like autism that requires parents to do so much to initiate their children's activities and yet for which they get so little response from their children. The relief of family burdens is as important a goal of treatment as the relief of the children's abnormal behaviour. Of course, the two goals go very much hand in hand as parents are likely to be helped by any improvement in their children's behaviour. Nevertheless, that is not enough on its own, as parents have doubts and worries that go beyond the immediate practicalities of the children's disturbed behaviour. Moreover, there is always the need for parents to strike a balance between what they do for their handicapped child and what they do for their other children as well as the space that they provide for themselves to lead their own lives.

IMPROVING LANGUAGE SKILLS

At the time that we started our study, the main emphasis in behavioural approaches to language training was on the direct teaching of specific elements of speech and of spoken language. There was a tendency to assume that all children could be taught all aspects of language as long as training was sufficiently persistent and intensive. There was no attempt to carry out any detailed, systematic evaluations of individual children's levels or patterns of handicaps. Our research, in parallel with similar findings from other studies (Howlin, 1986b), has pointed to the need for several alterations in the general direction of therapeutic interventions with respect to language. First, it has become widely appreciated that the purpose of words is social communication; hence it is social communication, rather than words as such, that should be the main therapeutic goal. Whatever their linguistic level, there needs to be a focus on the children's social usage of language skills. Our findings showed that it was indeed on the social usage that treatment made most difference. In accord with the ideas of the times, we put a lot of effort into the direct teaching of language but the benefits were quite modest. Nevertheless, the finding that the children could be helped to make much better use of their existing language is important and it is crucial that this be given a high priority in treatment. For the same reasons, it is necessary that as much attention be paid to the children's *understanding* of language as to their production of words. Also, it is necessary to extend communication training to modalities other than spoken language if it is clear that children are not making appreciable progress in speech. At the most basic level, this means that children should be helped to use pointing or demonstration to indicate their needs and wishes. Thought must be given to the use of augmented or alternative systems of communication such as sign language.

Second, it is clear that there are major advantages in planning treatment on the basis of detailed assessment of the children's developmental attainments. That is to say, it makes most sense to start with the child's current level of skill, moving on from there to whatever is the next appropriate phase, rather than to seek in mechanical fashion to get all children to produce spoken language. Thus, if autistic children are not currently using any words, it is particularly important to assess their level of language comprehension. If that is below, say, a 12 or 18 month level and the child's pattern of babble remains primitive and lacking cadences of speech, it is unlikely that much will be gained by speech training as such as that point. Instead, it may be better to start with a more modest aim of improving the child's use of demonstration and pointing. If, on the other hand, in spite of a lack of words, the child is producing speech-like patterns of babble and has comprehension that is above the 18 month level it may well be worthwhile attempting to establish spoken language. A further developmental consideration in the planning of treatment is that the timing and structuring of speech training should take account of the normal course of language development. It seems appropriate to start with those aspects of language that normally appear earliest and which seem easiest for young, normal children to learn.

Perhaps, two dilemmas stand out most strikingly in the planning of language therapy. The first concerns the decision on how far the focus should be on the direct teaching of language skills and how far on the provision of the social environment that is likely to facilitate spontaneous language development. Of course, the two are not mutually exclusive alternatives and probably a combination of the two is to be preferred. Certainly, there is no doubt that, ordinarily, language develops in a social context. Hence, it would seem highly desirable to do all that is possible to ensure that autistic children engage in the social encounters that usually serve to facilitate language development. On the other hand, autistic children stand out in terms of their limited ability to make use of social opportunities. Consequently, it seems desirable to promote the development of spoken language by the variety of direct teaching techniques that are available. It seems likely that this is important for two rather separate reasons. Because autistic children lack the normal to and fro chatter that is characteristic of even the very earliest stages of normal speech development, parents find it very difficult to know how to talk with their autistic children. There is a danger that parents either markedly reduce their interactions because they are so unrewarding and unproductive or, alternatively, that they use speech forms that are too complex for their children to understand. It seems helpful for parents to be given explicit guidance on the techniques that are appropriate to their children's level of language and to the particular handicaps shown by autistic children. Although the main limitations on autistic children's language development seem to stem from the severity of their basic biological handicap, it does seem that direct teaching may make some difference, albeit a modest one.

The second dilemma concerns the decision on when to introduce communication modalities other than spoken language. The research undertaken to date provides no very clear guidance on this point. Nevertheless, there would probably be agreement on two extremes. If children are already using some words, and especially if they have some phrase speech (even if it is echolalic in character), there is likely to be no need to rely on anything other than spoken language. That is not to say, of course, that children should not be given the benefits of using signs and demonstrations as ways of augmenting communication, but it is probable that they can learn to use spoken language as the main medium. At the other extreme, if children have a very severe handicap in the understanding of language (say below the 12 month level) it is unlikely that they will be able to master those varieties of sign language that incorporate complex grammatical rules. Very simple signing may be possible but probably it is too much to expect that children will be able to combine signs if their understanding is so impaired. On general grounds, then, it would seem that the greatest potential for the introduction of alternative modes of communication lies with the group of chidren who have some level of language comprehension that ought to be sufficient for at least the beginnings of language, yet have failed to develop spoken language in spite of efforts to help them to do so. Given such circumstances, research suggests that both the use of sign language (Kiernan, 1987) and other alternative modes of communication (Shane, 1987) can be helpful. However, most of the work has been with non-autistic children with language difficulties and we lack knowledge on how much can be achieved with autistic children. Certainly, case studies indicate that some autistic children can learn to use signs to an extent that is useful for communication (Kiernan, 1983). But, little is known as yet on the degree to which autistic children's use of sign suffers from the same deficits and limitations as those evident with spoken language. Our experience suggests that, at least to some extent, their use of signs does show the limited spontaneity, creativity and social usage that is evident with speech. On the other hand, it seems that some autistic children can communicate better with signs than they can with words.

IMPROVING SOCIAL RELATIONSHIPS AND SOCIAL COMPETENCE

Many of the considerations discussed in relation to language apply equally to the development of social relationships. Once more, it is important to take into account the children's developmental level and what is known about the normal course of social development. If the skills that are taught are inappropriate to the child's mental age, it is unlikely that they will persist to a useful extent beyond the time of the immediate treatment programme. However, it is also necessary to consider what is required for normal usage. For example, it has proved quite difficult to get young autistic children to show sustained eye gaze. But a disregard of normative data has often led to autistic children being trained to use levels of eye contact that would be excessive even in normal individuals (Mirenda *et al.* 1983).

It seems too obvious to state that social behaviour has a social purpose but that is crucial to an understanding of the problems faced by autistic children. Some studies relying on quantitative measures of specific, isolated behaviours such as frequency of eye gaze or number of social contacts have often failed to find deficits in autistic children. It is not so much that these behaviours are not within the repertoire of autistic children but, rather, it is that their social usage of these behaviours is abnormal. Autisic and non-autistic individuals differ in *how* they use eye to eye gaze, *how* they play, and *how* they interact with other people. If more effective intervention is to be forthcoming, attention needs to focus on the *integration* of socially related behaviour systems, rather than on single behaviours out of context. Intervention programmes have shown that although these specific behaviours can indeed be increased by behavioural techniques, they do not necessarily result in any substantial improvements in social interaction (Lord, 1984; Strain, 1981; Strain *et al.*, 1979, Young and Kerr, 1979). It is desirable to train children in the use of a repertoire of skills that can be adapted to the demands of a variety of social settings (Lord, 1984). It is possible to teach older adolescents, using role play techniques, how to cope adequately in shops or restaurants or in highly circumscribed social or work situations. The main limitation is not so much in the situation specificity as such. The autistic individuals often have little problem in transferring their clinic taught skills to real-life situations of a similar kind. The fundamental difficulty lies in the fact that no two social situations are ever identical, and autistic children are singularly lacking in the ability to discriminate and make use of social cues. Because of the ever changing demands of social situations it is almost impossible to teach appropriate 'rules' of behaviour that will ensure social competence. Nevertheless, it may be possible to improve social functioning by modifying environmental complexities and thereby reducing the cognitive demands of the situation. Lord's studies have shown that autistic children appear most socially 'normal' in situations where the linguistic and cognitive demands are well within the children's capabilities. An increase in the amount of structure or pre-dictability of social situations results in greatly improved interactions. Perhaps, therefore, rather than attempting to teach new skills, treatment might do better to concentrate on providing the child with an environment in which his inherent social skills are most likely to be fostered.

Once more, however, there are a variety of unresolved issues. Follow-up studies are consistent in showing the distressing extent to which, even in adult life, autistic individuals who gained conversational language nevertheless remained severely impaired in their social relationships. On the other hand. although very few gained anything approaching normality in social relationships, some do achieve a substantial degree of social competence. The question is, what could be done to improve the likelihood of this good outcome? It has been suggested that if intensive treatment could be started earlier the benefits would be markedly better. There is a logic to this argument in so far as normal children develop selective social attachments for the first time between 6 and 12 months of age, these selective attachments become well-established over the next few years, and it seems that to an important extent they lead on to later peer relationships (Bretherton and Waters, 1985). There are rather few autistic children who have received intensive treatment during the first 2 years of life and it is possible that more could be acieved if treatment gained an earlier start (Fenske *et al*; 1985). But, so far, claims of the benefits of early treatment outstrip the empirical evidence. It is not easy reliably to diagnose autism at that age and it may well be that some of the most dramatic changes occur in children who would not in any case have shown marked autistic handicaps. Controlled trials are needed and so far they have not been undertaken. Moreover, autistic children are often at their most unresponsive at that age and it is unclear whether or not treatment could overcome this lack of responsiveness.

It is clear that social relationships develop through social interaction. No one now supposes that autistic children are helped by standing back and waiting for them to make social approaches. Some form of social intrusion in order to bring about the desired social interaction is necessary. Our findings show that something can be achieved by this approach and that skilled intervention can result in what is, at first, a mechanical interaction becoming truly social in character. However, is this enough? It seems that autistic children are particularly lacking in an ability to discriminate socio-emotional cues (Rutter, 1983). One may ask whether treatment might be improved by an explicit focus on teaching them such discriminations and helping them to understand their meaning. At present, we lack an adequate understanding of how such discriminations are best taught and we lack knowledge on how much can be achieved by this approach. The same applies to autistic individuals' difficulty in appreciating other people's beliefs and intentions (Baron-Cohen et al., 1985, 1986); a difficulty that is likely to interfere with their adaptive responses to social situations.

It is striking that many of the more mildly handicapped autistic individuals develop a desire for friendships as they grow older, but this desire tends not to be accompanied by the skills required to bring about such friendships. Clinical experience suggests that something can be gained by social skills training at this stage; nevertheless, the benefits have been relatively modest. There has been relatively little investment in this aspect of therapeutic work and it remains uncertain whether more can be achieved than has been possible up to now. There is no difficulty in getting autistic individuals to engage in role playing but there are considerable problems in getting them to understand the social demands of varying social situations. It is possible that greater use might be made of peer groups in this connection—especially in the middle years of childhood.

DECREASING RITUALISTIC AND STEREOTYPED BEHAVIOURS

As long ago as 1970, Frith (1970b) suggested that autistic children's tendency to impose structure and order might constitute a basic cognitive deficit. Nevertheless, this suggestion was taken up by few other investigators and little research was undertaken at the time to determine whether or not that was the case. Like others, at one time we thought that at least part of the ritualistic and stereotyped behaviours shown by autistic children were secondary handicaps. We also believed that such behaviours could be prevented if adequate help were given with what seemed to be the more fundamental deficits such as language and social communication (Rutter and Sussenwein, 1971). The findings from this study indicate that it is possible markedly to reduce such ritualistic and stereotyped behaviours, but it seems rarely possible to eliminate the tendency to impose structure. Moreover, the evidence is not in keeping with the suggestion that this is simply a secondary 'neurotic' response to handicap. It may be that to some extent it is a means of the autistic individual dealing with his gross deficits in conceptualization, creativity and imagination. Certainly the lack of spontaneity and initiative is striking even in the oldest and least handicapped autistic individuals. On the other hand, the tendency to rigidity does not seem appreciably to diminish as conceptualization improves. More probably, the tendency to rigidity, stereotyped behaviour and imposition of order constitutes a handicap in its own right.

Whatever the root cause of these problems it is clear that they have a most deleterious effect on the autistic individual's ability to achieve an independent life and on the day to day functioning of the rest of the family. The failure to take any initiative, together with the distress at unplanned interruptions in daily routines, generally means that even the highest functioning autistic people are unable to cope with anything other than the most mundane of jobs. Indeed, it is the extreme disruption and agitation that may result from these obsessive-like problems that frequently lead to loss of jobs. If outbursts take place in public places there may even be trouble with the police.

Many of the routines, rituals and compulsive behaviours seen with autistic individuals appear to be closely similar to the obsessional phenomena seen in obsessive–compulsive disorders occurring in non-autistic people. It seems that in non-autistic individuals, such compulsions are probably best treated by the technique of response prevention (Bolton et al., 1983). However, our experience suggests that this is not usually an effective mode of intervention in autism. Many of the more handicapped autistic children and adolescents are not capable of understanding what is involved and hence are not able to cooperate satisfactorily with the procedure. Moreover, even in the older, less handicapped autistic individuals, response prevention has not seemed a very satisfactory method. It may be that the compulsions seen in autism, although superficially similar, do not derive from the same mechanisms as those that operate in the general run of obsessional disorders. Certainly, the routines and rituals of autistic individuals seem to have a strongly compulsive component but they do not appear to have a primarily anxiety reducing function and direct attempts to prevent their occurrence usually result in a marked increase in tension, agitation and sometimes aggression. Rather than viewing the behaviour as a specific maladaptive motor act that serves to reduce anxiety it is probably more appropriate to consider the behaviours as part of a more general tendency to impose a predictable structure, order and routine.

As far as treatment is concerned, four behavioural approaches have proved effective. The first, the principle of graded change, has been generally applicable. As discussed in chapter 6, very small alterations in routine are introduced, with each change sufficiently small that it is accepted by the child without protest. The changes are progressively extended so that ultimately they amount to a major change in routine. Usually, this approach does not entirely eliminate the child's need to impose routine on many elements of daily life but it does serve markedly to reduce this tendency and, more especially, to reduce its impact on everyday life patterns.

Because most autistic children are happiest in a routine existence, it is easy for families to behave in ways that foster the development of new rituals and compulsions. With younger children, it has seemed helpful to encourage parents to structure the children's environment in such a way as to ensure that a certain amount of change is deliberately programmed. In other words, there is a degree of routine and predictability (because autistic children tend to function best with this approach) but, equally, there is careful attention to ensure that every routine has numerous small variations so allowing a degree of flexibility and adaptability to changing conditions.

Third, it seems that routines and stereotyped behaviours are most likely to develop when children lack the ability to engage in constructive play or meaningful tasks. The imposition of maladaptive stereotyped features can be reduced by attempts to modify the routines into useful, and preferably sociable, activities. Examples of this approach were given in chapter 6.

Fourth, with older autistic individuals, it may often be helpful to teach them how to predict in advance changes in routine that are likely to occur. For example, encouraging them to listen to local radio traffic reports and weather forecasts may be helpful in enabling them to appreciate when there are going to be problems in travelling to work. They can also be taught to accept certain changes in staffing at work or in school routines. Nevertheless, it is never possible to anticipate all changes and when problems arise unpredictably, as they are bound to do from time to time, it is all too apparent how persistent are the imposition of order tendencies shown by autistic individuals.

Lastly, especially with autistic adolescents and young adults, it has sometimes been helpful to give them a low dose of one of the milder psychotropic drugs, such as thioridazine, in order to reduce their tension and anxiety. The drug has little or no effect on their tendency to react adversely to changes in routine but it does serve to keep their agitation within more manageable limits so that the severity of their outburst is not such as to lead to untoward social consequences. Although not systematically assessed, our experience is that this use of drugs is less effective in younger autistic children—perhaps because they do not have the understanding or skills to take advantage of the opportunities for successful coping provided by the reduction in agitation.

The development of routines, rituals and compulsions is only one side of the problem with autistic individuals. In adolescence and adult life especially, the difficulty stems at least as much from their inflexibility, inability to show initiative and take decisions, their lack of spontaneity and autonomy, and sometimes their general obsessive-like slowness. These as-it-were 'negative' aspects have proved much more difficult to alleviate and they remain a major therapeutic challenge.

NON-SPECIFIC BEHAVIOURAL PROBLEMS

Broadly speaking, the therapeutic approaches that are effective with non-specific behavioural problems in autistic individuals are closely similar to those that are effective in non-autistic people. It has been a marked limitation of many previous behavioural programmes that they have been based on a much too narrow view of the scope of behavioural approaches (usually based on operant principles). As discussed in earlier chapters, operant approaches are indeed very useful in the treatment of many types of behavioural problem. They have a wide applicability and there are few problems that do not benefit from a consideration of the environmental factors that serve to perpetuate or reduce the problem behaviours. Nevertheless, they are but one part of a very much broader therapeutic armamentarium of behavioural approaches.

The technique of graded change has already been mentioned with respect to stereotyped behaviours but it has also proved useful in the treatment of some types of fear as well as difficulties with bedtime and sleeping routines. The various methods of treating phobias that involve a combination of exposure to the feared object together with methods that allow adaptation to the fear-stimulus are usually effective. These include different approaches to desensitization, graded 'flooding' and exposure, the teaching of coping skills, and modelling. The conditioning techniques established for the treatment of bedwetting or of daytime urinary incontinence seem as appropriate for autistic individuals as for other children. These include the 'bell and pad' equipment that serves immediately to waken children when they start to wet and the specially devised potty which plays a cheerful tune when the child passes urine into it (designed to increase the child's awareness of his bladder functions). The various forms of social intrusion useful in the facilitation of social interaction have been discussed in considering these problems. Also, there are numerous ways in which the environment may be manipulated or structured in order to avoid the precipitants of the maladaptive behaviours or to encourage successful coping skills. Even the best of these behavioural techniques is not universally successful and there may be various practical reasons that limit their applicability in particular cases. The implication is that therapists need to have a broad range of techniques at their disposal and to use both creativity and ingenuity in considering how the techniques may best be employed to deal with the specific problems that present with any one child.

APPROPRIATE STRUCTURING OF THE ENVIRONMENT

In recent years, as a reaction against the limitations imposed by the segregation of handicapped children in highly specialized facilities, there has been an increasing emphasis on placing such children in as normal an environment as possible. The move against special schools and towards 'main-streaming' is part of that tendency. Of course, there can be no dispute about the desirability of providing children with the least restrictive environment possible. Nevertheless, it is important to appreciate that many of the 'normal' placements reported in the literature on handicapped children in regular schools have in fact provided very specialized facilities with high quality, specially trained staff. The supposed superiority of main-streaming over special schools and classes is far from demonstrated (Howlin, 1985). Moreover, the advantages are mainly to be seen with more mildly handicapped youngsters who can benefit from the type of group teaching ordinarily provided for normal children. Very few autistic children are able to do so; rather, they require a much more individualized approach. Of course, it is important to provide autistic children with the maximal opportunities for developing normal skills and activities but simply placing them in a normal environment may not be the best way of achieving that objective. Because autistic children lack the normal abilities to make sense of their environment and because they lack social reciprocity and social initiative, they are at a severe disadvantage in making use of the opportunities that are so successful in fostering development in normal children. In order to produce more normal behaviours in the autistic child the *effective* environment may need to be very different from that in which normal children flourish.

To a large extent, normal children learn *despite* attempts to teach them. They are remarkably impervious, for example, to attempts systematically to improve their linguistic or symbolic functioning. They learn when ready, as long as they are given the opportunity to do so, and not before. Also they are as likely to learn through imitation and modelling as through any form of direct teaching. More especially, normal children seem to profit from spontaneous active exploration and manipulation of their environment and too much direct interference or structuring by adults may well be counter-productive. In sharp contrast, autistic children show little personal initiative, rarely seek social contacts, and show little exploratory interest. Accordingly, they are likely to need a very different environment in order to promote learning. A parallel may be seen in the findings on deaf children who appear to make better progress if reared by deaf parents than if they are brought up by hearing parents in a normal enviroment (Meadow, Greenberg and Erting, 1983). At first sight, this would seem to be handicapping in that deaf parents have so many limitations themselves. But the rich environment provided by spoken language is of little use to the child whose hearing impairment means that he cannot discriminate the language sounds. The greater use of sign, gesture and demonstration by deaf parents may provide less complex language in an *objective* sense but *effectively* it provides a richer environment for the deaf child who is able to make sense of these communications in a way that he cannot with spoken langue.

In the case of autistic children, it appears that they require an environment that imposes clear but developmentally appropriate demands on them. A high degree of structure may be required both to promote the child's existing skills and to reduce the occurrence of maladaptive behaviours (Clark and Rutter, 1981; Schopler *et al.*, 1971; Volkmar *et al.*, 1985). Parents need to intrude and to structure interactions (in a way that would not ordinarily be necessary with normal children) if interaction and communication between parent and child is to take place. Because autistic children do not show a normal degree of spontaneous exploration and because they are limited in their understanding, much more deliberate teaching may be necessary. As with normal children, it is desirable that autistic children be happy and contented but this is not best achieved by leaving autistic children to their own devices. It is in an unstructured, permissive environment that autistic children are most likely socially to withdraw and to engage in solitary ritualistic or maladaptive behaviours. It is only by providing a degree of organization of the children's activities that autistic children can learn to engage in constructive play which they will subsequently find pleasurable. Of course, the degree of structure that is necessary will depend on the child's developmental level (in general, structure is most necessary with the youngest and most handicapped children) and according to the needs and behaviour of individual children. It is certainly not that one wishes to restrict autistic children's spontaneity and initiative but rather that a degree of structure is usually necessary for such initiative to develop.

These considerations have led to a heavy reliance on adults for the structuring of autistic children's social activities. This is because adults are better able than children to recognize how best to adapt to the handicapped children's problems and how best to provide what is needed to initiate social interactions. Nevertheless, if autistic children are to learn how to play with other children and to develop any kind of friendship patterns with peers of similar age, they must experience doing things with other children. To some extent, this can be achieved by supervised play with other children within the family setting, and in terms of supervised activities with other handicapped children in the special classes or schools attended by the autistic children. There are also advantages in providing for supervised activities with normal peers. Studies have shown that this may provide striking short term benefits if peers can be taught how to interact with autistic children and be given the appropriate rewards and encouragement for doing so (Lord, 1984; McHale et al., 1981a; Stokes and Baer 1977; et al., 1978). However, the lack of reciprocity and mutual reinforcement, that is so essential for normal peer relationships but which is so lacking in autistic children, eventually takes its toll. Thus normal children, whatever external reinforcers may be on offer, eventually become 'exhausted' by their efforts to maintain social interaction. That does not mean that it is not useful to engage the help of peers but it does mean that there are necessary limitations in what they can be expected to do.

No matter how successful the intervention programme, autistic children continue to have problems in functioning outside structured settings, in establishing independent use of skills, and in showing any personal initiative. The need for structure tends to affect even higher functioning autistic adults who may possess a high level of skill in certain areas. In most cases it is not their lack of skills as such that proves a limitation in the adult work environment; rather, it is their lack of inititative, flexibility and adaptability and especially the problems imposed by their need for predictable routine, order and structure. Often they are unable to put their abilities to practical use unless they are constantly monitored, supervised and checked. Because of this failure to develop autonomy and initiative, many intelligent autistic children who achieve good results in school and college nevertheless have great difficulties making progress when placed in a far less structured job situation. Few achieve the occupational level that their academic achievements would lead one to expect. This observation underlines the very great need for services during the crucial time of transition from school to work. Our therapeutic involvement with autistic individuals since the study came to an end, together with our work with other young people, has shown what a critical and difficult period this can be. Very few autistic individuals are ready to move on to work at the age of 16, 17 or 18 years when leaving school. On the other hand, many are able to cope with some form of work, possibly in a sheltered environment, by the time they reach their mid 20s. Services are least well developed for this in-between age group of young adults. The development of appropriate services remains an important challenge for the future. Some young people have benefited from special residential training designed to teach handicapped people work routines and work skills but few of these courses are well adapted to the particular needs of autistic individuals. In particular, many work training and assessment schemes function on the basis of trying people out in a variety of different settings requiring different skills. The aim is to see which sort of job is likely to suit the person best. The limitation with respect to autistic individuals is that they require quite a long time as a rule to adapt to new situations and are at their worst when they first encounter a new task or a new setting. A much longer time span is needed in order to assess what is likely to be possible.

It is also clear that there is a paucity of suitable work settings for autistic adults. Most of them have behavioural difficulties of a kind and severity that make it difficult for them to be readily accommodated in the training centres designed for mentally handicapped adults. Moreover, family and other considerations mean that some form of residential placement is necessary for many. A long stay hospital is inappropriate for the more mildly handicapped autistic individuals but only a minority manage in the ordinary run of hostels. On the other hand, the sheltered communities for handicapped persons, both autistic and non-autistic, provide a most satisfactory placement in many cases. In such a setting, the autistic adult has a substantial degree of autonomy and responsibility but also the necessary supervision, structure and predictability of routine that is required.

COORDINATION OF SERVICES

In discussing treatment implications so far, we have mainly concentrated on behavioural methods of treatment as these constituted the mainstay of our developmentally oriented treatment programme. It is clear, however, that the coordination of services must be a central concern in any treatment programme. Virtually all autistic children require some form of special educational treatment; this is so whether they are in a school or class specifically provided for the needs of autistic children, in some other kind of special educational facility or in an ordinary school. Autistic children have considerable difficulties in the understanding of concepts and special help is required in order to ensure that they understand the meaning and implications of what they have learned. Particularly when young, autistic children have great difficulties in understanding group teaching or group instructions and this, perhaps more than anything else, constitutes the main reason for special teaching. But, in addition, it is common for autistic children to have a wide scatter of skills—being average or even unusually talented in some directions but markedly retarded in others. It is important that schooling capitalize on the children's abilities while at the same time providing special help for areas of difficulty. Because the children's problems in learning apply as much to social situations and the everyday demands of ordinary living as to the three Rs and other school subjects, it is most important that the approaches employed at home and those used at school are mutually supportive and not pulling in opposite directions.

The role of social services is equally important. There are a variety of allowances that are available to parents of handicapped children but it is not always easy to gain access to the relevant information about these. Parents need to be helped to be aware of the financial supports for which they are eligible, and may also require assistance in claiming these. There are several organizations that provide excellent holidays for handicapped children. Ordinarily these are arranged through social services. They provide an enjoyable new set of activities for the children and what is often a much needed break for the families. Temporary residential care may also be needed at times of crisis when parents become ill or when family difficulties become unmanageable. As already discussed, the period of transition after school leaving is a particularly crucial time when the help of social services may be most important in providing the necessary training and also appropriate day or residential placements.

Up to now, no medical treatments that are specific for autism have been discovered. Enthusiastic claims continue to be made from time to time for vitamins, for diets or for drugs such as fenfluramine. However, although these may provide some help to individual children their benefits are modest at best, and they are not suitable for general inclusion in a treatment programme. It is a medical truism that any drug that is chemically active is likely to have side-effects as well as therapeutic benefits. This is particularly the case with the long term administration of powerful drugs in childhood. There are a few severely disturbed autistic children who need long term medication but these are the minority. For others, drugs may be occasionally beneficial for the symptomatic treatment of overactivity, sleep difficulties or agitation. Epilepsy develops during adolescence in about a quarter of autistic individuals. Sometimes there are only a few epileptic attacks but often they persist and anticonvulsant medication is required. Again, when deciding on the appropriate anticonvulsant it is important to bear in mind possibly beneficial or adverse affects on children's behaviour.

Although pharmacological treatments are only infrequently the mainstay of treatment, they do have an occasional place in the treatment of many autistic children. However, it is important that the medical aspects of treatment be well integrated with other therapeutic approaches. Moreover, it would be much too narrow to see medical aspects as confined to the use of drugs. Good quality paediatric care is as important with autistic children as with any other group of handicapped young people. Although it would be unusual for deafness or visual impairments to constitute the main basis of autistic problems, they can constitute important contributory factors. It is often quite difficult to obtain accurate assessments of the vision and hearing of autistic children but is essential that they have regular testing and that the responsible clinicians be alert to the possibility of the later development of visual or hearing impairments. Because autistic children have such extreme difficulty in expressing themselves, it is easy to overlook the development of physical disease. Skilled medical surveillance is essential for this reason as well as others.

FAMILY ISSUES

Finally, it is important that the results of our treatment evaluation showed the value of a home based approach. The short term evaluation in which treatment and control groups were followed prospectively over a 6 month period showed the clear benefits of the treatment programme. However, because the control group had received rather a mixed bag of, often inadequate, treatments, the findings left ambiguous whether the benefits of the treatment programme lay in what was done or in the intensity of therapeutic involvement. The longer term follow-up findings were crucial in indicating that the intensity and frequency of family involvement were most important elements in the programme. This was evident because the control group had received treatment that followed essentially the same principles as those that we employed, but with the contact limited to clinic attendances at relatively infrequent intervals.

There were several rather different elements of the home based approach that seemed crucial. First, home visits were often highly informative in indicating the practicalities of the home environment that needed to be taken into account in planning therapeutic interventions. Of course, quite a lot of information can be obtained by asking parents for careful descriptions during their clinic attendance but out experience is that the home visit is a much more satisfactory way of obtaining the kind of information that is needed.

Second, the approach provides a focus on the children's behaviour as it is manifest at home. Parents can often give very good descriptions of their children's behavioural problems but usually they are much less able to describe *how* difficulties arise and how they themselves respond to the child. Other research has shown the difficulties experienced by most people in providing accurate descriptions of sequences of behaviour and there are comparable problems in describing one's own role simply because in the heat of the moment it is quite difficult to be aware of how one reacts. Home visits can be very useful in enabling the therapists to observe what actually happens and to work out with the parents alternative ways of dealing with the problems.

Third, parents are the people who are likely to spend most time in one to one interaction with their children. Accordingly, they are in the best position to provide the optimal restructuring of the environment and the most appropriate consistent, immediate ways of dealing with their children's behavioural difficulties. It is for this reason that a prime emphasis was placed on using the parents' skills as one of the key factors in the treatment programme. As the results have shown, the parental role as co-therapist works well.

Fourth, the home based approach meant that there was a focused concern on the possible needs of the family for practical help. Attention was paid to such matters as baby-sitting arrangements, holiday provision, medical and dental care, and the various forms of financial and other assistance that may be available. Parents were encouraged to show initiative in making their own arrangements on these things and families were always put in touch with the relevant parental organization, the National Society for Autistic Children. Parents often received much support from contact with other parents who faced similar problems and, in addition, the National Society is an invaluable source of information on all matters related to the care and treatment of autistic children.

Fifth, the family orientation of the treatment programme meant that there was a concern for the family as a whole and not just for the handicapped child. We were at pains to keep burdens on parents to a minimum and we attempted to ensure, through discussion and practical arrangements, that parents and siblings were able to have interests, activities and sources of enjoyment of their own outside the care of their handicapped child.

Finally, we sought to be sensitive to the variety of worries, anxieties and feelings of guilt experienced by the parents. Of course, parents respond in an wide variety of ways to having a handicapped child and it is a mistake to assume that all will experience feelings of guilt or self-doubt. They do not. Nevertheless, bringing up a handicapped child is not an emotionally neutral event and most families experience psychological troubles of some degree at some time. Many are able to deal with these themselves without need for professional help but in other cases skilled counselling may be required. It is important to appreciate that the involvement of parents as co-therapists necessarily involves widening the scope of therapy. Advice cannot be restricted solely to the sort of intervention techniques that parents should use. Therapists need to be sensitive to the emotional and practical demands placed on parents by their role as co-therapists as well as those that are intrinsic to the raising of an autistic child. Guidance is often needed on how to distribute time most effectively in order to benefit the autistic child while at the same time living their own lives. Parents may alternate between despairing over the lack of progress by their autistic child and wishing to give up therapy altogether, and becoming overenthusiastic in giving up all other interests in order to help the one handicapped child. Parents are not simply tools of the therapists but are individuals in their own right and their needs have to be taken into account if intervention is to be successful. Worries over handling, over their other children, over the future, or over the possible causes of the condition are common; advice on these matters as well as on practical management is crucial. Again, the type of therapeutic intervention required will vary according to the nature of the problems involved and to the needs of particular parents. Some will be helped by behavioural programmes, some by accurate information, some by a more psychotherapeutic approach and the majority by a combination of these.

In attempting to create an environment that promotes optimal change in the children's behaviour, it is apparent that considerable changes in family functioning are required. As the results of the project made clear, it is much easier to effect such changes in families given direct help at home than through irregular outpatient attendance. It seems that parents are greatly helped by seeing management techniques being put into action in the home, rather than being left to translate theory into practice on their own. Of course, this approach is not cheap, in terms of either money or professional time. Although the cost is much less than that of inpatient or residential care it is nevertheless substantially greater than that of ordinary, occasional outpatient treatment. The benefits of a home based approach, therefore, need to be weighed against the expense of this type of programme. The research evaluation has shown the superiority of the home based programme but the question arises as to whether some less expensive approach based on the same principles might be equally effective. We have no systematic data on this matter, but since the study came to an end we have sought to provide a similar programme for a rather larger number of families with more limited resources.

One of our major aims has been to enlist the services of District Handicap Teams as much as possible. Children are still seen for assessment and diagnosis with one or two home visits being made to establish the nature of the problems and to explore the types of treatment approach that are likely to be most effective. Contacts are then made with the local referral agencies involved with the family and our aim is to try to work *through* them; giving them advice on how to deal with problem behaviours and how to foster development in other areas, rather than to intervene directly with families ourselves. The professional contacts involved are not restricted to any one discipline; at various times psychologists, psychiatrists, social workers, health visitors, teachers and family practitioners have all been involved as co-therapists in this way. The crucial requirement is not that they have any specialist knowledge or training either in autism or behavioural techniques, but that they are trusted and respected by the family, and are able to deal sensitively and practically with problem issues as they arise, making use of such additional professional expertise as they may require.

Chapter 14

Implications for Research and for Clinical Concepts

EVALUATIONS OF TREATMENT EFFICACY

The project findings have implications for the design of studies to evaluate the efficacy of treatment methods. Even today, the literature remains full of claims that this, that or the other treatment method is effective, with such claims being based on the children's response to treatment but without any comparable assessment of control groups treated in other ways. Within the behavioural literature, reliance tends to be placed on either the greater improvements that follow treatment compared to those in a no-treatment baseline period, or the pattern of changes within a single case as related to the use of multiple baselines or reversal designs. Such designs are indeed useful in pointing to the high probability that the treatment used was specifically responsible for the acceleration in behavioural change and that the benefits were greater than those that followed the previous period of no therapeutic intervention. Nevertheless, our findings are important in showing the rather marked difference in conclusions that follows the use of a controlled group comparison together with a longer period of follow-up. It is useful to consider why these different forms of therapeutic evaluation give somewhat different answers. The results as presented in the usual single case study form showed dramatic benefits for many children across a range of different behaviours. The case–control follow-up study showed benefits attributable to the treatment programme but the benefits were both more modest and more variable according to the particular type of behaviour studied. Benefits were most marked with the non-specific behavioural problems and least marked with language competence and general intelligence (there being no IQ benefits attributable to treatment).

Several rather different features account for this pattern of findings. First, all studies have shown huge individual variation in autistic children's progress. Some have remained severely handicapped and some improve tremendously. It is important to appreciate that these marked improvements occur with all forms of treatment and indeed they were notable in a previous era when very few children received treatment that would be considered at all adequate by present day standards (see Kanner, 1973). Accordingly, it must be expected that any treatment programme will have its dramatic 'successes', the improvements being due to the mildness of the children's handicaps rather than to anything to do with treatment as such. These dramatic improvements will be much more frequent if the group of children treated includes a high proportion with a good prognosis on the basis of their level pattern of initial handicaps. The only satisfactory way of determining whether the benefits are directly attributable to the treatment programme is to make a systematic comparison of matched groups of children treated in different ways.

Second, there is a crucial distinction between the therapeutic benefits as shown by changes in the children's behaviour in the treatment setting itself and the changes as seen in other settings or other social circumstances. It has been a universal finding that marked behavioural improvements in the treatment setting may be accompanied by little or no therapeutic gains in terms of the children's behaviour elsewhere. Our own research included examples of children showing marked improvements at home not at school. A somewhat related issue concerns the difference between the children's behaviour as elicited and as shown spontaneously. It is a common observation in therapeutic studies that the results in terms of children's spontaneous use of language are rather disappointing compared with the changes in children's language as produced through appropriate structuring and encouragement. The implication is that the outcome measures must span several settings and must include spontaneous as well as elicited behaviour.

Third, different measures tend to give different answers on the benefits of treatment. For example, standardized psychometric measures of language showed rather small, statistically non-significant, differences between treatment and control groups, whereas observational measures of the child's use of language showed substantially greater therapeutic benefits. Of course, these results do not contradict one another as each reflects a rather different aspect of language. The former evaluations show that treatment made little difference to the children's basic language competence or capacity, whereas the latter indicated that, in spite of that, the children in the treatment group were making rather better use of the language skills they possessed. There was also a difference between parental ratings and observational measures with respect to the timing of change. Direct observations showed that changes were at their maximum during the first 6 months of treatment, whereas parental ratings showed the main improvement to occur somewhat later. The implication is that, although there were indeed rather rapid specific behavioural changes, it took some time for these to be of sufficient magnitude and sufficient breadth to affect the overall parental perceptions of the degree of behavioural disturbance. In part, it is a matter of ratings being influenced by children's previously established behavioural 'reputation' (so introducing a misleading artifactual time lag), but in part it is that the parental ratings tend to be based on a rather wider range of behaviours. In so far as that is the case, the time lag is real in its indication that specific behavioural changes do not at first make much impact on the overall level of difficulty created. Nevertheless, the methodological point that arises is that observational measures are an essential part of the evaluation if there is to be avoidance of a premature conclusion that treatment is not being effective. Equally, however, parental ratings are necessary in order to get a more satisfactory measure of the value of the behavioural changes.

Fourth, conclusions on the efficacy of treatment were crucially influenced by the length of follow-up. However, the effects differed strikingly according to the particular behaviours in question. Thus, at the 6 month follow-up, the children in the treatment group showed significant improvements in the rate of non-specific maladaptive behaviours, compared to the control group. Differences between treated children and controls at 18 months were even greater. In this case, the initial picture on therapeutic benefits proved accurate but was an underestimate of the longer term gains. The results suggest that treatment of these behaviours is likely to result in fairly rapid behavioural changes if it is ultimately going to prove successful. Accordingly, if children do not show improvements within a relatively short period of time it would seem important to modify intervention programmes without delay.

The benefits of the treatment programme in the alleviation of ritualistic and compulsive behaviour were also evident at the 6 month stage but, in contrast to the non-specific behavioural problems, there was little further change between the 6 and 18 month follow-ups. The same conclusion about benefits being seen fairly quickly if they are going to occur applies. But, there is a difference in the sense that it seems there are greater limitations in the changes that are possible. Stereotyped and routinized behaviour is very much part of the autistic syndrome, and although it is possible markedly to diminish these problems they tend to persist in some degree.

The picture with respect to changes in language was different yet again. The therapeutic benefits for language were maximal at 6 months and were markedly lessened by the time of the 18 month follow-up. That is to say, the treatment programme was associated with quite marked gains in the children's use of language but these initial benefits were not followed by the continuing growth in language competence that was hoped for. The findings strongly suggest that the effect of treatment was to activate children's usage of language skills that were already partially available rather than to influence language competence as such. Of course, the benefits in terms of language usage were both real and worthwhile; nevertheless, the implications for ultimate language level were less optimistic than the initial therapeutic gains suggested. The findings underline the importance of an adequate length of follow-up in the evaluation of the treatment of chronically handicapping disorders.

Fifth, an over reliance on specific measures may lead to treatment claims being exaggerated or misleading. Autistic children's deficits in both com-munication and socialization are not primarily concerned with a lack of specific behaviours. Rather, problems lie in the integration of a complex set of behaviours for social purposes in social contexts. Thus, Lord (1984), reporting the results of a successful programme to increase peer relationships in autistic children, emphasized that in spite of the marked gains achieved in many specific social behaviours, the autistic children remained severely handicapped and were a long way from behaving normally with their peers. The same applied in this study when, despite the success of treatment in minimizing many abnormal behaviours, pervasive problems in communication and socialization remained. The characteristic failure to show empathy, understanding and reciprocity with respect to other people's feelings showed little improvement with intervention. Even those autistic individuals who were able eventually to develop a relatively wide range of social contacts, either through their work or through special interests such as music or railway groups, failed to form anything but the most superficial of relationships. As they grow older, many autistic individuals express the wish to be accepted and to do the sort of things that are appropriate for their age group. Thus they may want to leave home, get promotion at work or get married, but few have the social ability to achieve these goals. One or two young men have found girlfriends but even then their notions of what marriage entails remain somewhat hazy. Simon, for example, remarked that he 'wouldn't mind getting married' to his girlfriend (who was also mildly handicapped) but he expressed puzzlement as to how he could reconcile this with living at home with his parents as he always had done.

Finally, although comparative group data are necessary for the overall evaluation of the results of any treatment, the assessment of individual differences is also needed in order fully to understand the effects of treatment. For example, although group data indicated that intervention was valuable in increasing communicative speech, it was not true for all children in the group. Those autistic children with a severe and global language deficit made very little improvement whether or not they received special intervention. At the opposite extreme, children with some phrase speech, whether or not this was echolalic in nature, made good progress regardless of treatment and there were few long term differences between cases and controls for such children. The greatest benefits of treatment were found for those with more moderate degrees of language retardation. Without the treatment programme they tended to remain with little in the way of useful language but with treatment some useful communicative skills were usually obtained.

THERAPEUTIC MECHANISMS

As discussed in the previous chapter, the treatment programme involved a wide range of behavioural techniques together with counselling and other approaches. The need to incorporate a wide range of different treatment methods when dealing with the problems of autistic children has been highlighted in many other studies. Successful intervention programmes such as those by Schopler et al.. (1971, 1982), Marcus et al. (1978) and Koegel et al. (1982) have all employed similar broad based strategies. Inevitably, the complexity of the treatment programme in all these studies has meant that it has been impossible to determine which specific aspects of treatment were crucial for change. Like ours, all involved an individual approach to assessment and treatment, the systematic shaping of skills, and a careful restructuring of the child's environment in addition to the use of reinforcement and time out techniques.

It seems clear that a variety of different therapeutic mechanisms are likely to be involved in the changes leading to therapeutic benefits. For example, the processes involved in desensitization or graded change are rather different from those that underline operant approaches. Reinforcement is generally considered to be the most crucial element of operant treatment. Indeed, the guiding principle of behaviour modification procedures is that behaviour 'can be modified by its consequences' (Yule, 1980) and that 'any event or stimulus consequence that increases the strength or probability of the behaviour it follows is called a reinforcer' (Hall, 1971). Hence the basic tenet of operant conditioning theory is that if behaviours do increase in frequency they must be being reinforced in some way. Numerous studies have shown that approaches based on this principle do indeed work. Nevertheless, reinforcement is rarely the only behavioural technique applied in operant programmes. Furthermore, it appears from various intervention studies that careful restructuring of the environment is at least as important as reinforcement *per se*. Cheseldine and McConkey (1979), for example, found that parents do not necessarily need training in traditional behavioural techniques in order to increase the language skills of their children. Instead, simply setting parents specific language goals may result in marked improvements in the verbal interaction between children and their parents. Spradlin and Siegel (1982) suggested that, so far as language training is concerned, increasing the children's *opportunities* to use language may be more crucial than the use of traditional reinforcement techniques. Other work, too, has emphasized the need to establish functional competence when teaching new skills (Carr and Durand, 1985b; Goetz *et al.*, 1983; Litt and Schreibman, 1982. By this they mean that children's newly learned responses should have an immediate and direct effect on the environment that is not dependent on extrinsic reinforcers. Only if the child is able to manipulate his environment effectively by particular actions or verbalizations are these likely to be maintained and generalized. Furthermore, if functional competence can be achieved this is likely to result in a diminution of inappropriate behaviours that were previously used to achieve the same effect. Finally, data from Short's (1984) follow-up of the programmes initiated by Schopler *et al.* in the course of their TEACCH project indicated that improvements in children's behaviour were associated not with parents' use of reinforcement, which actually declined during treatment, but with the use of physical and verbal guidance provided by parents.

In other words, one of the essential features of treatment is to provide the necessary opportunities for children to learn how to communicate and how to develop relationships. When left to their own devices, autistic children tend not to interact socially and stereotyped behaviours and mannerisms are at a peak. Their social functioning and communicating tends to be much better when other people organize the situation in a planned way so that the child is engaged in interactions.

'Structure' tends to be the term that is applied to these planned circumstances, because other people decide, on the basis of the child's deficits and difficulties, what sort of setting is most likely to be helpful, rather than letting the children choose for themselves. The term does not imply rigidity nor does it involve coercion. The art, as well as the science, of appropriate environmental structuring requires that it not only brings about the desired social or communicative behaviours but also that it is pleasurable and rewarding to the child. Both naturalistic and experimental studies suggest that this structuring of the environment constitutes a crucial component of treatment. For example, Bartak and Rutter's (1973) comparison of autistic children's progress in three very different types of school found that the results were best in the highly structured unit employing formal educational techniques rather than in the permissive unit with much warm, positive encouragement of the children but little in the way of direction. Similarly, McHale et al. (1981) found that the communication skills of autistic children improved when teachers interacted with them under highly structured conditions. Numerous other studies of school and clinic based interventions concur in finding that simple restructuring of the environment so that social interactions and task involvement are brought about can have significant effects (Frankel and Graham, 1976; Lord, 1984; McHale et al., 1981; Schopler et al., 1971; Strain et al., 1979; Koegel et al., 1982; Volkmar et al., 1985). Experimental studies support the same conclusion (Currie and Brannigan, 1970; Clark and Rutter, 1981; Koegel and Covert, 1972; Lovaas et al., 1965; McConnell, 1967). It is clear that the era of permissive, non-intrusive approaches to treatment is over. There is no point in a 'waiting for them to flower' stance, as autistic children's deficits mean that they lack the skills to make use of their environment.

Treatment has both to create the opportunities and to ensure that autistic children engage in the necessary activities. What remains uncertain, however, is precisely how this should be done. What sort of situation is most likely to bring about the reciprocal social interchanges that constitute the basis for both language and social relationships? How can the situation be arranged so that autistic children respond appropriately to the other person; how can they learn to build social interchanges, and how can they be helped to develop empathy or learn how to discriminate and understand socio-emotional cues? Can empathy be taught and, if so, how? At this study has shown, we know a good deal about how to reduce or even eliminate maladaptive behaviours of many different kinds. What we know much less about is what is needed to foster more normal development when children have serious deficits in their capacities to make sense of their social environment. This remains one of the major challenges for therapeutic developments in the future.

IMPLICATIONS FOR CLINICAL CONCEPTS OF AUTISM

As discussed in chapter 2, there has been a steady mounting of evidence, from a wide variety of studies, that autism involves a set of basic cognitive deficits

(Rutter, 1983). The findings from our evaluation of treatment strongly support that concept. Many aspects of autistic children's behaviour showed marked, sometimes dramatic, improvements. Yet, the children's IQ scores remained generally stable, with no difference between treatment and control groups. It seems that treatment makes no difference to autistic children's general intelligence. Moreover, there was no association between the degree of behavioural chage and shifts in IQ. The lack of response to treatment, together with the lack of association between treatment and alterations in behaviour, suggests that the intellectual deficit constitutes a biological handicap. The finding from research that the IQ level is strongly associated with the risk of epileptic seizures developing during adolescence (Bartak and Rutter, 1976) provides even stronger evidence. It has sometimes been argued that autistic children's poor cognitive performance is a consequence of negativism (Jose and Cohen, 1980; Wallace, 1975) but experimental findings have shown clearly that cognitive task failure is a function of the complexity of the tasks involved rather than lack of motivation (Clark and Rutter, 1979; Volkmar, Hoder and Cohen, 1982).

Nevertheless, we did not find that IQ predicted outcome. Follow-up studies have been consistent in showing that severe mental handicap (an IQ below 50) is strongly associated with a poor prognosis, and that good social functioning in adult life is almost entirely restricted to those individuals with a non-verbal IQ in the normal range (Lotter, 1978; Rutter, 1970). However, the same investigations indicated that, within the normal range, IQ showed only a very weak association with outcome. It is likely that the lack of association between IQ and outcome in our study was a function of the fact that the treated children had a mean non-verbal IQ of 89, with none having an IQ below 60. Still, it is necessary to ask why IQ does not predict outcome in this range. The fact that it does not, indicates that autism cannot be thought of as just a variety of mental retardation (Rutter and Schopler, 1987). Autistic children differ from both normal and mentally retarded children of similar mental age in their relative failure to use meaning in their memory processes and in their limitations on tasks involving sequencing, coding, abstraction and conceptualization (Frith and Snowling, 1983; Hermelin, 1976; Hermelin and O'Connor, 1970).

The importance of specific deficits in language and language related skills was shown by the very limited impact that treatment made on language competence and by the predictive power asociated with the level of the children's initial language handicap. Our study, like those of others (e.g. Clements et al., 1982), showed that treatment can bring about improvements in certain aspects of linguistic performance but it makes very little difference to the basic language deficit. However, it would be misleading to see autistic children's problems as primarily linguistic in nature (Cromer, 1987; Rutter, 1983). Their main impairment does not involve grammar (i.e. it is not in the feature that is most distinctive of language); moreover, their handicap extends to non-verbal as well as verbal communication and to the thought processes as well as to the use of spoken language. Furthermore, it is not just a lack of language (or even an abnormality of language) that characterizes autism. Rather, it is a striking limitation in spontaneity and creativity in the production of language and in the use of language for social communication. The implication is that the basis of autistic children's deficit is not likely to be restricted to some element of language competence; similarly, the goals of treatment must go beyond attempts to increase vocabulary or grammar and to decrease echolalic usage. The aim must be to aid the development of spontaneous social communication—a far more difficult therapeutic objective.

This recognition has led investigators to pay greater attention to the social deficits associated with autism. Hobson (1986) found that autistic children were markedly impaired in their ability to discriminate socio-emotional cues (from which he inferred a lack of empathy) and Baron-Cohen et al. (1985, 1986) found that they had great difficulty on tasks involving the intepretation of other people's points of view (from which was inferred a deficit in appreciating the thinking of other people). Therapeutic studies have shown the parallels between communication and social functioning. Like others (Clark and Rutter, 1981; Lord, 1984; Lovaas, et al., 1973; McHale et al., 1980, 1981; Short, 1984) we found that treatment could bring about worthwhile improvements in various elements of social behaviour, but spontaneous social interactions with peers in unstructured settings showed far less improvement. Social intrusion and structuring do help and the therapeutic results *negate* the expectations of Tinbergen and Tinbergen (1972) that this would lead to increased withdrawal. The suggestion that the social deficits derive from social anxiety has no support. On the contrary, it was striking that many of the older autistic children sought interactions (albeit inappropriately) and caused parental embarrassment by their disinhibition and lack of sensitivity to other people's feelings. Treatment often succeeded in improving social involvement and in reducing socially unacceptable behaviours. What it failed to accomplish was to bring about a normal reciprocity in social interactions and a normal appreciation of socio-emotional cues. That remains a therapeutic challenge for the future, but the solution is likely to require a better understanding of the nature of this social deficit and the mechanisms involved in its operation.

Just as spontaneous reciprocal relationships with other people were particularly impaired and particularly resistant to treatment, so, too, the development of spontaneous imaginative play was quite restricted. Quantitative increases were obtained in the amount of toy play, as in the amount of social interaction, but there were few gains attributable to treatment in the complexity, spontaneity or creativity of play. Improvements in play tended to centre around activities structured by the parents and generally they related to specific play materials. Other studies have shown the same (Lord, 1984). The development of play is highly dependent on autistic children's level of cognitive and language development (McHale et al., 1980; Sigman et al., 1987; Wing and Gould, 1979); nevertheless, the association is not the same as that found in normal children. Ordinarily, imaginative and make-believe play is well established by the time children reach 30 months of age but autistic children with mental ages well above that level continue to lack the imagination and creativity that is so evident in the play of toddlers.

It is clear that the most striking deficits of autistic children centre around their cognitive, linguistic and social functioning, with the greatest handicap apparent in situations that demand an integration of *all these* domains. Thus, language is least affected in non-social contexts and most impaired when it has to be used for social communication. Cognitive development is most normal in the area of non-social, non-verbal tasks. Also, social skills are most limited in situations that make many social and cognitive demands on the child. Autistic children can exhibit surprisingly high levels of socially appropriate behaviour in highly structured interactions, planned and organized by others, but they tend to be at a loss in less predictable, less structured situations in which they have to provide a lead or interpret what is expected of them.

It may be that this problem is relevant to the oft-noted failure of autistic children to generalize therapeutic gains from one setting to others. Skills learned in one setting frequently fail to be used elsewhere. Training in multiple settings, or with several different therapists, using a range of activities and styles of working can do much to overcome this situation-specificity tendency (Egel, 1981; Koegel *et al.*, 1982; Stokes *et al.*, 1978). Autistic children are highly reliant on structure and if a new situation has a different organization they are likely to be 'thrown' and uncertain how to behave. But it is important to note that this failure to generalize does not apply to all skills. The educational study by Bartak and Rutter (1973) showed that autistic children who learned to read and write, or who gained an understanding of money, had no particular difficulty in using these skills whenever they were needed. It seems that the difference is that, once having gained these scholastic skills, it requires little understanding to see how to apply them in a new setting. That is markedly different from social situations, no two of which are identical. There is a constant need to perceive what is involved and to *adapt* the use of skills to changing situations. It is that adaptation that autistic children find so difficult. The main deficit may not involve a failure of generalization as such but rather a serious limitation in *conceptualization*. Autistic individuals are severely impaired in their ability to perceive and to interpret social situations and hence find great difficulty in making the necessary adaptations. It appears that treatment needs to focus on increasing these social conceptual skills, as well as on providing a range of therapeutic contexts to increase generalization.

However, that raises the further question of the nature and meaning of autistic children's apparent 'resistance to change' and this tendency to impose a stereotyped structure and order on their life. We have noted that this tendency usually remained present to an important degree even though specific routines and rituals had been markedly diminished or even eliminated. Nevertheless, an 'insistence on sameness' (the term originally employed by Kanner) does not seem to capture the essential element of the problem. Thus, it proved readily possible to reduce handicapping attachment objects from a large blanket to just a few threads, or from a heavy belt to a tiny fragment of leather. Of course, the careful grading of the change made this possible but is implausible to suppose that the autistic children had forgotten what the object looked like initially (their excellent rote memory has been the subject of frequent comment). Similarly, in treating autistic children's preoccupations and rituals, it has often been useful to build in an ever increasing list of exceptions to situations where the routine is imposed. Perhaps, it is not resistance to change as such that is the problem but rather resistance to unpredictable change.

Yet this does not seem an adequate explanation for the pervasive autistic tendency to impose a stereotyped structure and order, nor for the frequent development of compulsions and preoccupations of various sorts. It may well be that it reflects some kind of specific cognitive deficit (Frith, 1970a, b) although it is not at all clear just what this deficit might involve. The routines and rituals appear very similar to those seen in non-autistic obsessional disorders and, indeed, they are frequently referred to as 'obsessions'. Nevertheless, as already discussed, it seems likely that the mechanisms involved may be different, and that the treatment approaches that are effective are not the same. Our findings suggest that the principle of graded change is the most useful in tackling autistic children's 'obsessions'. However, it is evident that more research is required to delineate the processes involved in these stereotyped behaviours.

FUTURE PROGRESS IN TREATMENT

There has been great progress in the development of effective methods of treating the behavioural problems shown by autistic children. It is important that these methods be made generally available to autistic children and their families. Much that is worthwhile can be accomplished and there can be no excuse for failing to provide the help that is so much needed by parents facing the problems of rearing a handicapped child whose autistic deficits serve to make social interactions so unrewarding as well as creating a host of management difficulties. Yet, it is all too apparent that the great majority of autistic individuals remain handicapped throughout their lives. Treatment does not result in a 'cure' or anything approaching it. Is it likely that more can be accomplished in the future?

We suggest that there are three main routes that need to be followed. First, it is clear that autism has some kind of organic basis, although it remains uncertain just what that basis is. Until recently, our tools to investigate brain functioning were exceedingly limited but advances in brain imaging techniques have opened up new horizons. So far these techniques have not led to any elucidation of the nature of the biological basis of autism but they may do so in the future and it is important that this avenue be explored further. Equally, there have been important advances in genetic concepts and in methods of genetic study (including the new opportunities provided by molecular biology). It is evident that there is a substantial component to at least some cases of autism and it is crucial that this be studied further, making use of the new methods now available (Folstein and Rutter, 1987). While there are currently no 'breakthroughs' in the biochemical and pharmacological study of autism, these are fields of rapid progress and it is necessary that these advances be applied to autism. It may be expected that the next decade or so will see progress in the biological understanding of autism. Whether or not such progress will lead to improved methods of treatment will depend on what is discovered, but the potential is there.

Second, there has been great strides in the delineation of the nature of some aspects of the cognitive deficit in autism (Rutter, 1983). These have done much to identify the impairments in language and in thought processes. Also, they have begun to outline important features of the social handicap. It is necessary that more be done to aid understanding of the mechanism involved in this pervasive failure to develop close, mutually reciprocal relationships involving love or friendship. Equally, it is important that greater attention be paid to the possible processes underlying the stereotyped behaviours and imposition of structure and order. Interventions are best planned on the basis of an adequate appreciation of the nature of the abnormalities to be remedied.

Third, as discussed in detail throughout this book, there are various areas in which further therapeutic research is required to improve behavioural methods of intervention. In particular, attention needs to be paid to the indications for and value of non-verbal forms of communication; to the development of spontaneity and reciprocity in social communication and interactions; to aiding social conceptualization, and to the reduction of stereotyped and ritualistic behaviour. Much has been achieved but much more remains to be done. The nature of autism makes it imperative that these three research routes of biological investigation, of psychological study, and of therapeutic innovations go forward in harness, with each building on the knowledge stemming from the other two.

References

August, G., Stewart, M. and Tsai, L. (1983) The incidence of cognitive disabilities in the siblings of autistic children, *British Journal of Psychiatry*, **138**, 416–422.

Azrin, N. and Foxx, R. (1971) A rapid method of toilet training the institutionalized mentally retarded, *Journal of Applied Behaviour Analysis*, **4**, 89–99.

Azrin, N., Sneed, T. and Foxx, R. (1974) Dry bed training: Rapid elimination of childhood enuresis, *Behaviour Research and Therapy*, **12**, 147–156.

Baker, B., Heifetz, L. and Murphy, R. (1980) Behavioural training for parents of mentally retarded children: One year follow-up, *American Journal of Mental Deficiency*, **85**, 31–38.

Baker, M. and Nelson, K. (1984) Recasting and related conversational techniques for triggering syntactic advances by young children, *First Language*. **5**, 3–22.

Bandura, A. (1969) *Principles of Behaviour Modification*. New York: Holt, Rinehart & Winston.

Barnes, S., Gutfreund, M., Satterly, D. and Wells, G. (1983) Characteristics of adult speech which predict children's language development, *Journal of Child Language*, **10**, 65–84.

Baron-Cohen, S., Leslie, A. and Frith, U. (1985) Does the autistic child have 'A theory of mind'? *Cognition*, **21**, 37–46.

Baron-Cohen, S., Leslie, A. and Frith, U (1986) Mechanical, behavioural and intentional understanding of picture stories in autistic children, *British Journal of Developmental Psychology*, **4**, 113–125.

Bartak L., and Rutter, M. (1973) Special educational treatment of autistic children: A comparative study. I: Design of study and characteristics of units, *Journal of Child Psychology and Psychiatry*, **14**, 161–179.

Bartak, L. and Rutter, M. (1976) Differences between mentally retarded and normally intelligent autistic children, *Journal of Autism and Childhood Schizophrenia*, **6**, 109–120.

Bartolucci, G., Pierce, S. and Streiner, D. (1980) Cross-sectional studies of grammatical morphemes in autistic and mentally retarded children, *Journal of Autism and Developmental Disorders*, **10**, 39–50.

Baumeister, A. (1967) Learning abilities of the mentally retarded. In Baumeister, A. (ed.), *Mental Retardation: Appraisal, Education and Rehabilitation*. London: University of London Press.

Bender, L. (1953) Childhood schizophrenia, *Psychiatry Quarterly*, **27**, 663–681.

Berlin, I. (1978) Psychotherapeutic work with parents of psychotic children. In Rutter, M. and Schopler, E. (eds.), *Autism: A Reappraisal of Concepts and Treatment*. New York: Plenum.

Bettelheim, B. (1967) *The Empty Fortress: Infantile Autism and the Birth of the Self*. New York: Free Press.

Black, J.M. (1978) Families with handicapped children—who helps whom and how? *Child Care, Health and Development*, **4**, 239–245

Black, M., Freeman, B. and Montgomery, J. (1975) Systematic observation of play behaviour in autistic children, *Journal of Autism and Childhood Schizophrenia*, **5**, 363–372.

Boatman, M. and Szurek, S. (1960) A clinical study of childhood schizophrenia. In D. Jackson (ed.), *The Etiology of Schizophrenia*. New York: Basic Books.

Bolton, D., Collins, S. and Steinberg, D. (1983) The treatment of obsessive–compulsive disorder in adolescence: A report of 15 cases, *British Journal of Psychiatry*, **142**, 456–464.

Boniface, D. and Graham, P. (1979) The 3-year-old and his attachment to a special soft object, *Journal of Child Psychology and Psychiatry*, **20**, 217–224.

Bretherton, I. and Waters, E. (eds.) (1985) *Growing Points of Attachment Theory and Research*. Monographs of the Society for Research in Child Development. Serial no. 209, **50**, 601–616.

Bricker, W. and Bricker, D. (1972) Assessment and modification of verbal imitation with low functioning retarded children. *Journal of Speech and Hearing Research*, **15**, 690–698.

Brown, R. (1973) *A first language: The early stages*. London: George Allen & Unwin.

Browning, R. M. (1971) Treatment effects of a total behaviour modification program with five autistic children, *Behaviour Research and Therapy*, **9**, 319–328.

Byrne, E. and Cunningham, C. (1985) The effects of mentally handicapped children on families: A conceptual review, *Journal of Child Psychology and Psychiatry*, **26**, 847–864.

Campbell, M. (1978) Pharmacotherapy. In Rutter, M. and Schopler, E. (eds.), *Autism: A Reappraisal of Concepts and Treatment*. Plenum: New York, pp. 337–355.

Cantwell, D., Baker, L. and Rutter, M. (1978) A comparative study of infantile autism and specific developmental receptive language disorder. IV: Analysis of syntax and language function, *Journal of Child Psychology and Psychiatry*, **19**, 351–362.

Cantwell, D. P., Baker, L. and Rutter, M. (1979) Families of autistic and dysphasic children. I: Family life and interaction patterns, *Archives of General Psychiatry*, **36**, 682–688.

Cantwell, D., Howlin, P. and Rutter, M. (1977) The analysis of language level and language function, *British Journal of Disorders of Communication*, **12**, 119–135.

Carr, E. and Durand, V. (1985a) The social communicative basis of severe behavior problems in children. In Reiss, S. and Bootzin, R. (eds.), *Theoretical Issues in Behavior Therapy*. New York: Academic Press.

Carr, E. and Durand, V. M. (1985b) Reducing behaviour problems through functional communication training, *Journal of Applied Behaviour Analysis*, **18**, 111–126.

Carr, J. (1982) *Helping Your Handicapped Child*. London: Penguin.

Carr, J. (1984) Family processes and parent involvement. In Dobbing, J. (ed.), *Scientific Studies in Mental Retardation: Proceedings of First European Symposium*. London: Macmillan.

Charlop, M. (1983) The effects of echolalia on acquisition and generalization of receptive labelling in autistic children, *Journal of Applied Behaviour Analysis*, **16**, 111–126.

Cheseldine, S. and McConkey, R. (1979) Parental speech to young Down's Syndrome children: An intevention study, *American Journal of Mental Deficiency*, **83**, 612–620.

Chomsky, N. (1965) *Aspects of a Theory of Syntax*. Cambridge Mass.: MIT Press.

Clardy, E. (1951) A study of the development and course of schizophrenia in children, *Psychiatry Quarterly*, **25**, 81–90.

Clark, H. and Clark, E. (1977) *Psychology and Language: An Introduction to Linguistics*. New York: Harcourt Brace.

Clark, P. and Rutter, M. (1977) Compliance and resistance in autistic children, *Journal of Autism and Childhood Schizophrenia*, **7**, 33–48.

Clark, P. and Rutter, M. (1979) Task difficulty and task performance in autistic children, *Journal of Child Psychology and Psychiatry*, **20**, 271–285.

Clark, P. and Rutter, M. (1981) Autistic children's responses to structure and interpersonal demands, *Journal of Autism and Developmental Disorders*, **11**, 201–217.

Clements, J. (1985) Training parents of mentally handicapped children, *Newsletter: Association for Child Psychology and Psychiatry*, **7**, 2–9.

Clements, J., Bidder, R., Gardner, S., Bryant, G. and Gray, O. (1980) A home advisory service for pre-school children with developmental delays, *Child: Care, Health and Development*, **6**, 25–33.

Clements, J., Evans, C., Jones, C., Osborne, K. and Upton, G. (1982) Evaluation of home based language training programme with several mentally handicapped children, *Behaviour Research and Therapy*, **20**, 243–249.

Cromer, R. (1980) Normal language development: recent progress. In Hersov, L., Berger, M. and Nicol, A. (eds.) *Language and Language Disorders in Childhood*. New York: Pergamon Press, pp. 1–21.

Cromer, R. (1987) Language acquisition. Lanaguage disorder and cognitive development. In Yule, W. and Rutter, M. (eds.), *Language Development and Disorders. Clinics in Developmental Medicine* London and Oxford: MacKeith Press/Blackwell.

Cross, T. G. (1977) Mothers' speech adjustments: The contribution of selected child listener variables. In Snow, C., and Ferguson, C. (eds.), *Talking to Children: Language Input and Acquisitions*. Cambridge: University of Cambridge Press.

Currie, K. and Brannigan, C. (1970) Behavioural analysis and modification with an autistic child. In Hutt, S. and Hutt, C. (eds.), *Behaviour Studies in Psychiatry*. Oxford: Pergamon.

Danaher, B. (1974) Theoretical foundations and clinical applications of the Premack principle: review and critique, *Behavior Therapy*, **5**, 307–323.

Delacato, C. H. (1974) *The Ultimate Stranger: The Autistic Child*. New York: Doubleday.

DeMyer, M. K. (1979) *Parents and Children in Autism*. New York: John Wiley.

DeMyer, M., Barton, S., DeMyer, W., Norton, J.A., Allen, J. and Steele, R. (1973) Prognosis in autism: A follow up study, *Journal of Autism and Childhood Schizophrenia*, **3**, 199–246.

DeMyer, M.K., Barton, S., Alpern, G.D., Kimberlin, C., Allen, J., Yang, E. and Steele, R. (1974) The measured intelligence of autistic children, *Journal of Autism and Childhood Schizophrenia*, **4**, 42–60.

De Villiers, J. and De Villiers, P. (1973) A cross sectional study of the acquisition of grammatical morphemes in child speech, *Journal of Psycholinguistic Research*, **2**, 267–278.

Dewey, M. and Everard, P. (1974) The near normal autistic adolescent, *Journal of Autism and Childhood Schizophrenia*, **4**, 348–356.

Deykin, E. and MacMahon, B. (1979) The incidence of seizures among children with autistic symptoms, *American Journal of Psychiatry*, **136**, 1310–1312.

Doll, E. A. (1965) *Vineland Social Maturity Scale*. Circle Pines, Minn.: American Guidelines Service.

Dornberg, N. (1978) Some negative effects on family integration of health and education services, *Rehabilitation Literature*, **39**, 107–110.

Douglas, J. W. B., Lawson, A., Cooper, J. E. and Cooper, E. (1968) Family interaction and the activities of young children. Method of assessment, *Journal of Child Psychology and Psychiatry*, **9**, 157–171.

Douglas, J. and Richman, N. (1984) *My Child Won't Sleep*. Harmondsworth, Middlesex: Penguin.

Egel, A.L. (1981) Reinforcer variation: Implications of motivating developmentally disabled children, *Journal of Applied Behavior Analysis*, **14**, 345–350.

Egel, A., Koegel, R. and Schreibman, L. (1980) Review of educational treatment procedures for autistic children. In Mann, L. and Sabatino, D. (eds.), *The Fourth Review of Special Education*. New York: Grune and Stratton.

Eisenberg, L. (1956) The autistic child in adolescence, *American Journal of Psychiatry*, **112**, 607–612.

Elgar, S. (1966) Teaching autistic children. In Wing, J. K. (ed.), *Early Childhood Autism: Clinical, Educational and Social Aspects*. Oxford: Pergamon.

Eysenck, H. (ed.) (1960) *Behaviour Therapy and the Neuroses*. New York: Pergamon.

Fay, W. and Schuler, A. (1980) *Emerging Language in Autistic Children*. London: Edward Arnold.

Fenske, E. C., Zalenski, S., Krantz, P. J. and McClannahan, L. E. (1985) Age at intervention and treatment outcome for autistic children in a comprehensive intervention program, *Analysis and Intervention in Developmental Disorders*, **5**, 49–58.

Ferster, C. B. and DeMyer, M. K. (1961) The development of performances in autistic children in an automatically controlled environment, *Journal of Chronic Diseases*, **13**, 312–345.

Ferster, C. B. and DeMyer, M. K. (1962) A method for the experimental analysis of the behavior of autistic children, *American Journal of Orthopsychiatry*, **32**, 89–98.

Folstein, S. and Rutter, M. (1977) Infantile autism: A genetic study of 21 twin pairs, *Journal of Child Psychology and Psychiatry*, **18**, 297–321.

Folstein, S. and Rutter, M. (1987) Autism: Familial Aggregation and Genetic Implications, *Journal of Autism and Developmental Disorders* (in press).

Frankel, F. and Graham, V. (1976) Systematic observation of classroom behavior of retarded and autistic pre-school children, *American Journal of Mental Deficiency*, **81**, 73–84.

Frith, U. (1969) Emphasis and meaning in recall in normal and autistic children, *Language and Speech*, **12**, 29–38.

Frith, U. (1970a) Studies in pattern detection. I: Immediate recall of auditory sequences, *Journal of Abnormal Psychology*, **76**, 413–420.

Frith, U. (1970b) Studies in pattern detection. II: Reproduction and production of colour sequences, *Journal of Experimental Child Psychology*, **10**, 120–135.

Frith, U. (1971) Spontaneous patterns produced by autistic normal and subnormal children. In Rutter, M. (ed.), *Infantile Autism: Concepts, Characteristics and Treatment*. London: Churchill Livingstone.

Frith, U. (1972) Cognitive mechanisms in autism: Experiment with color and tone sequence production, *Journal of Autism and Childhood Schizophrenia*, **2**, 160–173.

Frith, U., and Snowling, M. (1983) Reading for meaning and reading for sound in autistic and dyslexic children, *British Journal of Developmental Psychology*, **1**, 329–342.

Fulwood, D. (1981) Mum or supermum? *Australian Citizen Limited*, **August**, 241–247.

Furrow, D., Nelson, K. and Benedict, H. (1979) Mother's speech to children and syntactic development: Some simple relationships, *Journal of Child Language*, **6**, 423–442.

Gajzago, C. and Prior, M. (1974) Two cases of 'Recovery' in Kanner Syndrome, *Archives of General Psychiatry*, **31**, 264–268.

Gardner, J. (1976) Three aspects of childhood autism. PhD thesis, University of Leicester.

Gath, A. (1974) Siblings' reaction to mental handicap: A comparison of the brothers and sisters of mongol children, *Journal of Child Psychology and Psychiatry*, **15**, 187–198.

Gath, A. (1978) *Down's Syndrome and the Family: The Early Years*. London: Academic Press.

Gelfand, D. M. and Hartmann, D. P. (1975) *Child Behavior Analysis and Therapy*. New York: Pergamon.

Gleitman, L., Newport, E. and Gleitman, H. (1984) The current status of the Motherese hypothesis, *Journal of Child Language*, **11**, 43–80.

Goetz, L., Schuler, A. and Sailor, W. (1983) Motivational considerations in teaching language to severely handicapped students. In Hersen, M., Van Hasselt, V. and

Matson, J. (eds.), *Behaviour Therapy for the Developmentally and Physically Disabled*. New York: Academic Press.

Goldfarb, W. (1961) *Childhood Schizophrenia*. Cambridge, Mass.: Harvard University Press.

Goldfarb, W. (1974) *Growth and Change of Schizophrenic Children*. New York: Wiley.

Gray, B.B. and Ryan, B.P. (1973) *A Language Program for the Non Language Child*. Champaign, Ill.: Research Press.

Guess, D., Sailor, W. and Baer, D.M. (1974) To teach language to retarded children. In Schiefelbusch, R.L. and Lloyd, L.L. (eds.), *Language Perspectives—Acquisition, Retardation and Intervention*. London: Macmillan.

Guess, D., Sailor, W. and Baer, D. (1976) *Functional Speech and Language Training for the Severely Handicapped. Part I: Persons and Things*. Lawrence, Kans. H & H. Enterprises.

Hall, R.V. (1971) *Managing Behavior*. Lawrence, Kans.: H. & H. Enterprises.

Halpern, W.I. (1970) The schooling of autistic children: Preliminary findings, *American Journal of Orthopsychiatry*, **40**, 665–671.

Harris, J. and Wolchick, S. (1982) Teaching speech skills to non-verbal children and their parents. In Steffen, J. and Karoly, P. (eds.), *Autism and Severe Psychopathology: Advances in Child Behavioural Analysis and Therapy*, Volume 2. Lexington, Mass.: Lexington Books, pp. 289–314.

Hemsley, R. and Carr, J. (1980) Methods of increasing behaviour with the severely retarded. In Yule, W. and Carr, J. (eds.), *Behaviour Modification for the Severely Retarded*. London: Croom Helm.

Hemsley, R., Howlin, P., Berger, M., Hersov, L., Holbrook, D., Rutter, M. and Yule, W. (1978) Treating autistic children in a family context. In Rutter, M. and Schopler, E. (eds.), *Autism: Reappraisal of Concepts and Treatment*. New York: Plenum.

Hermelin, B. (1976) Coding the sense modalities. In Wing, L. (ed.), *Early Childhood Autism* (2nd edn), London: Pergamon, pp. 135–168.

Hermelin, B. and Frith, U. (1971) Psychological studies of childhood autism. Can autistic children make sense of what they see and hear? *Journal of Special Education*, **5**, 1107–1117.

Hermelin, B. and O'Connor, N. (1970) *Psychological Experiments with Autistic Children*. London: Pergamon.

Hewett, F. (1965) Teaching speech to an autistic child through operant conditioning, *American Journal of Orthopsychiatry*, **35**, 927–936.

Hingtgen, J.N., Coulter, S.K. and Churchill, D.W. (1967) Intensive reinforcement of imitative behavior in mute autistic children, *Archives of General Psychiatry*, **17**, 36–43.

Hobson, R.P. (1982) The autistic child's knowledge of persons. Paper presented at Symposium on Affective and Social Understanding, Durham, September 1982.

Hobson, R.P. (1983) The autistic child's recognition of age-related features of people, animals and things, *British Journal of Developmental Psychology*, **1**, 343–352.

Hobson, R.P. (1986) The autistic child's appraisal of expressions of emotion. *Journal of Child Psychology and Psychiatry*, **27**, 321–342.

Holland, J. (1981) The Lancaster Portage Project, *Health Visitor*, **54**, 486–488.

Holmes, N., Hemsley, R., Rickett, J. and Likierman, H. (1982) Parents as cotherapists: Their perceptions of a home-based behavioral treatment for autistic children. *Journal of Autism and Developmental Disorders*, **12**, 331–342.

Horsborough, K., Cross, T. and Ball, J. (1985) Conversational interactions between mothers and their autistic, dysphasic and normal children. In Cross, T. and Riach, L. (eds.) *Proceedings of the Second National Child Development Conference. ACER*.

Howlin, P. (1979) Training parents to modify the language of their autistic children: a home based approach. Unpublished PhD thesis, University of London.

Howlin, P. (1980) Language training with the severely retarded. In Yule, W. and Carr, J. (eds.), *Behaviour Modification with the Severely Retarded*. London: Croom Helm.

Howlin, P. (1981a) The effectiveness of operant language training with autistic children, *Journal of Autism and Developmental Disorders,* **11**, 89–106.

Howlin, P. (1981b) The results of a home-based language training programme with autistic children, *British Journal of Disorders of Communication,* **16**, 21–29.

Howlin, P. (1984a) Parents as therapists: A review. In Miller, D. (ed.), *Remediating Children's Language.* London: Croom Helm.

Howlin, P. (1984b) The acquisition of grammatical morphemes in autistic children: A replication of the findings of Bartolucci et al 1980, *Journal of Autism and Developmental Disorders,* **14**, 127–136.

Howlin, P. (1985) Special educational treatment. In Rutter, M. and Hersov, L. (eds.), *Child and Adolescent Psychiatry* (2nd edn). Oxford: Blackwell.

Howlin, P. (1986) An overview of social behaviour in autism. In Schopler, E. and Mesibov, G. (eds.), *Social Behaviour in Autism.* New York: Plenum

Howlin, P. (1987a) Behavioural approaches. In Yule, W. and Rutter, M. (eds.), *Lanaguage Development and Disorders. Clinics in Developmental Medicine,* London and Oxford: MacKeith Press/Blackwell.

Howlin, P. (1987b) The treatment of obsessions and compulsions. In Corbett, J. (ed.), *Proceedings of the Symposium on Behaviour Disorders and Mental Retardation.* London: Royal Society of Medicine.

Howlin, P., Cantwell, D., Marchant, R., Berger, M. and Rutter, M. (1973a) Analyzing mothers' speech to young autistic children: A methodological study, *Journal of Anbormal Child Psychology,* **1**, 317–339.

Howlin, P., Marchant, R., Rutter, M., Berger, M., Hersov, L. and Yule, W. (1973b) A home-based approach to the treatment of autistic children, *Journal of Autism and Childhood Schizophrenia,* **4**, 308–336.

Howlin, P. and Rutter, M. (1987) The verbal interaction between autistic children and their mothers: A preliminary Causal Analysis Journal of Child Psychology and Psychiatry. (In press)

Jeffree, D. M. and Cashdan, A. (1971) Severely subnormal children and their parents: An experiment in language improvement, *British Journal of Educational Psychology,* **4**, 184–194.

Jensen, G. D. and Womack, M. S. (1967) Operant conditioning techniques applied in the treatment of an autistic child, *American Journal of Orthopsychiatry,* **37**, 30–34.

Jones, M. C. (1924) The elimination of children's fears, *Journal of Experimental Psychology,* **7**, 382–390.

Jose, P. and Cohen, D. (1980) The effects of unfamiliar tasks or teachers on autistic children's negativism, *Journal of American Academy of Child Psychiatry,* **19**, 78–89.

Kahn, J. V. (1977) A comparison of manual and oral language training with mute retarded children, *Mental Retardation,* **15**, 21–23.

Kanner, L. (1943) Autistic disturbances of affective contact, *Nervous Child,* **2**, 217–250.

Kanner, L. (1951) The conception of wholes and parts in early infantile autism, *American Journal of Psychiatry,* **108**, 23–26.

Kanner, L. (1954) To what extent is early infantile autism determined by constitutional inadequacies. Reprinted in Kanner, L. (1973), *Childhood Psychosis: Initial Studies and New Insights.* Washington: Winston.

Kanner, L. (1964) *A History of the Cure and Study of the Mentally Retarded.* Springfield, Ill. C. C. Thomas.

Kanner, L. (1971) Follow up study of eleven autistic children originally reported in 1943. *Journal of Autism and Childhood Schizophrenia,* **1**, 119–145.

Kanner, L. (1973) *Childhood Psychosis: Initial Studies and New Insights.* Washington: Winston.

Kiernan, C. (1983) The use of non-social communication techniques with autistic individuals. *Journal of Child Psychology and Psychiatry,* **24**, 339–376.

Kiernan, C. (1987) Non-vocal communication systems: A critical survey. In Yulc, W. and

Rutter, M. (eds.), *Language Development and Disorders. Clinics in Developmental Medicine.* London and Oxford: MacKeith Press/Blackwell.

Klee, T. and Fitzgerald, M. (1985) The relation between grammatical development and mean length of utterance in morphemes. *Journal of Child Language,* 12, 251–270.

Koegel, R. and Covert, A. (1972) The relationship of self stimulation to learning in autistic children, *Journal of Applied Behavior Analysis,* 5, 381–388.

Koegel, R. and Rincover, A. (1974) Treatment of psychiatric children in a classroom environment, *Journal of Applied Behavior Analysis,* 7, 45–49.

Koegel, R. and Rincover, A. (1976) Some detrimental effects of using extra stimuli to guide learning in normal and autistic children. *Journal of Abnormal Child Psychology,* 4, 59–61.

Koegel, R., Rincover, A. and Egel, A. (eds.) (1982) *Educating and Understanding Autistic Children.* Houston; Tex.: College Press.

La Greca, A. (1981) Social behaviour and social perception in learning disabled children: A review with implications for social skills training, *Journal of Pediatric Psychology,* 6, 395–416.

Langdell, T. (1978) Recognition of faces: An approach to the study of autism, *Journal of Child Psychology and Psychiatry,* 19, 255–268.

Lepper, M. (1981) Intrinsic and extrinsic motivation in children with autism. In Collins, W. (ed.), *Aspects of the Development of Competence.* Hillsdale, Erlbaum NJ: pp. 155–214.

Ling, D. and Ling, A. H. (1974) Communication development in the first three years of life, *Journal of Speech and Hearing Research,* 17, 146–159.

Litt, M. and Schreibman, L. (1982) Stimulus specific reinforcement in the acquisition of receptive labels by autistic children, *Journal of Analysis and Intervention in Development Disabilities,* 1, 171–186.

Lord, C. (1984) The development of peer relationships in children with autism. In Morrison, F., McHale, F., Lord, C. and Keating, D. *Applied Developmental Psychology I.* New York: Academic Press, pp. 165—229.

Lotter, V. (1974) Factors related to outcome in autistic children, *Journal of Autism and Childhood Schizophrenia,* 4, 263–277.

Lotter, V. (1978) Follow up studies. In Rutter, M. and Schopler, E. (eds.), *Autism: A Reappraisal of Concepts and Treatment.* New York: Plenum, pp. 475–495.

Lovaas, O. (1966) A program for the establishment of speech in psychotic children. In Wing, J. K. (ed.), *Early Childhood Autism: Clinical, Educational and Social Aspects.* Oxford: Pergamon.

Lovaas, O. (1977) *The Autistic Child: Language Development through Behaviour Modification.* New York: Wiley.

Lovaas, O. (1978) Parents as therapists for autistic children. In Rutter, M. and Schopler, E. (eds.), *Autism: A Reappraisal of Concepts and Treatment.* New York: Plenum.

Lovaas, O., Freitag, F., Gold, U. and Kassorla, I. (1965) Experimental studies in childhood schizophrenia. Analysis of self destructive behaviour. *Journal of Experimental Child Psychology,* 2, 76–84.

Lovaas, O., Koegel, R., Simmons, J.Q. and Stevens, J. (1973) Some generalizations and follow up measures on autistic children in behavior therapy, *Journal of Applied Behavior Analysis,* 6, 131–165.

Lovaas, O., Schaeffer, B. and Simmons, J.Q. (1965) Experimental studies in childhood schizophrenia: Building social behaviour in autistic children by use of electric shock, *Journal of Experimental Research in Personality,* 1, 99–109.

McConichie, M. R. (1974) Developing syntax in retarded children: Two individual case studies with parents as therapists. Unpublished M. Phil thesis. University of London.

McConnell, O. (1967) Control of eye contact in an autistic child, *Journal of Child Psychology and Psychiatry,* 8, 249–255.

McCubbin, H., Joy, C., Cauble, A., Correau, J., Patterson, J. and Needle, R. (1980) Family stress and coping: A decade review, *Journal of Marriage and the Family*, **42**, 855–871.

McCullagh, P. and Nelder J. (1983) Generalized Linear Models ... Monographs on Statistics & Applied Probability. London: Chapman Hall.

McDonagh, T.S. and McNamara, J.R. (1973) Design criteria relationships in behavior therapy with children, *Journal of Child Psychology and Psychiatry*, **14**, 271–282.

McHale, S. (1983) Social interactions of autistic and non-handicapped children during free play, *American Journal of Orthopsychiatry*, **53**, 81.

McHale. S., Olley, J., Marcus, L. and Simeonsson, R. (1981) Non handicapped peers as tutors for autistic children, *Exceptional Children*, **48**, 263–265.

McHale, S. and Simeonsson, R. (1980) Effects of interaction on non-handicapped children's attitudes towards autistic children, *American Journal of Mental Deficiency*, **85**, 18–25.

McHale, S., Simeonsson, R., Marcus, L. and Olley, J. (1980) The social and symbolic quality of autistic children's communication, *Journal of Autism and Developmental Disorders*, **10**, 299–314.

Mahalski, P. (1983) The incidence of attachment objects and oral habits at bedtime in two longitudinal samples of children age 1.5 to 7 years, *Journal of Child Psychology and Psychiatry*, **24**, 283–296.

Marchant, R., Howlin, P., Yule, W. and Rutter, M. (1974) Graded change in the treatment of the behaviour of autistic children, *Journal of Child Psychology and Psychiatry*, **15**, 221–227.

Marcus, L., Lansing, M., Andrews, C. and Schopler, E. (1978) Improvement of teaching effectiveness in parents of autistic children, *Journal of American Academy of Child Psychiatry*, **17**, 625–639.

Marks, I. (1975) Behavioural treatment of phobic and obsessive–compulsive disorders: A critical appraisal. In Hersen, M., Eisler, R. and Miller, P. (eds.), *Progress in Behaviour Modification*. New York: Academic Press.

Marshall, G.R. (1966) Toilet training of an autistic eight-year-old through conditioning therapy: A case report, *Behavioural Research and Therapy*, **4**, 242–245.

Marshall, N. and Hegrenes, J.R. (1970) Programmed communication therapy for autistic, mentally retarded children, *Journal of Speech and Hearing Disorders*, **35**, 70–83.

Martlew, M. (1987) Prelinguistic conversation. In Yule, W. and Rutter, M. (eds.), *Language Development and Disorders. Clinics in Development Medicine*. London and Oxford: MacKeith Press/Blackwell.

Martin, G.L., England, G., Kaprowy, E., Kilgour, K. and Pilek, V. (1968) Operant conditioning of kindergarten class behaviour in autistic children, *Behaviour Research and Therapy*, **6**, 281–294.

Mathis, M.I. (1971) Training of a 'disturbed' boy using the mother as therapist: A case study, *Behavior Therapy*, **2**, 233–239.

Meadow, K., Greenberg, M. and Erting, C. (1983) Attachment behaviour of deaf children with deaf parents, *Journal of American Academy of Child Psychiatry*, **22**, 23–28.

Meadow, K., Greenberg, M., Erting, C. and Carmichael, H. (1981) Interactions of deaf mothers and deaf pre-school children: Comparisons with three other groups of deaf and hearing dyads, *American Annals of the Deaf*, **126**, 454–468.

Mecham, M.J. (1958) *Verbal Language Development Scale*. Beverly Hills, Calif.: Western Psychological Services.

Minton, J., Campbell, M., Green, W., Jennings, S. and Samit, C. (1982) Cognitive assessment of siblings of autistic children, *Journal of American Academy of Child Psychiatry*, **21**, 256–261.

Mirenda, P., Donnelan, A. and Yoder, N. (1983) Gaze behavior: A new look at an old problem, *Journal of Autism and Developmental Disorders*, **13**, 397–409.

Mishler, E. and Waxler, N. (1965) Family interaction processes and schizophrenia: A review of current theories, *Merrill Palmer Quarterly*, 11, 269–316.

Mittler, P. (1979) Patterns of partnership between parents and professionals, *Teaching and Training*, 17, 111–116.

Mittler, P., Gillies, S. and Jukes, E. (1966) Prognosis in psychotic children. Report of follow up study, *Journal of Mental Deficiency Research*, 10, 73–83.

Mittler, P. and Mittler, H. (1983) Partnerships with parents: An overview. In Mittler, P. and McConichie, H. (eds.), *Parents, Professionals and Mentally Handicapped People*. London: Croom Helm.

Morris, R. and Kratochwill, T. (1983a) *The Practise of Child Therapy*. Oxford: Pergamon.

Morris, R. and Kratochwill, T. (1983b) *Treating Children's Fears and Phobias*. Oxford: Pergamon.

Murphy, G. (1982) Sensory reinforcement in the mentally handicapped and autistic child: A review. *Journal of Autism and Developmental Disorders*, 12, 265–278.

Murphy, G. (1987) Direct observation as an assessment tool in functional analysis and treatment. In Hogg, J. and Raynes, N. (eds.), *Assessment in Mental Handicap: A Guide to Tests, Batteries and Check Lists*. London: Croom Helm.

Murphy, G. and Wilson, B. (1985) *Self Injurious Behaviour*. Bristol: BIMH Publications.

Nelson, K. (1977) Facilitating children's syntax acquisition, *Developmental Psychology*, 13, 101–107.

Nelson, K. (1983) (Ed.) Children's Language, 4, Hillside, New Jersey: Erlbaum.

Nelson, R. O. and Evans, I. M. (1968) The combination of learning principles and speech therapy techniques in the treatment of non-communicating children, *Journal of Child Psychology and Psychiatry*, 9, 111–124.

Newport, E., Gleitman, H. and Gleitman, L. (1977) Mother, I'd rather do it myself: Some effects and non effects of maternal speech style. In Snow, C. and Ferguson, C. (eds.), *Talking to Children*. Cambridge: Cambridge University Press.

Ney, P., Palvesky, A. E. and Markely, J. (1971) Relative effectiveness of operant conditioning and play therapy in childhood schizophrenia, *Journal of Autism and Childhood Schizophrenia*, 1, 337–349.

O'Gorman, G. (1970) *The Nature of Childhood Autism*, second edition. London: Butterworth.

O'Leary, K. (1980) Pills or skills for hyperactive children, *Journal of Applied Behavior Analysis*, 13, 191–204.

Patterson, G. (1982) *Coercive Family Process*. Eugene, Oreg.: Castalia Publishing Company.

Patterson, G. R. and Brodsky, G. (1966) A behaviour modification programme for a child with multiple problem behaviours, *Journal of Child Psychology and Psychiatry*, 7, 277–295.

Patterson, G., Cobb, J. and Ray, R. (1973) A social engineering technology for re-training the families of aggressive boys. In Adams, H. and Unikel, I. (eds.), *Issues and Trends in Behavior Therapy*. Springfield, Ill.: C. C. Thomas.

Patterson, G. and Reid, J. (1973) Intervention for families of aggressive boys: A replication study, *Behavioural Research and Therapy*, 10, 168–185.

Paul, R. and Cohen, D. (1984) Outcomes of severe disorders of language acquisition, *Journal of Autism and Developmental Disorders*, 14, 405–422.

Paul, R., Cohen, D. and Caparulo, B. (1983) A longitudinal study of patients with severe developmental disorders of language learning, *Journal of American Academy of Child Psychiatry*, 22, 525–534.

Pawlicki, R. (1970) Behavior-therapy research with children: A critical review, *Canadian Journal of Behavioural Sciences*, 2, 163–173.

Piggott, L. R., Gdowski, C. L., Villanueva, D., Fischhoff, J. and Frohman, C. F. (1986) Brief communication: Side effects of fenfluramine in autistic children. *Journal of the American Academy of Child Psychiatry*, 25, 2, 287–289.

Premack, D. (1959) Towards empirical behavior laws. I: Positive reinforcement, *Psychological Review*, **66**, 219–233.

Prior, M. and Griffin, M. (1985) *Hyperactivity: Diagnosis and Management*. London: Heinemann.

Prizant, B. and Duchan, J. (1981) The functions of immediate echolalia in autistic children, *Journal of Speech and Hearing Disorders*, **22**, 241–246.

Reynell, J. (1969) *Reynell Developmental Language Scales*. Windsor, England: NFER Publishing Company.

Reynell, J. (1977) *Reynell Developmental Language Scales* (revised). Windsor, England: NFER Publishing Company.

Richardson, S., Dohrenwend, B. and Klein, D. (1965) *Interviewing: Its Forms and Functions*. London: Basic Books.

Ricks, D. M. (1975) Verbal communication in pre-verbal normal and autistic children. In O'Conner, M. (ed.), *Language, Cognitive Deficits and Retardation*. London: Butterworths.

Riguet, C., Taylor, N., Benaroya, S. and Klein, L. (1981) Symbolic play in autistic, Downs and normal children of equivalent mental age, *Journal of Autism and Developmental Disorders*, **11**, 439–443.

Rimland, B., Calloway, E. and Dreyfus, P. (1978) The effects of high doses of Vitamin B₆ on autistic children: A double blind crossover study. *American Journal of Psychiatry*, **135**, 472–475.

Risley, T. R. and Baer, D. M. (1973) Operant behavior modification: The deliberate development of behavior. In Caldwell, B. C. and Riccuitti, H. N. (eds.), *Review of Child Development Research. 3: Child Development and Social Policy*. Chicago: University of Chicago Press.

Risley, T. and Wolf, M. (1967) Establishing functional speech in echolalic children, *Behaviour Research and Therapy*, **5**, 73–88.

Ritvo, E. R., Freeman, D. J., Geller, E. and Yuwiler, A. (1983) Effects of fenfluramine on 14 autistic outpatients. *Journal of the American Academy of Child Psychiatry*, **22**, 549–558.

Rosenthal, J., Massie, H. and Wulff, K. (1980) A comparison of cognitive development in normal and psychotic children in the first 2 years of life from home movies, *Journal of Autism and Developmental Disorders*, **10**, 433–444.

Rutter, M. (1970) Autistic children. Infancy to adulthood, *Seminars in Psychiatry*, **2**, 435–450.

Rutter, M. (1971) The description and classification of infantile autism. In Churchill, D. W., Alpern, G. D. and DeMyer, M. K. (eds.), *Infantile Autism*. Springfield, Ill.: C. C. Thomas.

Rutter, M. (1972) Childhood schizophrenia reconsidered, *Journal of Autism and Childhood Schizophrenia*, **2**, 315–337.

Rutter, M. (1978) Language disorder and infantile autism. In Rutter, M. and Schopler, E. (eds.), *Autism: A Reappraisal of Concepts and Treatment*. New York: Plenum.

Rutter, M. (1979) Language, cognition and autism. In Katzman, R. (ed.), *Congenital and Acquired Cognitive Disorders*. New York: Raven Press.

Rutter, M. (1980) Language training with autistic children. How does it work and what does it achieve. In Hersov, L. A., Berger, M. and Nichol, R. (eds.), *Language and Language Disorders in Children*. Oxford: Pergamon Press.

Rutter, M. (1983) Cognitive deficits in the pathogenesis of autism, *Journal of Child Psychology and Psychiatry*, **24**, 513–533.

Rutter, M. (1985a) Infantile autism and other pervasive developmental disorders. In Rutter, M. and Hersov, L. (eds.), *Child and Adolescent Psychiatry (2nd edn)*. Oxford: Blackwell.

Rutter, M. (1985b) Family and school influences in cognitive development, *Journal of Child Psychology and Psychiatry*, **26**, 349–368.

Rutter, M. (1985c) The treatment of autistic children, *Journal of Child Psychology and Psychiatry*, **26**, 193–214.

Rutter, M. and Bartak, L. (1973) Special education treatment of autistic children: A comparative study. II: Follow-up findings and implications for services, *Journal of Child Psychology and Psychiatry*, **14**, 241–270.

Rutter, M. and Graham, P. (1968) The reliability and validity of the psychiatric assessment of the child, *British Journal of Psychiatry*, **114**, 563–579.

Rutter, M., Graham, P. and Yule, W. (1970) *A Neuropsychiatric Study of Childhood*. Clinics in Developmental Medicine no. 35/36. London: Heinemann.

Rutter, M., Greenfield, D. and Lockyer, L. (1967) A five to fifteen year follow-up study of infantile psychosis. II: Social and behavioural outcome, *British Journal of Psychiatry*, **113**, 1183–1199.

Rutter, M. and Lockyer, L. (1967) A five to fifteen year follow up study of infantile psychosis. I. Description of sample, *British Journal of Psychiatry*, **113**, 1169–1182.

Rutter, M. and Lord, C. (1987) Language impairment associated with psychiatric disturbance. In Rutter, M. and Yule, W. (eds.), *Language Development and Disorder. Clinics in Developmental Medicine*. London and Oxford: MacKeith Press/Blackwell.

Rutter, M. and Schopler E. (1987) Autism and pervasive developmental disorders: Concepts and diagnostic issues. In Rutter, M., Tuma, A. and Lann, I. (eds.), *Assessment and Classification in Child and Adolescent Psychiatry*. New York: Guildford Press.

Rutter, M. and Sussenwein, F. (1971) A developmental and behavioural approach to the treatment of preschool autistic children, *Journal of Autism and Childhood Schizophrenia*, **1**, 376–397.

Rutter, M., Tizard, J. and Whitmore, K. (eds.) (1970) *Education, Health and Behaviour*. London: Longman.

Scherer, N. and Olswang, L. (1984) Role of mothers' expansions in stimulating children's language production, *Journal of Speech and Hearing Research*, **27**, 387–396.

Schopler, E. (1971) Effects of treatment structure on development in autistic children, *Archives in General Psychiatry*, **24**, 415–421.

Schopler, E. (1983) New developments in the definition and diagnosis of autism. In Lahey, B. B. and Kazdin, A. E. (eds.), *Advances in Clinical Child Psychology*, vol. 6. Plenum Press: New York, pp. 93–127.

Schopler, E., Brehm, S. S., Kinsbourne, M. and Reichler, R. J. (1971) Effects of treatment structure on development in autistic children, *Archives of General Psychiatry*, **20**, 174–181.

Schopler, E. and Reichler, R. J. (1971a) Developmental therapy by parents with their own autistic child. In Rutter, M. (ed.), *Infantile Autism: Concepts, Characteristics and Treatment*. London: Churchill Livingstone.

Schopler, E. and Reichler, R. J. (1971b) Parents as co-therapists in the treatment of psychotic children, *Journal of Autism and Childhood Schizophrenia*, **1**, 87–102.

Schopler, E., Mesibov, G. and Baker, A. (1982) Evaluation of treatment for autistic children and their parents, *Journal of American Academy of Child Psychiatry*, **21**, 262–267.

Schwartz, R., Chapman, K., Prelock, P., Terrel, B. and Rowan, L. (1985) Facilitation of early syntax through discourse structure, *Journal of Child Language*, **12**, 1, 13–36.

Shaffer, D. (1985) Nocturnal enuresis: Its investigation and treatment. In Shaffer, D., Ehrhardt, A. and Greenhill, L. (eds.), *The Clinical Guide to Child Psychiatry*. New York: The Free Press.

Shane, H. (1981) Decision making in early augmentative communication system use. In Schiefelbusch, R. and Bricker, D. (eds.), *Early Language: Acquisition and Intervention*. Baltimore, Md.: University Park Press.

Shane, H. (1987) Trends in Communication aid technology for the severely speech impaired system, In Yule, W., Rutter and M. (eds.), *Language Development and*

Disorders. Clinics in Developmental Medicine. London and Oxford: MacKeith Press/Blackwell.

Shapiro, M. B. (1966) The single case in clinical psychological research, *Journal of Genetic Psychology*, **74**, 3–23.

Short, A. (1984) Short term treatment outcome using parents as co-therapists for their own autistic children, *Journal of Child Psychology and Psychiatry*, **25**, 443–458.

Sigman, M., Ungerer, J., Mundy, P. and Sherman, T. (1987) Cognitive functioning in autistic children. In Cohen, D., Donnelan, A. and Paul, R. (eds.), *Handbook of Autism and Atypical Development*. New York: Wiley. (In press)

Simeonsson, R. and McHale, S. (1981) Research on handicapped children: Sibling relationships. *Child: Care, Health and Development*, **7**, 153–171.

Singer, M. T. and Wynne, L. (1963) Differentiating characteristics of parents of childhood schizophrenics, childhood neurotics and young adult schizophrenics, *American Journal of Psychiatry*, **120**, 234–243.

Skinner B. F. (1957) Verbal Behaviour. New York: Appleton Century Crofts.

Skuse, D. (1984) Extreme deprivation in early childhood: Theoretical issues and a comparative review, *Journal of Child Psychology and Psychiatry*, **25**, 543–572.

Sloane, H. N., Johnston, M. K. and Harris, F. R. (1968) Remedial procedures for teaching verbal behavior to speech deficient or defective young children. In Sloane, H. N. and MacAulay, B. D. (eds.), *Operant Procedures in Remedial Speech and Language Training*. New York: Houghton Mifflin.

Sloane, H. N. and MacAulay, B. D. (1968) *Operant Procedures in Remedial Speech and Language Training*. New York: Houghton Mifflin.

Slobin, D. I. (1973) Cognitive pre-requisites for the development of grammar. In Ferguson, C. A. and Slobin, D. I. (eds.), *Studies of Child Language Development*. New York: Holt, Rinehart & Winston.

Spence, J. (1980) *Social Skills Training with Children and Adolescents: A Counsellor's Manual*. Windsor: NFER.

Spradlin, J. and Siegel, G. (1982) Language training in natural and clinical environments, *Journal of Speech and Hearing Disorders*, **47**, 2–6.

Stark, J., Giddan, J. J. and Meisel, M. (1968) Increasing verbal behaviour in an autistic child, *Journal of Speech and Hearing Disorders*, **33**, 42–47.

Stokes, T. and Baer, D. (1977) An implicit technology of generalization, *Journal of Applied Behavior Analysis*, **10**, 349–368.

Stokes, T., Douce, C., Rowbury, T. and Baer, D. (1978) Peer facilitation of generalization in a pre-school setting. *Journal of Abnormal Child Psychiatry*, **6**, 203–209.

Strain, P. (1981) Peer-mediated treatment of exceptional children's withdrawal. *Journal of Exceptional Education Quarterly*, **1**, 93–105.

Strain, P., Kerr, M. and Ragland, E. (1979) Effects of peer mediated social initiations of prompting/reinforcement procedures on the social behavior of autistic children, *Journal of Autism and Developmental Disorders*, **9**, 41–54.

Stutsman, R. (1948) *Guide for Administering the Merrill Palmer Scale of Mental Tests*. New York: Harcourt Brace & World.

Szurek, S. and Berlin, I. (1956) Elements of psychotherapeutics with the schizophrenic child and his parents, *Psychiatry*, **19**, 1–9.

Tiegerman, E. and Primavera, L. (1984) Imitating the autistic child: Facilitating communicative gaze behavior, *Journal of Autism and Developmental Disorders*, **14**, 27–38.

Tinbergen, E. and Tinbergen, N. (1972) Early childhood autism, an ethological approach. *Advances in Ethology. 10: Supplement to Journal of Comparative Ethology*. Paul Parry: Verlag.

Tinbergen, N. and Tinbergen, E. (1988) *'Autistic' Children: New Hope for a Cure*. London: Allen & Unwin.

Tsoi, M. and Yule, W. (1980) Building up new behaviours in shaping, prompting and fading. In Yule, W. and Carr, J. (eds.), *Behaviour Modification for the Mentally Handicapped.* London: Croom Helm, pp. 69–78.

Ullman, L. P. and Krasner, L. (eds.) (1965) *Case Studies in Behavior Modifications.* New York: Holt, Rinehart & Winston.

Ungerer, J. and Sigman, M. (1981) Symbolic play and language comprehension in autistic children, *Journal of American Academy of Child Psychiatry*, 20, 318–337.

Uzgiris, I. (1981) Experience in the social context. Imitation and play. In Bricker, R. and Schiefelbusch, D. (eds.), *Early Language: Acquisition and Intervention.* Baltimore, Md.: University Park Press.

Van Engeland, H., Bodnar, F. and Bolhuis, G. (1985) Some qualitative aspects of the social behaviour of autistic children: An ethological approach, *Journal of Child Psychology and Psychiatry*, 26, 879–894.

Van Hasselt, V., Herson, M., Whitehill, M. and Bellack, A. (1979) Social skill assessment and training for children: An evaluative review, *Behaviour Research and Therapy*, 17, 413–437.

Volkmar, F. R. and Cohen, D. J. (1982) A hierarchical analysis of patterns of non-compliance in autistic and behavior-disturbed children. *Journal of Autism and Developmental Disorders*, 12, 35–42.

Volkmar, F., Hoder, E. and Cohen, D. (1985) Compliance, 'negatiuism' and the effects of treatment structure in autism: an naturalistic study, *Journal of Child Psychology and Psychiatry*, 26, 865–878.

Wahler, R. and Leske, F. (1973) Accurate and inaccurate observer summary reports: Reinforcement theory interpretation and investigation, *Journal of Nervous and Mental Disorders*, 156, 386–394.

Wallace, B. (1975) Negativism in verbal and non-verbal responses of autistic children, *Journal of Abnormal Psychology*, 84, 138–143.

Wells, G. and Guttfreund, M. (1986) The conversational requirements for language learning. In Rutter, M., Yule, W. and Bax, M. (eds.), *Language Development and Disorders.* Clinics in Developmental Medicine. London: Blackwell Scientific/SIMP.

Werry, J., Carlielle, and Fitzpatrick, B. (1983) Rhythmic motor activities (stereotypies) in children under five: Etiology and prevention, *Journal of American Academy of Child Psychology*, 22, 329–336.

Wetzel, R. J., Baker, J., Rooney, M. and Martin, M. (1966) Outpatient treatment of autisic behaviour, *Behaviour Research and Therapy*, 4, 169–177.

Wikler, L. (1978) Chronic stresses of families of mentally retarded children, *Family Relations*, 30, 281–288.

Wing, L. (1969) The handicaps of autistic children: A comparative study, *Journal of Child Psychology and Psychiatry*, 10, 1–40.

Wing, L. (ed.) (1976) *Early Childhood Autism* (2nd edn). London: Pergamon.

Wing, L. (1980) *Autistic Children: A Guide for Parents.* London: Constable.

Wing, L. and Gould, J. (1979) Severe impairments of social interaction and associated abnormalities in children: Epidemiology and classification, *Journal of Autism and Developmental Disorders*, 9, 11–29.

Wing, L., Gould, J., Yeates, S. and Brierly, L (1977) Symbolic play in severely mentally retarded and in autistic children, *Journal of Child Psychology and Psychiatry*, 18, 167–178.

Winnicott, D. W. (1953) Transitional objects and transitional phenomena, *International Journal of Psychiatry*, 34, 89–97.

Wolchick, S. (1983) Language patterns of parents of young autistic and normal children, *Journal of Autism and Developmental Disorders*, 13, 167–180.

Wolchick, S. and Harris, S. (1982) Environments of autistic and normal children matched for language age: A preliminary investigation, *Journal of Autism and Developmental Disorders*, 12, 43–54.

Wolf, M., Risley, T., Johnston, M., Harris, F. and Allen, E. (1967) Application of operant conditioning procedures to the behaviour problems of an autistic child: A follow up and extension, *Behaviour Research and Therapy*, **5**, 103–111.

Wolf, M. M., Risley, T. R. and Mees, H. I. (1964) Applications of operant conditioning procedures to the behaviour problems of an autistic child, *Behaviour Research and Therapy*, **2**, 305–312.

Wolpe, J. (1958) *Psychotherapy by Reciprocal Inhibition*. Stanford, CA: Stanford University Press.

Young, C. and Kerr, M. (1979) The effects of a retarded child's social imitations on the behaviour of severely retarded school age peers, *Education and Training of the Mentally Retarded*, **14**, 185–190.

Yule, W. (1980) Identifying problems—functional analysis and observation and recording techniques. In Yule, W. and Carr, J. (eds.), *Behaviour Modification for the Mentally Handicapped*. London: Croom Helm, pp. 15–32.

Yule, W. (1985) Behavioural approaches. In Rutter, M. and Hersov, L. (eds.), *Child and Adolescent Psychiatry: Modern Approaches* (2nd edn). Oxford: Blackwell.

Yule, W. and Berger, M. (1972) Behaviour modification principles and speech delay. In Rutter, M. L. and Martin, J. A. M. (eds.), *The Child with Delayed Speech*. Clinics in Developmental Medicine, no. 43. Spastics International Medical Publications. London: William Heinemann.

Yule, W. and Berger, M. (1975) Communication, language and behavioural modification. In Kiernan, C. and Woodward, F. (eds.), *Behaviour Modifications with the Severely Retarded*. Amsterdam: Associated Scientific Publications.

Yule, W. and Carr, J. (eds.) (1980) *Behaviour Modification for the Mentally Handicapped*. London: Croom Helm.

Zigler, E. (1981) A plea to end the use of the patterning treatment for retarded children, *American Journal of Orthopsychiatry*, **51**, 388–390.

Appendix

APPENDIX 3.1
INDIVIDUAL DETAILS OF CHILDREN IN EXPERIMENTAL GROUP

Name	Age first diagnosed	Age treatment begun	IQ[a]	Language level	Mecham scores	Social class[a]
(1) Thomas	2 yr 10 m	4 yr 5 m	124	No speech	4 m	I
(2) Ben	7 yr 0 m	7 yr 1 m	82	No speech	1 yr 4 m	I
(3) Alex	4 yr 8 m	4 y 8m	73	Few words	1 yr 4 m	II
(4) Matthew	4 yr 8 m	4 yr 9 m	98	Words/echoed phrases	2yr 6 m	II
(5) Wayne	6 yr 9m	9 yr 10 m	77	Few word approximations	1 yr 4 m	V
(6) Stevie	4 yr 1 m	8 y 3 m	97	Sentences	3 yr 0 m	III m
(7) Simon	8 yr 5 m	9 yr 10 m	89 (WISC)	Sentences	8 yr 0 m	I
(8) Duncan	4 yr 1 m	4 yr 10 m	104	Words and occasional phrases	1 yr 10 m	III nm
(9) Jamie	3 yr 5 m	7 yr 10 m	67	No speech	1 yr 0 m	II
(10) Martin	3 yr 2 m	3 yr 4 m	105	No speech	1 yr 4 m	I
(11) Patrick	4 yr 11 m	5 yr 4 m	66	No speech	7 m	III m
(12) Kevin	4 yr 5 m	5 yr 2 m	100	Words/ occasional phrases	2 yr 1 m	III nm
(13) Peter	4 yr 1 m	4 yr 3 m	94	Phrases—mostly echolalic	2 yr 2 m	III nm
(14) Gary	3 yr 10 m	3 yr 10 m	60	No speech	1 yr 1 m	V
(15) Graham	5 yr 11 m	10 y 7 m	106 (WISC)	Words	2 yr 1 m	I
(16) Sam	6 yr 5 m	6 yr 5 m	74	Words and phrases	2 yr 8 m	IV

NOTES
(a) Non-verbal IQ tested on Merrill Palmer scale unless otherwise indicated.
(b) Social class according to Registrar General's definitions.

APPENDIX 3.2
INDIVIDUAL DETAILS OF CHILDREN IN SHORT-TERM CONTROL GROUP

Name	Age	IQ	Language-Level	Mecham scores	Social class
(1) Joe	7 yr 3 m.	60	Gestures only	1 yr 4m.	V
(2) Peter	7 yr 4 m.	72	None (odd words in past)	1 yr 4m.	II
(3) Anthony	8 yr 2 m.	82	Sentences	8 yr 6 m.	II
(4) David	8 yr 9 m.	81	Sentences	6 yr 6 m.	II
(5) James	11 yr 11m.	130 (WISC)	Sentences/phrases	4 yr 2 m.	III nm
(6) Andrew	5 yr 11 m.	62	Words	2 yr 3 m.	I
(7) Jeremy	3 yr 4 m.	130	None	5 m	IIInm
(8) Martin	3 yr 8 m.	115	Phrases	2 yr 4 m.	IV
(9) Christopher	7 yr 0 m.	68	Phrases	2 yr 9 m.	I
(10) Jimmy	4 yr 8 m.	86	None	1 yr 5 m.	I
(11) Stevie	5 yr 0 m.	98	Occasional words	1 yr 9 m.	IV
(12) Michael	3 yr 5 m.	80	None	6 m.	IV
(13) Simon	7 yr 3 m.	77	Phrases	2 yr 5 m	II
(14) Roland	6 yr 0 m	96	None (occasional words in past)	1 yr 7 m	II

NOTE

(*a*) Non-verbal IQ assessed on Merrill Palmer scale unless otherwise indicated.

APPENDIX 3.3
INDIVIDUAL DETAILS OF CHILDREN IN LONG-TERM CONTROL GROUP

Name	Age first diagnosed	Age at FU	IQ[a]	Language	Mecham scores	Social class
(1) Philip	3 yr 5 m.	8 yr 4 m.	115	None	4 m.	I
(2) Andrew	5 yr 11 m.	13 yr 2 m.	60	None	1 yr 4 m.	III nm
(3) Russell	3 yr 1 m.	8 yr 0 m.	81	Words and and occasional echoed phrase	1 yr 4 m.	IV
(4) Jonathon	6 yr 0 m.	11 yr 9 m.	85	Words and echoed phrases	2 yr 6 m.	I
(5) Ricky	8 yr 2 m.	14 yr 5 m.	72 (WISC PF)	Odd words	1 yr 4 m.	III nm
(6) Tony	1 yr 6 m.	10 yr 8 m.	68	Phrases	2 yr 6 m.	I
(7) Robin	8 yr 1 m.	10 yr 11 m.	80 (WISC PF)	Sentences	6 yr 0 m.	I
(8) Charles	4 yr 8 m.	8 y 7 m.	100	Occasional words and phrases	1 yr 4 m.	III nm
(9) Matthew	3 yr 5 m.	5 yr 0m.	122	None	10 m.	I
(10) Derek	4 yr 11 m.	10 yr 5 m.	108	None	7 m.	I
(11) Terence	5 yr 0 m.	9 yr 5 m.	87	None	7 m.	II
(12) David	5 yr 7 m.	9 yr 3 m.	72	Words— occasional echoes	1 yr 6 m.	II
(13) Peter	5 yr 0 m.	9 yr 1 m.	85	Words/echoed phrases	1 yr 11 m.	I
(14) Alex	4 yr 1 m.	13 yr 9 m.	109	None	1 yr 6 m.	I
(15) Robbie	5 yr 4 m.	11 yr 9 m.	80	Words	1 yr 6 m.	I
(16) Vernon	5 yr 4 m.	12 yr 3 m.	89	Words/echoed phrases	3 yr 4 m.	IV

NOTE

(a) Non-verbal IQ assessed Merrill Palmer scale unless otherwise indicated.

APPENDIX 3.4
LANGUAGE AND BEHAVIOUR
RATINGS USED IN MATCHING CASES AND LONG-TERM
CONTROLS

All items were based on 5 point scale: 0 = no problem, 4 = marked problem.
Ratings of children reached 90% agreement between independent raters.

Areas assessed:

(1) Language level		(Maximum severity score = 20)
	Rating	*Level*
Use of speech	0	Uses complete sentences
	1	Uses phrase speech
	2	Uses mainly single words
	3	Uses sounds communicatively
	4	No speech or communicative use of sounds
Language function	0	Chats spontaneously
	1	Occasional spontaneous comment/questions
	2	Uses speech in response to prompts, or to make wants known
	3	Uses speech only if prompted
	4	No speech
Echolalia	0	None
	1	Occasional (i.e. only if does not understand question)
	2	Frequent
	3	Most of speech is echolalic
	4	No speech
Comprehension	0	Understands at least 2–3 commands in sequence
	1	Understands single instructions (including prepositions, etc.)
	2	Understands single words
	3	Understands words with additional non-verbal cues
	4	No understanding of speech
Response to gesture	0	Responds to subtle facial cues
	1	Responds to complex gesture/mine
	2	Responds to simple signs
	3	Responds to pointing only
	4	No response
(2) Social Responsiveness		(Maximum severity score = 16)
Responses to parents	0	Spontaneously shows affection. Responds to other's moods
	1	Shows affection, but infrequently
	2	Doesn't demonstrate affection, but likes cuddles, etc.

	Rating	*Level*
	3	Only rarely enjoys physical contact
	4	Dislikes physical contact
Social discrimination	0	Differentiates well between parents and others
	1	Shows less than normal differentiation
	2	Lacks normal shyness of strangers
	3	Little discrimination between parents and others
	4	No discrimination—will approach anyone
Social interaction	0	Normal interest in strangers
	1	Limited interest, poor eye contact
	2	No interest, avoids eye contact
	3	Dislikes strangers until gets to know them; avoids eye contact
	4	Withdraws from, very distressed by strangers
Relationship with peers	0	Plays cooperatively; has special friend
	1	Plays simple group games (e.g. cards, lotto)
	2	Simple chasing, rough and tumble games; may show parallel play
	3	Observes other children, does not joint in
	4	Ignores or withdraws from other children
(3) Play		(Maximum severity score = 8)
Plays with toys	0	Complex constructional toys
	1	Simple constructional toys
	2	Rolls balls, cars along
	3	Toys used mainly in ritualistic way
	4	No play, exclusively ritualistic use of objects
Imaginative play	0	Complex pretend games (e.g. 'mothers and fathers')
	1	Simple pretend play (e.g. being car or animal)
	2	Plays with dolls, tea sets, etc., as if real
	3	Holds dolls, etc., occasionally as if real
	4	No imaginative play
(4) Abnormal 'autistic' behaviours	All rated as:	(Maximum severiety score = 28)
Abnormal response to stimuli	0	None
Resistance to change	1	Very infrequent dubious abnormality (1 per week or less)
Object attachment		
Rituals	2	Occasional, or in specific circumstances only
Obsessions		
Stereotypies/mannerisms	3	Frequent: several times per week
Phobias	4	Very disruptive, occurs at least daily

	Rating	*Level*
(5) Disruptive behaviours	All Rated (Maximum severity score = 16)
Tantrums/Screaming	as:	
	0	None
Aggression	1	Very rare (less than 1 per month)
Destructiveness	2	Occasional (less than 1 per week)
Self-injury	3	Frequent (several times per week)
	4	Very disruptive (at least 1 per day)
(6) Developmental problems		(Maximum severity score = 12)
Feeding	0	No problem
	1	Some faddiness only
	2	Many problems, strong dislikes of certain foods
	3	Very restricted range of foods eaten
	4	Only one or two foods (e.g. exclusively hamburgers and biscuits) eaten
Sleeping	0	No problem
	1	Occasional disturbed nights
	2	Goes to sleep late and disturbs parents in evening but then sleeps through night
	3	Wakes at least once per night
	4	Difficulty in going to sleep and wakes in the night
Toileting	0	No problem
	1	Occasional accidents
	2	Nocturnal enuresis only
	3	Wets day and night
	4	Wets and soils
(7) Activity level and mood		(Maximum severity score = 12)
Activity level	0	Normal
	1	Slightly underactive
	2	Slightly overactive
	3	Markedly inactive — difficult to engage in any activity
	4	Markedly overactive—constantly 'on the go'.
Concentration	0	Concentrates well on many tasks
	1	Concentrates on some tasks for at least 10–15 minutes
	2	Concentrates mainly on activities of obsessional interest
	3	Rarely spends more than 1–2 minutes in any activity
	4	Constantly moving from one activity to another
Mood	0	Generally happy, appropriate affect
	1	Usually happy, but often shows inappropriate affect (e.g. laughs if people are sad)

Rating	level
2	Labile—sudden mood changes
3	Often distressed without reason
4	Usually miserable and unhappy

APPENDIX 3.5
DETAILS OF SCORING ON PARENTAL INTERVIEW

Since the schedule was over 100 pages in length it is not duplicated here. Examples of scoring, therefore, are given below. Items were generally rated on 3 to 5 point scales (see examples below) although for some areas, notably language, play and social behaviour, broader scales were necessary. In each case a score of 0 indicates no problem. A high score indicates severe problems. For example:

(1)	*Rituals*	0 None
		1 Infrequent and very mild
		2 Definite rituals, but not very frequent
		3 Marked and frequent rituals interfering considerably with daily activities

(2)	*Enuresis*	0 Absent
		1 Occasional (i.e. less than 1 incident per month)
		2 1 per month to 1 per week
		3 Twice or more times per week
		4 Daily

(3)	*Level of functional speech*	0 Spontaneous phrase speech (of 4+ words)
		1 Phrase speech but only in response to prompts and questions; not spontaneous
		2 Use of 3-word phrases
		3 Use of 2-word phrases
		4 Wide use of single words (to label, ask for objects, etc.)
		5 Single words only as commands (e.g. 'No' 'dinner')
		6 No functional speech

DEFINITIONS OF GLOBAL CATEGORIES USED IN INTERVIEW SCHEDULE

Language level and usage (14 items)

Score obtained	*Level*
90+	No speech
71–90	Meaningful sounds, 1–10 single word utterances
51–70	Infrequent but communicative single or 2 word utterances
31–50	Communicative speech of 2+ words but infrequent
11–30	Fairly frequent and adequate use of communicative speech
0–10	Few problems

Gestural communication (3 items)

Score obtained	*Level*
18+	No speech and no gesture
15–17	No speech and only associated motor gestures to convey needs

12–14	Can use basic gestures but avoids communicating in this way if possible
9–11	Uses 1–2 basic gestures (points, claps, waves) spontaneously
6–8	Uses basic gestures spontaneously
3–5	Uses most basic gestures frequently (claps, waves, nods, etc.) but little facial expressiveness
0–2	No gesture necessary because communicates by speech and uses some expressive hand/facial gestures

Language problems (18 items)

Score obtained	Level
80+	No speech
71–80	Some single words, but speech really below echolalic/ metaphorical level
61–70	Single words predominantly, some echoes, some spontaneous
51–60	Some phrase speech but this mainly echolalic
41–50	Phrase speech but up to 50% echolalia/jargon
31–40	Some appropriate phrase speech; 25–50% echolalic
21–30	Appropriate phrase speech—less than 25% echolalia or jargon
11–20	Mainly appropriate speech—only occasional echolalia
0–10	Good appropriate speech—echolalia rare, although may show some pronoun reversal

Response to speech (5 items)

Score obtained	Level
14–15	Little or no apparent comprehension of speech
12–13	Some response to simple commands but response variable
9–11	Responds to simple commands if given additional cues
6–8	Able to respond to single word commands
3–5	Comprehension of instructions involving 1–2 basic ideas
0–2	Responds to most commands; can obey instructions containing more than 2 ideas

General social responsiveness (11 items)

Score obtained	Level
31+	Little response or affection shown either to parents or to others
21–30	Some degree of responsiveness to parents but unresponsive or uninhibited with strangers
11–20	Responsive to parents, but can be disruptive with other adults/children
6–10	Responsive to parents, occasional problems with other adults/children
3–5	Responsive to parents—little trouble with other adults, but poor interaction with children
0–2	Good response to parents; reacts well with other adults/children

Response to Parents (6 items)

Score Obtained	Level
12+	Little response to parents. No discrimination between them and other adults
11–12	Some discrimination between parents and other adults, but shows little affection and will avoid physical or eye contact
9–10	Shows discrimination between parents and others. Prefers them to strangers but response to affection and physical contact variable
6–8	Enjoys cuddles and physical contact at least some of the time but no obvious affection for parents in other ways
3–5	Responds to affection when given, but less responsive than normal child to absence, etc., of parents
1–2	Shows affection—hugs and cuddles—but does not initiate this. Always glad to see parents
0	Normal response. Spontaneously shows affection—responds to parents' moods, etc.

Response to other adults (2 items)

Score obtained	Level
10–12	Very little response to anyone. Generally seems oblivious of their presence
8–9	Extremely uninhibited with strangers. No discrimination between them and others whom he knows well
6–7	Very upset by presence of strangers
4–5	Less inhibited than normal with strangers. May cause some embarrassment but not unduly disruptive.
2–3	Shyer than normal with strangers. Withdraws from, but not upset by people he does not know. Relaxes as he got to know them
0–1	No problem with strangers except perhaps for overshyness

Response to peers (3 items)

Score obtained	Level
9–10	Becomes very upset by other children. Disrupts their games or shows hostility to them
7–8	Withdraws from other children
5–6	Will join in with simple games but only with adult encouragement and supervision
3–4	Plays simple games with other children without too much encouragement (chases them, etc.)
1–2	Plays quite complex games with other children—card games, etc. Needs little adult supervision
0	Plays well in many games. Has special friend

Play (13 items)

Score obtained	Level
31+	Little use of objects except for ritualistic purposes

26–30	Some appropriate use of simple constructional toys, but only with encouragement
21–25	Will use constructional equipment spontaneously but no imaginative use of objects
16–20	Good with constructional materials and some rudimentary play with other objects—pushes cars, etc.
11–15	Good at constructional tasks, and some imaginative use of dolls, cooking utensils, etc.
6–10	Concentrates well on variety of tasks. Simple pretend play with dolls, etc. Draws imaginatively. Pretends to be things (e.g. animals) himself
0–5	Concentrates well on many activities. Joins in pretend games

Abnormal response to stimuli (12 items)

Score obtained	Level
11+	Abnormally sensitive to touch/sound sight of objects. Causes frequent disruption to other activities because of this
8–10	Frequent touching/looking at particular objects. This distracts him while out/working, etc.
5–7	Has particular interest in one sensory modality. Can be disruptive/distracting
2–4	Mild but not too frequent interest in one sensory modality
0–1	No problem or very dubious abnormal interest

Obsessions/rituals (11 items)

Score obtained	Level
20+	Many obsessions and rituals. Great dislike of changes of any kind
16–19	Many obsessions and rituals but will tolerate change if this does not interfere with these.
11–15	Has number of obsessions and rituals. Can be deflected from these with careful handling, but they do disrupt family life
6–10	Has one or more serious obsession/attachment but no severe rituals. Still some disruption to family life
1–5	Mild obsessions or rituals but these do not disrupt family activities unduly
0	No problem

Mannerisms (3 items)

Score obtained	Level
7+	Very frequent and lead to exclusion of most other activities. Child very upset if restrained
5–6	Very frequent. Some upset if stopped. Tend to make child conspicuous in public
3–4	Frequent mannerisms but child can be diverted from them if given other occupation.
1–2	Occasional/mild mannerisms. Not conspicuous
0	No problem

Activity (3 items)

Score obtained	Level
9–10	Markedly overactive. Clumsiness leads to a lot of destructive behaviour
7–8	Overactive much of time. Frequently knocks things over
5–6	Overactive unless given things to do, but this not too difficult to deal with
3–4	Mild overactivity. Slight clumsiness
1–2	Rather *underactive*, difficult to get him to do much
0	No problem

Mood (4 items)

Score obtained	Level
9–10	Very labile and unpredictable moods. Generally seems unhappy and miserable. Frequently shows inappropriate affect
7–8	Often unhappy and changeable in mood
5–6	Swings quickly from one mood to another but not predominantly unhappy
3–4	Occasional unexpected bouts of tearfulness or laughter not related to circumstances
1–2	Little expression of mood, but not particularly unhappy and only rarely shows inappropriate affect
0	Usually happy and shows appropriate affect

General behaviour problems (13 items)

Score obtained	Level
21+	Frequent difficulties in 5 or more behaviour areas
16–20	Frequent difficulties in 3 or more behaviour areas
11–15	Frequent difficulties in 1–2 areas, and several less frequent behavioural difficulties
6–10	At least weekly problems in 1–2 areas
1–5	Occasional problems in 1–2 areas
0	None

Social problems (10 items)

Score obtained	Level
21+	Frequent difficulties in many situations. Can hardly ever be taken out
16–20	Difficult in many social situations. Frequently has to be withdrawn when company visits—these avoided if possible
11–15	Is taken out on visits, etc., but these often end in disruption
6–10	Often goes out with parents. Occasionally disruptive and has to be taken away
1–5	Occasional problems in control but is taken out a lot
0	No problem

Skills (5 items)

Score obtained	Level
20	No pre-reading/number skills
15–19	Very simple pre-reading *or* pre-number skills (2–3 year level approx.)
10–14	Simple pre-reading and pre number skills (3–4 year level approx.)
5–9	Number work or reading/writing at about 5–6 year level
2–4	Number work and reading/writing at about 5–6 year level
0–1	Number work and reading/writing at 7+ level

APPENDIX 3.6
DEFINITIONS OF CATEGORIES USED IN THE ASSESSMENT OF CHILDREN'S LANGUAGE

Morpheme Analysis

The measure of syntactical complexity used were the inflections:

	Interrater reliability
'ing' present progressive (running, jumping, etc.)	(95%)
's' plural (cats, dogs, etc.)	(97%)
'ed' past regular (jumped, danced, etc.)	(100%)
's' possessive (Mary's, Mummy's, etc.)	(100%)
's' present (runs, jumps, etc.)	(100%)

Other morphemes used were

Past irregular (went, saw, etc.)	(100%)
Pronouns (he, she, they, etc.)	(95%)
Pronoun case (him, her, etc.)	(92%)
Pronoun possessive (his, hers, etc.)	(93%)
Articles (a, an, the)	(96%)
Prepositions (in, on, by, etc.)	(97%)

Transformational Analysis

Transformation rules included were

The imperative (i.e. deletion of subject: 'Make it go', Run!' etc.)	(78%)
Question inversion (i.e. reversal of subject–verb order: 'Can I go?' 'Will it go?' etc.	(83%)
'Wh' questions (i.e. 'Wh' word + reversal: 'What is he?' 'Who are you?' etc.)	(100%)
Negative (i.e. insertion of *not*: 'I will not go', 'I am not eating', etc.)	(100%)
'Do' support (i.e. the use of 'do' to strengthen declarative sentence: 'He does like it', 'I do think so'	(100%)
Infinitive (i.e. use of to + uninflected verb form: 'I want to go', 'I hope to leave')	(100%)

Children's use of auxiliary verbs and the copula 'to be' were also included. More complex transformations such as passives, truncated questions, etc., were not selected for analysis, since initial pilot work indicated that examples of these rules occurred very rarely in the speech of the autistic children studied.

Complexity of Phrase Utterance

In addition to children's use of specific structures, the general complexity of phrase utterances was analysed. Phrase structures rated were:

(1) Complex sentences (simple sentences plus additional clauses, e.g. 'Mummy told me to go, so I didn't' (99%)
(2) Simple sentences (noun phrase plus verb phrase, e.g. 'The big dog ran away') (98%)
(3) Noun phrases (big dog, blue ball, etc.) (97%)
(4) Verb phrases (e.g. 'running away, 'going home') (96%)
(5) Prepositional phrases ('on the mat', 'in the cup', etc.) (96%)

For each child using at least 2-word utterances, the number of correct phrases, morphemes and transformations used was calculated. Counts were also kept of the number of obligatory contexts in which the rules should have been used, so that percentages of correct usage could be determined. Calculations of children's use of syntactical rules were based only on transcripts of non-echolalic speech. Echolalic utterances were excluded from the analysis. Mean morpheme length of utterance was calculated according to Brown (1973) (Reliability = 97%)

APPENDIX 3.7
CATEGORIES USED IN ANALYSIS OF CHILDREN'S FUNCTIONAL
SPEECH (examples taken from actual transcripts; inter-rater reliabilities
in parenthesis)

A. Echolalic and Autistic Utterances

1. *Immediate Repetitions of Self* (100%). Utterances in which the child
    repeats himself, either exactly or with slight variations. Repetitions need
    not follow the original utterance without a break; occasionally other
    interpolated remarks can occur.

    e.g. Child   'Going to be black clouds
         Mother   'Come on lets do some painting'
         Child   'Ooh, ooh, be black clouds
                  Going to be black clouds'

2. *Immediate Repetitions of Others* (100%)
    (a)   *Exact*   Mother 'Ask the lady her name'
                            Child 'Ask the lady her name'
    (b)   *Reduction*   Mother 'Have you got any pink ones?'
                            Child 'Pink ones'
    (c)   *Expansion*   Child adds to utterance by mother.
         e.g.   Mother 'That's quarter to'
                            Child 'Quarter to three'

3. *Delayed Stereotyped Echoes* (92%). Utterances that the child has
    heard previously and is repeating verbatim. Often the intonation, or
    type of voice used, is not the child's normal one, so that it sounds as if
    someone else were speaking. Such remarks may often be grammatically
    more complex than the child's spontaneous utterances.

    e.g. 'Hello everyone and welcome to the Tony Blackburn Show', or
    (child to himself) 'Mustn't tease her. Mustn't tease the dog'

4. *Action Accompaniments and Thinking Aloud* (94%). Utterances in
    which the child is apparently talking to himself and making no attempt
    to communicate; may or may not occur in conjunction with a particular
    activity.

    e.g. Child (still blowing bubbles) 'Up Up. The bubble is going up
                                  Don't go down. Don't break bubble'

5. *Metaphorical or Telegraphic Utterances* (100%). Utterances in which
    the usage is idiosyncratic and whose meaning cannot be interpreted e.g.
    'Alove from me', 'Boot 50', 'A grandma pie'.

B. Socialized Utterances

6. *Prompted Echoes* (100%). These are repetitions of mothers speech but in response to a prompt from mother.

    e.g. Mother (teaching child to name pictures in a book) 'Ball'
    Child 'Ball'

Prompted echoes may be exact, reduced, or expanded (see definitions for inappropriate echoes). In addition *mitigated* echoes may occur, in which child makes appropriate changes in number or person when he repeats mother.

    e.g. Mother   'Is it because you don't like it?'
    Child   'Because I don't like it'
    Extensions to mother's speech may also occur.
    e.g. Mother   'You go to school with Diana, and Tommy and P . . .'
    Child   'And Peter'.

7. *Questions* (99%). Attempts by child to elicit information from mother. May be marked by intonation or by syntactic structure.

    e.g. 'You've got a set of Kings, no?'
    'Now it is whose turn'?
    'That's Mummy?' (for 'is that Mummy?')

8. *Answers* (100%) Childs responses to mother's questions or prompts.

    e.g. Mother   'Who can you see!'   Child   'The plank'
    Mother   'And at night you go to?'   Child   'Bed'

9. *Spontaneous Remarks* (92%). Voluntary comments or remarks by the child e.g. 'That's a milk lorry'. 'I want to play'.

10. *Directions or Commands* (94%). Utterances in which the child is directing or telling the mother to do something.

    e.g. (while playing cards) 'Your turn'
    'Gimme that'

11. *Automatic Language* (98%). Includes exclamations, and other 'intra-verbal' utterances (Skinner, 1957)

    e.g. 'Hello', 'Please', 'Excuse me', 'Go to hell', etc.
    Also included in this category are reading nursery rhymes, repeating the alphabet, or strings of numbers.

12. *Other* (98%). Includes reading, doing arithmetical calculations, and telling stories.

C. Non-Verbal and Incomprehensible Remarks

13. *Non-Verbal.* Grunts, groans, screams, etc. Also humming a tune without words (singing with words present was scored as 'Automatic')

14. *Incomprehensible.* Utterances which it was impossible to code because of being totally incomprehensible.

APPENDIX 3.8
DEFINITIONS OF CATEGORIES USED IN MOTHERS' SPEECH
ANALYSIS

(All examples are taken from actual transcripts)

Utterances Used in Response to Child's Speech or for the Purpose of Eliciting Speech from the Child (i.e. language directed utterances)

(1) *Questions* Syntactically marked by 'Wh' or other question word, by subject–verb inversion, or marked by intonation. Only scored if mother is obviously trying to elicit some sort of answer from the child. Utterances that were syntactically marked as questions but which in fact functioned as commands or directions to the child—e.g. 'Would you put that down?' 'Will you stop doing that?'—were scored as *directions*.

(2) *Answers* Must be preceded by a question.

(3) *Imitation*
    (a) *Exact* Exact repetition of child's utterance.
    (b) *Mitigated* Repetition of child's utterances but with appropriate change in pronoun, noun or verb number.
    (c) *Reduction* Partial repetition of child's utterance. For example,
    Child   'Why don't you go and mend the window'
    Mother   'Mend the window'
    (d) *Expansion* Repetition of child's utterances with additions. For example
    Child   Want Peter Rabbit'
    Mother   'You want Peter Rabbit do you, all right then'

(4) *Correction* A response by the mother which by intonation or content clearly implies that what the child has said is incorrect.
Corrections may be of:
    (a) *Syntax* For example,
    Child asking for biscuit   'You want a biscuit?'
    Mother   '*Who* wants a biscuit?' or '*I want* a biscuit'

    or

    Child   'He's a naughty little girl'
    Mother   'No, it's *she's* a naughty girl'
    (b) *Semantics* For example,
    Child   'It's hot-raining'
    Mother   'No it's called steam'.
    (c) *Articulation* For example,
    Child   'Tree cars'
    Mother   'No, three cars'.
    (d) *Fact* For example

Child   'We went to Granpy's yesterday'

Mother   'Ooh you fibber, we went to the beach'.

(5)   *Directed mimicry* Instructing child to say something using a direct marker such as the word 'say', e.g. 'Say bye-bye'.

(6)   *Prompting* Urging child to say something but with no direct marker. Instead prompt is given by tone or content, or by mother supplying part of the response. For example, 'Was it a *bus* you went to school on?' (Mother's intonation implies she expects child to respond with the word bus.) Or 'Who comes with you? Mrs. Ha...' (for Mrs Harris).

(7)   *Direct reinforcement* Word or comment by mother which indicates that she is listening to the child, or approves what he says, e.g. 'Right', 'That's good', 'Oh you did that nicely'.

General Comments and Utterances in Response to Child's Activities (non-language directed remarks)

(8)   *Directions, demands or suggestions* For example, 'Let's play Leggo', 'Aren't you going to come and kiss me better?'

(9)   *General statements or comments* When no response expected by mother. 'Isn't it a lovely day!' 'Isn't she a good girl!'

(10)   *Indirect modelling* Story telling, reading, reciting nursery rhymes, counting, singing, etc.

(11)   *Remarks of approval or affection* (Obviously no response expected.) 'You're a nice boy aren't you?' 'That's a very good boy'.

(12)   *Remarks implying criticism or disapproval* (Obviously no answer expected.) For example, 'You must not throw bricks at Nicola', 'What did you do *that* for?'

Speech not Classified in Above Categories

(13)   *Interjections* For example, 'Oh dear', 'Hello there'.

(14)   *Incomprehensible utterances* Either part or whole of utterance inaudible.

APPENDIX 3.9

MOTHER'S SPEECH CATEGORIES INTERRATER RELIABILITY AT BEGINNING OF PROJECT AND 2 YEARS LATER

Category	% agreement prior to treatment (based on ratings of 9 × $\frac{1}{2}$ hr transcripts)	% agreement after 2 years (based on ratings of 4 × $\frac{1}{2}$ hr transcripts)
(1) Questions	92	98
(2) Answers	100	100
(3) Echo (exact)	93	98
(4) Echo (mitigated)	100	98
(5) Reduction	100	100
(6) Expansion	98	100
(7) Directed mimicry	100	100
(8) Prompt	94	97
(9) Correction	96	96
(10) Reinforcement	89	94
(11) Direction	92	93
(12) Statement	87	95
(13) Approval	83	91
(14) Disapproval	86	90
(15) Indirect modelling	92	100
(16) Interjections	85	100
(17) Incomprehensible	100	100

APPENDIX 3.10
STABILITY OF MOTHER'S SPEECH PATTERNS OVER TIME
(Average period between recordings = 4 weeks)

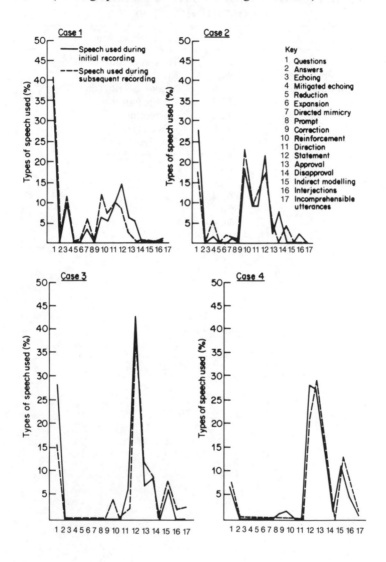

APPENDIX 3.11

RELIABILITY OF CATEGORIES USED IN THE OBSERVATION OF MOTHERS' BEHAVIOUR AND IN THE ASSESSMENT OF MOTHERS' COMMUNICATION

Behaviour	%	Communication	%
Ignoring child	85.2	Total speech to child	95.7
Interacting with observer	94.6	Praise	83.0
Interacting with other	88.8	Negative/criticism	92.6
No interaction	91.7	Confirmation	86.6
Out of room	72.6	Correction	96.4
Own task	97.8	Directions	92.1
Attention to child	83.4	Positive Tone	76.3
Total Contact with Child	86.5	Negative Tone	96.0
Neutral contact	68.3		
Directing contact	85.9		
Negative contact	65.4		
Positive contact	70.0		
Smiles	99.9		
Gesture	100.0		

APPENDIX 3.12
RELIABILITY OF CATEGORIES USED IN THE OBSERVATION OF CHILDREN'S BEHAVIOUR AND IN THE ASSESSMENT OF CHILDREN'S COMMUNICATION

Behaviour	%	Communication	%
Not occupied	97.1	Total utterances	98.8
Task alone	97.4	Non-communicative verbalizations	89.2
Task with mother	98.6	Communicative verbalizations	58.3
Play alone	94.6	Non-communicative words	97.7
Play with mother	93.5	Communicative words	76.6
Rituals/stereotypies	79.4	Non-communicatie phrases	86.1
Object attachment	86.8	Communicative phrases	89.9
Out of room	95.1	Cries/distress	48.7
Disruptive/aggressive	100.0	Gesture	100.0
Non-cooperative	88.9		

APPENDIX 11.1
PRESENT PLACEMENT OF CASES AND LONG TERM CONTROLS

Cases

Thomas	Residential community for autistic adults
Ben	Residential community for autistic adults
Alex	Residential unit for the severely subnormal
Matthew	Residential community for autistic adults/adolescents
Wayne	Residential community for autistic adults/adolescents
Stevie	Residential community for autistic adults/adolescents
Simon	Sheltered employment (Care Village). Lives at home
Duncan	School for autistic children
Jamie	Residential hospital for the severely subnormal
Martin	Private school
Patrick	Residential community for autistic adults
Kevin	School for children with severe mental retardation
Peter	School for autistic children
Graham	Adult training centre. Lives at home
Sam	Residential unit for individuals with mixed handicaps
Gary	School for children with severe mental retardation

Controls

Philip	Residential hospital unit for the severely subnormal
Andrew	Residential unit for autistic individuals
Russell	Sheltered employment. Living at home
Jonathon	Residential unit for individuals with mixed handicaps
Ricky	Residential hospital for the severely retarded
Tony	Residential unit for autistic adults/adolescents
Robin	In employment. Living at home
Charles	Residential unit for individuals with mixed handicaps
Matthew	School for mixed handicaps
Derek	Residential unit for individuals with mixed/language handicaps
Terence	Residential hospital for the severely subnormal
David	At home, no special provision
Peter	Residential unit for the severely subnormal
Alex	Lost contact
Robbie	Residential unit for individuals with mixed handicaps
Vernon	Residential unit for autistic adults/adolescents

Index